BACK
TO
SCHOOL

FOR GROWN-UPS

First published in North America in 2010 by Barron's Educational Series, Inc.

All inquiries should be addressed to:

Barron's Educational Series, Inc.

250 Wireless Boulevard

Hauppauge, New York 11788

www.barronseduc.com

Library of Congress Control Number: 2009936831

ISBN-13: 978-0-7641-6271-8

ISBN-10: 0-7641-6271-3

Conceived, designed, and produced by

Quid Publishing

Level 4, Sheridan House

114 Western Road

Hove

BN3 1DD

England

www.quidpublishing.com

Design by: Lindsey Johns

Printed in Singapore

9 8 7 6 5 4 3 2 1

Dedications

Stephen:

My thanks to Joanne for her patient support and Nick King for his careful research.

Ian:

With apologies to the teachers who tried so hard to make me appreciate this stuff the first time around.

	LESSON 1 (09:00–10:30)	LESSON 2 (10:30–12:00)

MONDAY — Earth Sciences (p12)
- **When** Was Earth Formed?
- **Why** Have There Been Ice Ages?
- **What** Is a Continent?
- **Who** Was Alfred Wegener?
- **Where** Is Krakatoa?

MONDAY — History (p22)
- **Where** Is the Cradle of Civilization?
- **When** Was Writing Developed?
- **Why** Did Socrates Poison Himself?
- **What** Happened to the Romans?
- **Who** Invented Gunpowder?

TUESDAY — Science (p58)
- **When** Was the Big Bang?
- **Who** Was Albert Einstein?
- **What** Is Light?
- **Where** Is the Limit of the Universe?
- **Why** Are Time and Space the Same Thing?

TUESDAY — Art (p68)
- **Where** Are the Oldest Cave Paintings?
- **What** Is the Bayeux Tapestry?
- **When** Was the Renaissance?
- **Who** Painted the *Mona Lisa*?
- **Why** Were the Impressionists Initially Unpopular?

WEDNESDAY — Civics (p104)
- **What** Is a Constitution?
- **Who** Was George Washington?
- **Where** Is the World's Oldest Capital City?
- **When** Was the United Nations Formed?
- **Why** Did Karl Marx Write *Das Kapital*?

WEDNESDAY — Earth Sciences (p114)
- **Why** Do Animals Migrate?
- **Who** Found the Source of the Nile?
- **Where** Is the Great Barrier Reef?
- **What** Is the Driest Place on Earth?
- **When** Was the Grand Canyon Formed?

THURSDAY — Literature (p150)
- **When** Did Tolstoy Write *War and Peace*?
- **Who** Was Eric Arthur Blair?
- **What** Is Moby-Dick?
- **Why** Are Books Sometimes Banned?
- **Where** Is the World's Most Comprehensive Library?

THURSDAY — History (p160)
- **Where** Was the Bubonic Plague From?
- **Why** Was the Magna Carta Important?
- **When** Was the Printing Press Invented?
- **What** Did Columbus Do in 1492?
- **Who** Was Thomas Paine?

FRIDAY — Religion (p196)
- **Why** Is Zeus also Jupiter?
- **Where** Does Hinduism Come From?
- **When** Did Buddha Live?
- **What** Does Pantheism Mean?
- **Who** Were the Fathers of Western Philosophy?

FRIDAY — Science (p206)
- **When** Did the Dinosaurs Die Out?
- **Who** Was Carl Linnaeus?
- **Why** Is Evolution Controversial?
- **What** Is DNA?
- **Where** Do *Homo sapiens* Come From?

Mathematics	**When** Was the Abacus Invented?	**Religion**	**What** Is a Monotheistic Religion?	**TEST ONE**
	What Is a Prime Number?		**Who** Was Abraham?	
	Where Does Zero Come From?		**When** Was the Bible Written?	
	Who Was Fibonacci?		**Where** Is Mecca?	
p32	**Why** Is Pi Also a Number?	p42	**Why** Does the Pope Live in the Vatican?	p52

Mathematics	**Why** Does 1 + 1 = 2?	**Literature**	**When** Were the Norse Sagas Created?	**TEST TWO**
	When does $4(x + 3)^2 + 5 = \sqrt{9}(2 + 6 + 7 + 8)$?		**Why** Don't All Poems Rhyme?	
	What Is Calculus?		**Who** Was Shakespeare?	
	Who Was Pythagoras?		**Where** Does Haiku Come From?	
p78	**Where** Was the Metric System Invented?	p88	**What** Is a Stanza?	p98

Science	**What** Is Alchemy?	**Phys Ed**	**When** Did the Olympics Begin?	**TEST THREE**
	Who Was Marie Curie?		**Who** Broke the Four-Minute Mile Barrier?	
	Where Do Diamonds Come From?		**Why** Are Soccer Balls Round?	
	When Does a Solid Become a Liquid?		**Where** Was Wrestling Invented?	
p124	**Why** Is Water a Solvent?	p134	**What** Is the Fastest Swim Stroke?	p144

Art	**Who** Took the First Photograph?	**Civics**	**Why** Do We Vote?	**TEST FOUR**
	Why Did Van Gogh Cut Off His Ear?		**Where** Do Laws Come From?	
	What Is Pop Art?		**What** Is the Separation of Powers?	
	Where Is the World's Largest Gallery?		**Who** Is Nelson Mandela?	
p170	**When** Will La Sagrada Familia Be Finished?	p180	**When** Was the Age of Revolution?	p190

Earth Sciences	**When** Did the Worst Earthquake Happen?	**History**	**What** Started World War I?	**TEST FIVE**
	Why Is Tourism So Important?		**Who** Was the Worst Dictator of the Twentieth Century?	
	Who Was Gerardus Mercator?		**Why** Was an Atomic Bomb Dropped on Hiroshima?	
	Where Is the World's Largest City?		**Where** Was the First Female Head of Government Elected?	
p216	**What** Is Climate Change?	p226	**When** Did the Cold War End?	p236

Introduction

What did you learn in school? You should have learned about the great works of art; the literature that shaped society; the political leaders who changed the world and the historical events they were part of; the key geographical facts that help us to understand the earth, as well as the scientific knowledge that examines our world and the universe beyond. You *should* have learned all that and more, but you probably have more detailed memories of your first sweetheart and the long summer vacations.

* *Why did Van Gogh cut off his ear? (p. 172)*

Who were the fathers of Western philosophy? (p. 204) *

Back to School for Grown-Ups captures the knowledge that eluded you at school, brings it right up to date, and tells you everything you need to know in clear, concise language. Each key area of knowledge is divided into individual lessons, and each of the lessons is subdivided into questions based on the five Ws: who, what, when, where, and why? For example, "Why did Socrates poison himself?" and "What is Pop Art?" From each question several aspects are explored, helping you to develop a crosscurricular understanding, like linking references to Marxism with the Industrial Revolution and the start of World War I.

Each lesson also includes related and sometimes unusual information in the form of fact and quotes. These should help you to remember each lesson and, as an added extra, to impress your friends. With the clear summaries and quick quizzes to challenge your new knowledge, this is one school book that you will actually enjoy reading. You can start from the beginning and work to the end, pick your favorite topics, or take a "lucky dip" and see what you find out.

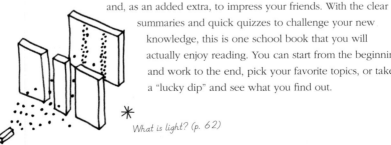

* *What is light? (p. 62)*

How to use this book

So that you get the most out of **Back to School for Grown-Ups**, the sample spreads
below show the book's different features and how to navigate your way around them.
Remember: You can read the book from cover to cover, or just dip in and out.

Each "Lesson"
comprises five
questions: Who,
What, When,
Where, and Why?

Short "Fact" boxes
introduce unusual
and/or interesting
snippets of trivia so
that you can impress
your friends.

Lesson spread

Photographs and
illustrations are
used throughout
as visual aids.

Check that you
understood everything
with the short-and-
snappy summary.

Quotations from
famous individuals
enrich the text
and give different
perspectives

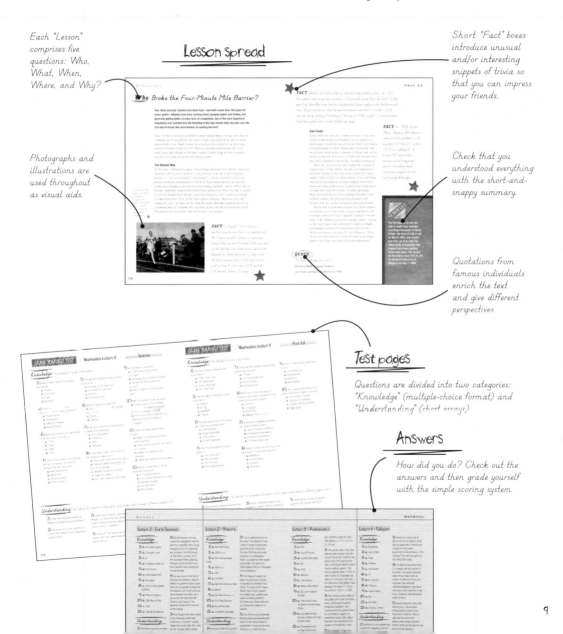

Test pages

Questions are divided into two categories:
"Knowledge" (multiple-choice format) and
"Understanding" (short essays)

Answers

How did you do? Check out the
answers and then grade yourself
with the simple scoring system.

Monday

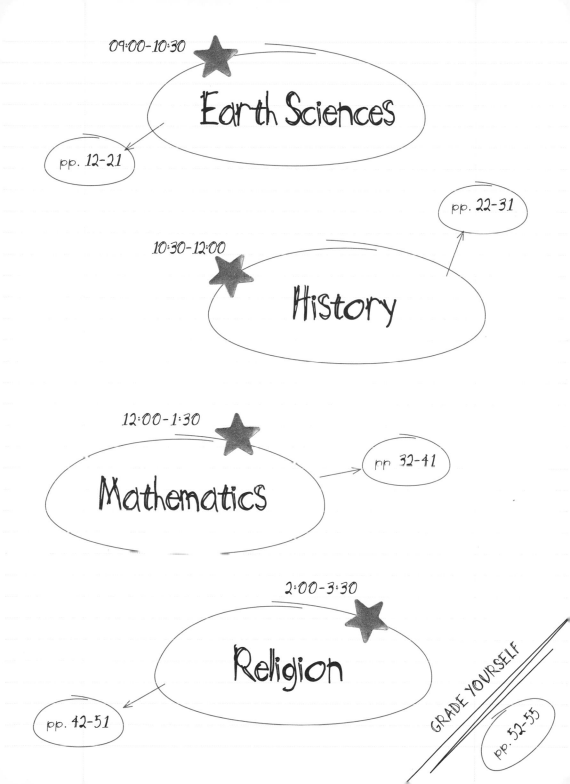

09:00-10:30

Earth Sciences

pp. 12-21

pp. 22-31

10:30-12:00

History

12:00-1:30

Mathematics

pp 32-41

2:00-3:30

Religion

pp. 42-51

GRADE YOURSELF

pp. 52-55

When Was Earth Formed?

When we look at the natural landscape—plains and rivers, lakes and mountains—it's difficult to imagine that there was a time when none of this existed, but that is certainly the case. In fact, the process of formation is still happening beneath our feet; for planet Earth, which was once a ball of molten matter, is still cooling and, although the outer layer is now hard and crunchy, it still has a chewy center.

If you accept the vast and convincing body of scientific knowledge, Earth wasn't created in a day or a week but over a period of hundreds of millions of years. The story of Earth, and of the entire solar system, begins more than 4.6 billion (4,600,000,000) years ago. At that time, clouds of interstellar gas and dust had formed throughout the universe. These clouds consisted of hydrogen and helium created in the big bang (which we will learn about in our first lesson tomorrow morning), together with heavier elements forged from protons and neutrons in the nuclear furnaces of early stars. Within each cloud, all this material was being drawn together by gravity. Possibly given a kick start by a supernova—the explosion of a nearby star—the cloud, or nebula, that was to become our solar system became a rotating flattened disk in which the particles started to clump together. A star formed in the center of the disk and the material in the rest of the cloud formed into bands at various distances from this star. Within the bands, the material then gradually coalesced to form balls of molten matter and gas, and so the planets came into being, orbiting around the Sun. Earth is one of these planets.

FACT: Early in its history, before it had begun to cool, Earth was struck a glancing blow by a large object, possibly an errant planet. The impact may have increased Earth's speed of spin, as well as tilting the planet in its orbit. This tilt relative to the Sun is the reason we have seasons. What's more, the impact knocked a dollop of molten rock off Earth, and this formed a new body orbiting our planet: the Moon.

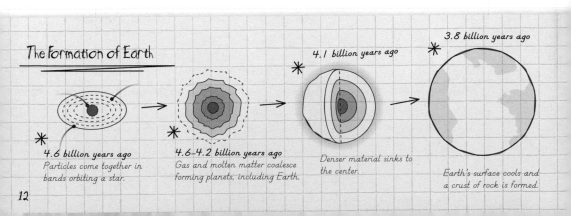

The Formation of Earth

3.8 billion years ago

4.1 billion years ago

4.6 billion years ago
Particles come together in bands orbiting a star.

4.6–4.2 billion years ago
Gas and molten matter coalesce forming planets, including Earth.

Denser material sinks to the center.

Earth's surface cools and a crust of rock is formed.

FACT: *Earth may be about halfway through its life. In another five billion years or so, as it burns up its fuel supply, the Sun will contract and then grow hugely to become a red giant, vaporizing this planet before shrinking back to become a white dwarf star.*

SUMMARY

Earth was formed from hydrogen, helium, and heavier elements that came together in an interstellar cloud some 4.6 billion years ago. Although the surface of the planet has cooled enough to form an outer crust, the majority of the planet remains a ball of molten rock.

Growing and Cooling

As Earth grew, the gravity it exerted increased, and for 500 million years the planet was bombarded with chunks of matter that imparted energy and kept it molten. In this liquid ball, the heavier material sank to the middle and the lighter matter floated. The planet attracted gases, forming an atmosphere containing water vapor, and the surface cooled, forming a solid crust.

That was about 4.1 billion years ago, so we might expect to find rocks that are that old, but in fact another heavy bombardment by meteoroids, asteroids, comets, and general debris caused it all to become molten again. That ended about 3.8 billion years ago, the crust solidified for a second time, and there are rock formations that date from this period.

Today's Earth

Earth's structure reflects its history. The dense inner core, a hot ball of nickel and iron some 1,520 miles (2,450 km) across, is hot enough to be molten but is under such enormous pressure that it remains solid. Around this is an outer core of liquid metal about 1,240 miles (2,000 km) thick. It is the rotation of the liquid outer core around the solid inner core that gives Earth its magnetic field.

Next comes the lighter material of the mantle, a layer of semimolten rock 1,775 miles (2,855 km) thick, made up of silicon compounds and containing magnesium and iron. On top of this is the hard crust, up to 40 miles (64 km) thick in places, and as little as 3 miles (5 km) thick in parts of the ocean bed. Like the mantle, the crust is made of silicate rocks and a range of minerals.

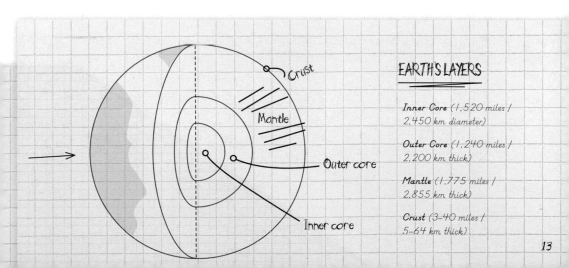

Crust

Mantle

Outer core

Inner core

EARTH'S LAYERS

Inner Core (1,520 miles / 2,450 km diameter)

Outer Core (1,240 miles / 2,200 km thick)

Mantle (1,775 miles / 2,855 km thick)

Crust (3–40 miles / 5–64 km thick)

Why Have There Been Ice Ages?

With all the talk of global warming, you may wonder how Earth's temperature has varied throughout its history. In fact, there have been periods when the average temperature was much higher than it is now, when hardly a trace of snow or ice could be found anywhere on the planet, and there have been times when it was much lower and great ice sheets covered much of the world. So what causes these wide fluctuations in global temperature?

It may surprise you to learn that Earth is currently experiencing what is probably its fifth great ice age; although fortunately we are in a warmer part of that ice age—a period known as an interglacial—when the great ice caps and glacial fields have retreated, if only temporarily.

The first person to suggest that ice fields had once been much more extensive than they are now was the Swiss-German geologist Jean de Charpentier, who was working in the Alps in the early nineteenth century, studying the origins of large scattered boulders known as "erratics." At the time, they were thought to be meteorites, but he realized that they were made of the same rock as the surrounding mountains and concluded that they had been moved by glaciers that had since melted. We now know that he was right. Another glaciologist, a Swiss-American named Louis Agassiz, not only agreed with him but also put forward evidence to suggest that much of the globe had at one time been covered with thick ice. Earth scientists have since built up a very detailed picture of the planet's climatic history.

In the last three billion years, there have probably been five major ice ages, the first taking place more than two billion years ago. Some 850 million years ago an event known as "Snowball Earth" began, a period of severe cold lasting about 220 million years in which the whole of the globe was covered in ice. The third ice age lasted from 460 to 430 million years ago, the fourth from 350 to 260 million years ago, and this current fifth ice age started about 20 million years ago. Temperatures rise and fall throughout an ice age, producing glacial and interglacial periods, and this one reached its coldest about three million years ago. An interglacial began about 10,000 years ago, and this continues today.

FACT: *Supremely adapted to the cold, woolly mammoths existed between about 300,000 and 12,000 years ago and roamed the tundra of northern Eurasia and America toward the end of the last deep freeze. They were hunted by the earliest modern humans and feature in European cave paintings. The oldest known ivory carving, found in southwestern Germany in 2007, is a 35,000-year-old statuette of a woolly mammoth.*

The deep-frozen carcasses of complete mammoths have been found in Siberia.

FACT: *The end of the second ice age seems to have coincided with the evolution of a wealth of complex single-celled and multicelled organisms, although whether there is a causal link between these events, and what this might be, remains a matter for some debate.*

So What Causes Ice Ages?

The mechanisms that cause ice ages and determine their progress are complex, and several factors are undoubtedly at work. These include fluctuations in energy output from the Sun, changes in Earth's distance from the Sun, and, importantly, the movements of the tectonic plates. The positions and elevations of the world's landmasses affect wind patterns and the circulation of warm air over the globe, but their effect on ocean currents is even greater. It may be that the landmasses have periodically cut off the circulation of currents to the poles, causing the temperatures there to fall. Once ice sheets start to form, they reinforce the cooling process by increasing the reflection of the Sun's energy back into space, and temperatures continue to drop. The concentration of carbon dioxide (CO_2) in the atmosphere is also known to have a major impact on global temperatures, as this "greenhouse gas" reduces the radiation of energy from Earth, so it is likely that falls and rises in CO_2 levels are factors in starting and ending ice ages. The movements of Earth's tectonic plates can affect carbon dioxide levels, because active volcanoes release CO_2, and the uplifting of mountain ranges such as the Himalayas leads to increased erosion and weathering of silicate rocks, a process that tends to absorb carbon dioxide. We have undoubtedly played our part, too, and the current trend toward global warming as a result of human activity promises to end the current ice age with a bang.

FACT: *Although human societies existed during the last glacial period, it wasn't until the temperatures began to rise that settled ways of life developed. Within a few thousand years of the start of this interglacial, the first human civilizations began to flourish in the more hospitable environment.*

SUMMARY

There have probably been five major ice ages in Earth's history, with ice sometimes enshrouding the whole globe. They are caused by a complex web of factors including the Sun's energy output, Earth's distance from the Sun, and tectonic movement.

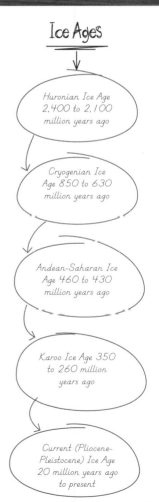

Ice Ages

Huronian Ice Age 2,400 to 2,100 million years ago

Cryogenian Ice Age 850 to 630 million years ago

Andean-Saharan Ice Age 460 to 430 million years ago

Karoo Ice Age 350 to 260 million years ago

Current (Pliocene-Pleistocene) Ice Age 20 million years ago to present

What *Is a Continent?*

The answer to the question "What is a continent?" may seem obvious. A continent is a landmass so large that you can go a long way without falling off the edge. We commonly speak of the seven continents—North and South America, Africa, Antarctica, Australia, Asia, and Europe—and we think of them as permanent and stationary. But what if there haven't always been seven? What if they can join together, change shape, move apart, and migrate around the globe? What then is a continent?

As we shall see (pp. 18–19), Alfred Wegener and others believed that the continents moved but couldn't work out how they plowed through the ocean floor. The solution was provided by research that began in the 1950s and showed that they don't move across the ocean floor—they move *with* the ocean floor. The only thing wrong with Wegener's theory of continental drift was that it's not just the continents that are drifting. Everything is on the move. The ground beneath our feet is just a thin crust floating on a semisolid layer of mantle, called the asthenosphere, and this crust consists of several sections that move independently. These are now known as tectonic plates (from the Greek word for "builder"), and some of the plates include much thicker areas of crust. These are what we know as continents.

FACT: *Geologists have shown that all the landmasses were indeed once joined together in the single supercontinent that Wegener called Pangaea, but it wasn't the first time this had happened. It is thought that Earth's continents also came together a billion years ago, breaking apart 400 million years later, and then reassembling to form Pangaea about 250 million years ago.*

Earth's TECTONIC PLATES

Unlike Earth's continents, there is no definite answer to the question, "How many tectonic plates are there on Earth?" The diagram below shows seventeen of the largest plates, and the directions in which they are moving.

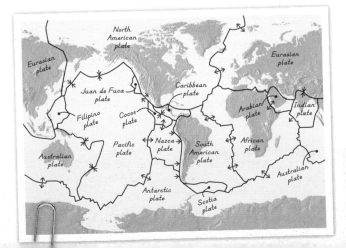

FACT: *The idea that the continents move because of convection currents in the mantle was put forward by the British geologist Arthur Holmes in 1944, and it was an important step in developing the theory of plate tectonics.*

Divergent Boundary As two tectonic plates move apart, liquid magma rises up through the gap that opens between them, creating new crust.

So Why Do They Move?

These discoveries came initially from studies of the ocean floor that showed that ridges of new rock are being formed on the seabed in mid-ocean. By the 1960s it was accepted that these underwater ridges, which can be more than 2 miles (3 km) high and 1,200 miles (1,930 km) wide, occur at the boundaries between the plates. The new rock is being formed from molten material welling up at the joints as the plates themselves move apart as the result of convection currents in the semimolten layer beneath. The lines at which plates are moving apart are known as divergent or constructive boundaries.

Convergent Subductive Boundary At a subduction zone, one plate slides down beneath the edge of the other. As it is pushed down, the rock melts.

Where Do They Go?

The next question is that if new crust is being created, where can the old crust move to? At first it was thought that the planet might be getting larger, but it is now known that where an oceanic plate pushes against another oceanic plate or a continent, one slides down beneath the other, forcing the oceanic crust down into the asthenosphere and causing it to become molten again. This form of "convergent" boundary is called a subduction zone, and it creates a deep oceanic trench. Convergent boundaries also occur where continental plates are colliding, and here the forces cause the land to buckle and rise. This is happening in northern India, for example, where the Indo-Australian and Eurasian plates are colliding, resulting in the formation of the Himalayan mountain range, which is still rising. A third kind of boundary—a transformational boundary—occurs where two plates are sliding against each other. It is at the edges of the tectonic plates that most of Earth's spectacular geological events, such as earthquakes (see pp. 216–217) and volcanic eruptions (see pp. 20–21), take place.

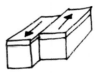

Convergent Collision Boundary Where two continental plates collide, the edges of the plates are pushed upward, buckling and folding to create mountain ranges.

Transformational Boundary Where two plates are moving horizontally past each other, crust is neither created nor destroyed, but the friction can cause stresses to build up.

SUMMARY

Continents are the thickest parts of the tectonic plates that make up Earth's crust. These plates are floating on the semi-molten rock of the mantle, and over geological time they move relative to each other.

Who Was Alfred Wegener?

The last picture taken of Alfred Wegener before his fateful trip to Greenland.

If you have never heard of Alfred L. Wegener, then you're missing a key piece in the jigsaw of our understanding of the planet. He came up with a vital theory of how the world came to be the way it is today and, most important, he did so by bringing together evidence from many different branches of science. His "interdisciplinary" thinking helped shape the way that research is conducted today.

Alfred Lothar Wegener was born in Berlin, Germany, in 1880, the fifth child of theologist and classical linguist Richard Wegener. He went to university in Berlin and earned a PhD in astronomy. Working as an astronomer at Berlin's public observatory, he became interested in the atmosphere, and then in weather and climate, which led him to join a research expedition to Greenland in 1906. There he tested his theories about meteorology and geophysics and developed the use of balloons to track Arctic air currents. He made a second expedition to Greenland in 1912 while a tutor at the University of Marburg, Germany.

After World War I, in which he was wounded, Wegener returned to Marburg before accepting, in 1924, a professorship in meteorology and geophysics at the University of Graz, in Austria. Throughout this time Wegener was constantly making connections between all the disciplines that he studied—geography, geology, meteorology, polar exploration, paleontology—and this is what gave his research its strength.

QUOTE:

"Does not the east coast of South America exactly fit the west coast of Africa, as if they were once connected?" Alfred L. Wegener, in a letter to his future wife, December 1910

FACT: The Alfred Wegener Institute for Polar and Marine Research was founded in Germany in 1980 in memory of the great Arctic explorer and scientist. Its mission is to conduct research into ocean-ice-atmosphere interactions, animal and plant life in the Arctic and Antarctic, and the evolution of the polar continents and seas. Global climate change is a central focus of the research.

QUOTE:

"Scientists still do not appear to understand sufficiently that all Earth sciences must contribute evidence toward unveiling the state of our planet in earlier times..." Alfred L. Wegener, The Origin of Continents and Oceans, 1929

FACT: *Wegener made his last expedition to Greenland in 1930, where he set up permanent research stations. Concerned for the safety of two of his team at the station in the middle of the ice cap, he and two companions made a hazardous journey to bring them supplies. He celebrated his fiftieth birthday there before setting off on the return trip with Rasmus Villumsen, a 22-year-old Greenlander. They didn't make it. Wegener's body was discovered in the snow the following spring, and Villumsen was never found.*

Continental Drift

Early in his career, Wegener became convinced that Africa and South America had once been part of a single landmass. The idea wasn't new—many people had noticed the similarity between the coastlines of the two continents—but Wegener brought together many different kinds of evidence. It was known from fossil evidence that many identical organisms had existed on both continents, but others explained this by suggesting the past existence of land bridges. By comparing the rock formations in South Africa and Brazil he showed that these, too, matched exactly, and that there were matches between other landmasses, such as the Scottish Highlands and the Appalachian mountains of eastern North America. He also discovered fossils of plants in the Arctic that could only have grown much closer to the equator, lending support to his idea that the continents had moved. In 1915 he published his findings in *The Origin of Continents and Oceans*, claiming that about 300 million years ago the continents had all been joined in a supercontinent that he called Pangaea (from the Greek meaning "all Earth"). He proposed that the landmass then broke up and the parts had been moving apart ever since. He was convinced that this process was responsible for creating mountain ranges, volcanoes, and earthquakes.

*

Wegener proposed, quite correctly, that all the landmasses had once been part of a "supercontinent" and had since moved apart.

But How?

There was just one flaw in Wegener's argument—he couldn't explain how huge landmasses could move across the surface of the planet. He and his supporters postulated Earth's rotation and the Moon's tidal pull; but these forces are not strong enough to send continents plowing through the solid rock that was thought to make up Earth's crust. Wegener's theory met opposition and even ridicule; by the time of his death in 1930 it had largely been put aside by the scientific community. It took another thirty years before the actual process that causes the continents to move was discovered, and Wegener's theory of continental drift was proved correct.

SUMMARY

Alfred L. Wegener (1880–1930) was a German astronomer, geologist, meteorologist, and Arctic explorer who proposed that Earth's landmasses were once all joined together. He provided strong evidence for this, drawn from many different branches of science, but his theory was rejected at the time because no one could explain how the landmasses could move.

Where Is Krakatoa?

Krakatoa is one of the world's most infamous volcanoes. In August 1883, it erupted with such force that the sound was heard almost 3,000 miles (4,800 km) away. The explosion blasted some 5 cubic miles (21 cubic km) of rock and ash into the air, demolished two-thirds of the island, and created devastating tsunamis that killed more than 36,000 people. This monster lies in the Indian Ocean, between the Indonesian islands of Sumatra and Java, but why here exactly?

The eruption of Krakatoa in 1883 reduced the conical peak, well known to sailors, to little more than a pile of rubble.

There are many different kinds of volcano, but they all occur where a hole or split in Earth's crust allows molten rock (called magma when it is below the crust, and lava when it is above), ash, and gases to escape from the mantle below. The extruded material can then build up to create a conical mountain or a broad, shieldlike formation. Volcanic activity usually happens at the boundary between two tectonic plates. Where the plates are moving apart, such as at the rift in a mid-ocean ridge, the magma wells up through the gap and the event is rarely dramatic; but in a subduction zone, where one plate is sliding down beneath another and being melted by the intense heat below, volcanoes can be violent. Volcanoes here form as a result of ruptures in the edge of the upper plate, and when the molten rock escapes, it can do so under enormous pressure, releasing a huge amount of energy. The explosion at Krakatoa, for example, was more than 10,000 times more powerful than the nuclear bomb that destroyed Hiroshima, Japan.

Why Is It Here?

Indonesia has some 130 active volcanoes—more than any other country—and this is because it lies on a subduction zone at the boundary between two tectonic plates, where the Indo-Australian plate is being pushed down beneath the Eurasian plate. In a satellite image, we can see the dark line where one dips below the other, forming what is known as the Sunda, or sometimes Java, Trench. The Indonesian islands and their volcanoes form a parallel arc to the north of the trench.

FACT: Some volcanoes form far from the edges of tectonic plates, at "hotspots" where plumes of exceptionally hot mantle force their way through the crust. These mantle plumes appear to remain in the same position while the tectonic plates move over them, and this can lead to the formation of a line of volcanoes. It is thought that the Hawaiian island chain was formed in this way.

FACT: The word "volcano" comes from Vulcan, the Roman god of fire. Romans believed Mount Etna, on the east coast of Sicily, was Vulcan's forge. At more than 2 miles (3 km) high, it is Europe's largest active volcano, and one of the most active in the world, being in a state of almost continual eruption.

FACT: *If you were watching movies in the late 1960s, you might remember* **Krakatoa: East of Java**, *which revolves around the dramatic eruption. Don't use the film's title to find your way to the volcano, however. Krakatoa is actually west of Java. The active volcano to the east of Java is Mount Tambora, which in 1815 produced the largest eruption in recorded history and had such an impact on global weather that it caused the northern hemisphere's worst famine of the nineteenth century.*

The Ring of Fire

The Sunda Trench is an extension of a belt of intense volcanic and seismic activity around the Pacific Ocean, known as the Ring of Fire. The Pacific plate is being pushed westward, and this has created several convergent boundaries that produce volcanic activity (shown in red on the map).

In the east, the movements of the smaller Nazca and Cocos plates have created volcanoes in Chile and Central America. In the northeast, the Aleutian Islands, which run in an arc to the west of Alaska, are mainly volcanic in origin, and volcanoes are found from Kamchatka in the northwest of the Pacific down through Japan and the Philippines all the way south to New Zealand.

The Ring of Fire

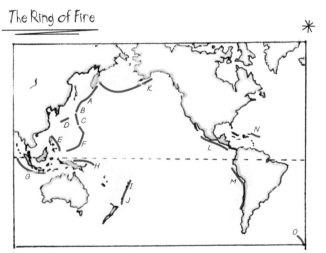

The Pacific plate and the smaller tectonic plates around it are all on the move, producing regions of intense geological activity where volcanoes and earthquakes occur.

A —Kurile trench
B —Japan trench
C —Izu Bonin trench
D —Ryukyu trench
E —Philippine trench
F —Marianas trench
G —Java (Sunda) trench
H —Bougainville trench
I —Tonga trench
J —Kermadec trench
K —Aleutian trench
L —Middle American trench
M —Peru–Chile trench
N —Puerto Rico trench
O —South Sandwich trench

SUMMARY Krakatoa was a large volcano in Indonesia—although it's been much smaller since 1883, when it blew itself to bits in one of the largest explosions on record. Volcanoes are formed when molten rock, or magma, is forced up through Earth's crust. This usually occurs when two tectonic plates come together and one is forced down beneath the other, causing fissures in the upper plate through which the magma can erupt. This is what is happening in the Sunda Trench.

Where Is the Cradle of Civilization?

Very early human history is difficult for historians to present with any degree of certainty. Our very earliest ancestors seem to have sprung from Africa, moving as small migrant bands in stages better measured in generations than miles. These bands were nomadic in character, a lifestyle best able to adapt to changing climates and topographies. By the time when distinct civilizations can be discerned, the human race had migrated across much of the globe. This has prompted a vigorous debate about the extent to which we can truly identify a single cradle of civilization.

The transition from nomadic to settled culture was a gradual one. In order to sustain a successful settled culture, one giving rise to a sustainable civilization, certain conditions had to exist. Essentially, these can be narrowed to three aspects: soils and wild plants suitable for agriculture; a mild and predictable climate; and an accessible supply of water. This combination of factors allowed the development of agriculture, eliminating the need to move from place to place in search of food sources.

Farm Foundations

The conditions for successful agriculture alone are not sufficient for a civilization to emerge. Successful agriculture produces a regular surplus, which in turn allows a proportion of the community to exist without being engaged in food production. The surplus also encourages trade: seeking profit from the surplus, or using it as an opportunity to exchange one commodity for other goods. With this development, a whole series of corresponding aspects began to emerge. A community that had groups engaged in different tasks began to establish a social order. Groups established a hierarchy, with one group considering itself to be superior to another. This hierarchy in early human civilizations often had three prominent groups: a warrior class, a religious class, and a trading class. The clarity of distinction between these groups and their relative importance varied from society to society, but all can be observed in early civilizations.

FACT: Mesopotamia translates as "the land between the rivers," referring to lands bordering the Tigris and Euphrates Rivers. This river system is located in a region that includes modern-day Iraq, as well as parts of Turkey, Iran, and Syria.

Among the first domesticated crops were the three cereals: emmer, einkorn, and barley.

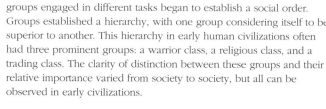

SUMMARY

The usual answer—and the one you may have been given in school—is that the Fertile Crescent was the cradle of civilization. A different view is that there were multiple cradles, as similar stages of development occurred on a global basis. The other main contenders are the river valleys of Mesoamerica, the Indus River valley in modern-day Pakistan, and the similarly suitable landscape of the Yellow River in China.

Fertile Beginnings

The location that holds the strongest traditional claim to being the cradle of civilization is the area sometimes known as the Fertile Crescent. The Fertile Crescent is a region centered on the Tigris and Euphrates Rivers. It was here, in around 3500 B.C.E., that the first Mesopotamian civilizations were born. These civilizations established a social order based on urban communities that were able to exist because of the surplus created by the surrounding agricultural communities. In the towns and cities, different early industrial processes were invented, in particular the manufacture of pottery and metal artifacts. The urban areas were also the first repositories of written communication, giving rise to another form of social distinction: those who were literate and those who were illiterate.

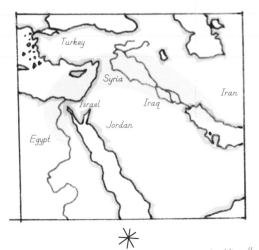

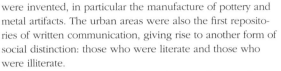

The Fertile Crescent is traditionally held to be the cradle of civilization. Located in the ancient Middle East, it incorporated the region between the Rivers Tigris and Euphrates.

The Sumerians were the first civilization of the Fertile Crescent. Agricultural villages that had existed for a considerable period began to coalesce as an increasingly complex network of irrigation canals demanded ever-greater levels of communication and cooperation. The success of this effort allowed urban areas to expand, the sure sign of a civilization. This success brought significant benefits and problems. The Fertile Crescent has a largely flat topography, which is wonderful for agriculture—and for invading armies. Successful nomadic cultures found great appeal in the treasures and delights of sedentary civilizations. Invaders destroyed, and then created, as they came to recognize the benefits of sustaining the civilizations that produced wealth and comfort. Perhaps reflecting the insecurity of their position, the Sumerians are known to have built complex and elaborately decorated temples presided over by a range of grim and forbidding gods.

From the Fertile Crescent, the hallmarks of civilization spread outward to other similarly favored areas, such as the Nile Valley. The Mesopotamian and Egyptian civilizations developed in distinctly different ways, but both were sufficiently successful to be sustainable in their own right and able to stimulate offshoot civilizations in the southern Mediterranean, eastern Africa, and along the Indus River.

FACT: *Mesopotamia is believed to be the birthplace of both the wheel (in the fifth millennium B.C.E.) and writing (in the fourth millennium B.C.E.), changing the course of human development.*

When Was Writing Developed?

Does writing have divine origins? It would certainly seem that it was believed by ancient societies, scattered in diverse locations across the globe, to be a gift of the gods. This belief tells us a great deal about the potency of the written word and the significance invested in it from the earliest era of human civilization. Unfortunately, it does not provide us with a date for the origin of writing. For that we need to turn to archeological evidence.

Dating the origin of written communication depends upon establishing a definition of writing. As far back as the seventh millennium B.C.E., in the early Neolithic period, there is evidence for the emergence of systems for recording data. Utilizing the resources present in the environment, the earliest writing surfaces were probably tanned animal hide, wooden tablets, or clay tokens. The strongest evidence favors clay tokens, but that may simply be because clay has proved to be more durable in resisting the erosion of time.

In order to accept this as the point at which writing was developed, we have to accept the broadest definition of writing as a symbolic recording of information. Rows of carefully aligned symbols have been discovered that date back as far as the fifth millennium B.C.E. The care and organization of the symbols certainly provides an impression of a form of text, but any translation is largely guesswork, and it could be argued that these symbols lack the coherence and continuity to justify the term "writing." In other words, they can be defined as essentially mnemonic or ideographic systems with a specific use and context.

SUMMARY

We can be sure that writing was developed in different forms across the globe, each time in response to the demands of trade, faith, and government in the earliest civilizations. The earliest origin is uncertain and difficult to define, but Mesopotamia in the fourth millennium B.C.E. is probably near the mark.

QUOTE:

"He who controls the present, controls the past. He who controls the past, controls the future."
George Orwell (1903–1950), author and essayist

FACT: *In ancient Egypt, Thoth was worshipped as the creator of writing, through the power to convert speech into a material object.*

* Thoth

Sumerian Tablet
(c. 2,600 B.C.E.)

The First Writing System

If we reject the earliest occurrences of symbol systems and instead define writing as a cultural tool, acknowledged and valued across a society, then the date of origin shifts to the late fourth millennium B.C.E. The early Mesopotamian civilizations can probably claim the distinction of developing the first form of writing. In virtually every case, the society attributed the origin of writing to a deity. This similarity indicates that there was no single point of inspiration but that writing was the product of a long developmental process.

FACT: *The Sumerians believed that writing was the creation of the god Enlil, whereas the Assyrians and Babylonians believed that the god Nabu was the scribe of the gods, recording their deeds and judgments, and that writing was his invention.*

The evolution of writing may have been driven by the needs of commerce. Sumerian clay tokens discovered in the city of Uruk have been interpreted as being concerned with the goods manufactured in, or for, the temple. Clay tokens may also have been employed to record harvest quantities, the number of animals in a flock, or the amount due in taxation. In all of these cases, a recognizable and agreed symbolism would have been invaluable, but this does not necessarily equate to writing as we understand it.

The supposed mythological origins of writing also show us that writing, in its earliest form, was associated with religious and political authority. To record and categorize knowledge was to possess power. Writing extends memory; it creates history. The writers of history are as much definers of the present and future as they are recorders of the past. For an agriculturalist or trader, counting systems may have been of much greater significance than writing, but to a political or religious elite writing offers power and influence.

Pictographic Alphabets

Hieroglyphics also emerged in the same period as proto-cuneiform ("wedge shaped," from the Latin *cuneus*, meaning "wedge") systems. The most famous are those of the ancient Egyptians. This pictorial system of recording was also developed in Mesoamerican societies, and picture-writing was employed by many indigenous societies until contact and conquest by Europeans.

A form of pictographic writing is also evident in the earliest forms of Chinese script, developed in the second millennium B.C.E. These were often etched onto animal bones or turtle shells. They became increasingly abstract and stylized. Indeed, the Chinese developed a standardized and widely employed form of writing that has retained a high degree of consistency across the millennia. Many of the characters used in the Lishu script in the first millennium B.C.E. are identical to characters employed in the modern Chinese language.

The ancient Egyptian hieroglyphs for "fig."

Why Did Socrates Poison Himself?

There are two short, contradictory answers to this question. The first has it that Socrates was a scruffy old Greek of limited personal charm who got caught out by his own arrogance. The second proposes that he was one of the foremost philosophers of the ancient world, and was prepared to sacrifice his life on a point of principle.

In either case, certain facts are clear. In 399 B.C.E., Socrates was sentenced to death by a jury of his Athenian peers. He was escorted to a nearby prison, where the sentence was to be carried out. There, in accordance with Athenian law, he drank the "state poison," commonly held to mean hemlock, and walked about his cell until his legs became numb. By that stage, the poison had taken hold and death was inevitable. He is believed to have been seventy years old at his demise.

The Socratic Method

The trial of Socrates had been brought about because of the accusations of three other Athenian citizens. They accused Socrates of "refusing to recognize the gods recognized by the state" and of "corrupting the youth" of the city. These accusations stemmed from the philosophy of Socrates and from the actions of some of his students.

* SOCRATES accused of "corrupting the youth of the city"

QUOTE:

"Crito, we owe a cock to Asclepius. Please, don't forget to pay the debt." The final words of Socrates (c. 469–399 B.C.E.)

Hemlock *

FACT: Hemlock (**Conium maculatum**) is a member of the same family as parsley. It is possible that it was employed in executions because it leaves the victim lucid almost until the point of death.

The philosophy of Socrates is known to us chiefly through the works of his most famous student, Plato. Plato constructed a series of "dialogues" in which Socrates exemplified a style of teaching that has become known as the Socratic method. This is a form of inquiry that employs a sequence of questions, not so much to elicit individual responses as to arrive at a point of fundamental insight. It can be taxing for the questioner and very wearing for the person being questioned, as trite or commonplace defenses are stripped away layer by layer. Naturally, such a method did not make Socrates universally popular. In a relatively small community, where Socrates would stand accused before his peers, such a practice, although perhaps admirable, was highly dangerous, as his trial was to demonstrate.

Trial and Sentence

Socrates was skeptical at best about the value of democracy. Athens at the time was a powerful city-state in which a form of democracy, available to adult male citizens, was highly cherished. This made Socrates a figure of suspicion for some in the city. It made it easy for his accusers in court to link him with the actions of two of his students, who had briefly overthrown the democratic government of the city.

FACT: The size of the jury made debate among the jurors impossible. In accordance with prevailing legal practice the jurors simply registered their judgment by placing a token marked "guilty" or "not guilty" in an urn.

A jury of 500 citizens was formed. It heard each of the accusers for one hour and then, to balance the case, Socrates was allotted three hours in his defense. At the end of the trial, the jury decided by a slim majority—280 to 220—that Socrates was guilty; though his margin of defeat offered some hope for a lenient sentence.

Socrates' accusers spoke in favor of the death penalty, but he had the right to suggest his own punishment. Perhaps foolishly, he did not propose the severe but life-preserving option of exile. Instead, he first of all suggested that he should be rewarded for his actions, and then changed the proposal to one of a modest fine. The jury was clearly unimpressed and determined that death was the appropriate outcome.

This final drama in the life of Socrates was recorded by Plato. Although he was not present, Plato employed the evidence of witnesses to recreate the scene through the narrative voice of a fictional character, Phaedo. The text evokes the strong emotions of Socrates' followers as the sentence was carried to its conclusion. It helped to seal the almost mythic status of Socrates who, like many public figures who have followed him, was perhaps more universally revered in death than in life.

SUMMARY

Charged with "refusing to recognize the gods recognized by the state" and of "corrupting the youth" of Athens, the philosopher Socrates was found guilty by a jury of his fellow citizens. His conduct during his trial, whether born of principle or arrogance, enraged the jurors, who imposed the death penalty through the traditional means of the "state poison."

What *Happened to the Romans?*

They came, they saw, they conquered—and then they fell. That, in short, is the history of the Romans. The role of Julius Caesar, the growth of the Roman world as it moved from republic to nominal republic to fully fledged empire, these are all well known. Shakespeare, historical novels, and television miniseries have made the delicious, corrupt, and bloody height of Rome famous. What happened after that is less highly valued and is often skipped over in school.

At its height it spanned the Mediterranean basin, thrusting its border to the edges of the Scottish Highlands, along the rivers Rhine and Danube, and up against the hostile and dangerous empires of the East. However, historians are divided about the causes of the fall of the Roman Empire.

The Roman forum (Forum Romanum) was a complex of temples, triumphal monuments, and political buildings that lay at the heart of Rome and the Roman world.

Killer Blows

One school of thought argues that the Roman Empire collapsed as a consequence of three killer blows struck in the space of under seventy years. In 395 C.E., Honorius and Arcadius, the sons of the emperor Theodosius, divided the empire in two. In doing so they drastically cut the potential of the empire to meet the multitude of difficulties that faced it. Trade was hampered, revenues from taxation declined, and, most important, the pool of men from which the military could draw was cut. The second blow came in 429, when the Vandals began a ten-year invasion of North Africa. Since the days of the republic, North Africa had been of great strategic importance to the Romans. Egypt in particular was considered the Roman world's "breadbasket," especially important for keeping the population of Rome fed on cheap bread and compliant to the will of its rulers. Finally, in 461, the emperor Majorian was murdered. He had been preparing for the reconquest of North Africa. His untimely death and the subsequent disputes regarding the succession led to any sense of unity being lost forever.

*FACT: Perhaps the most famous account of the collapse is **The Decline and Fall of the Roman Empire**, by the English historian Edward Gibbon. Published in 1776 and running to six volumes, it was regarded by many British people as a chilling portent of the potential future for their own empire.*

A seventeenth-century work by Anthony van Dyck, showing Saint Ambrose, the bishop of Milan, in conflict with Emperor Theodosius I, the last ruler of a unified Roman Empire.

FACT: *The most famous example of the Roman Empire's shift to a defensive stance is Hadrian's Wall, which sits near the border between modern-day England and Scotland. Built in 122 C.E., it was 12–15 feet (3.5–4.5 m) high and ran for 80 miles (130 km), operating as the border crossing for some 300 years.*

The Long View

The second school of thought takes a much longer view and argues that what happened to the Romans was an extended period of decline inherent in its initial growth. This perspective gives more emphasis to structural causes than to the individual hammer blows of fate. Indeed, some historians supporting this idea point out that the Roman army remained formidable and often victorious in battle almost to the very end.

The success of the Roman Empire was founded on the wealth provided by aggressive conquest. A successful military was essential to a vibrant empire, but it also contained the seeds of its destruction. The legions that poured the spoils of war to the heart of the empire were fundamentally loyal to their commanders. The emperor and people of Rome may have been the rallying cry, but it was the great generals who held the purse strings and employed the legions in their own vicious political struggles. Thus the Roman Empire lived with the terrible tension of both needing and fearing the legions.

As the empire reached what appeared to be its natural physical limit, the policy of the emperors shifted from expanding the borders to securing them. The legions became increasingly defensive in posture. Along the borders the legionnaires settled, becoming soldier-farmers. In the heart of the empire, wealthy landowners and merchants resisted the old concept of the political elite serving its time in the army as an act of service. They also resisted the drain of manpower and encouraged the absorption of barbarians into the military instead. This process of assimilation added an ethnic dimension to the long history of legion fighting legion to further the ambitions of the generals. In 406, the Suevi, Alans, and Vandals crossed the Rhine to be followed by others, with the Ostrogoths finally settling in Italy toward the end of the fifth century.

FACT:

The eastern (Byzantine) Roman Empire flourished and then sustained itself until 1453, when Constantinople fell to the army of the Ottoman Turks.

SUMMARY

Whichever perspective one favors, the outcome is the same. The Roman Empire in the West was at an end by the start of the sixth century. At least, the military and political entity that we call the Romans was at an end; the intellectual, literary, religious, and legal legacy of the Romans survived and thrives to the present day. Go to the centers of government and admire the architecture, much of it inspired by the Romans. Consider the notions of empire, democracy, constitutional law, and language and you will quickly identify the heritage of Rome. What happened to the Romans? Nothing. They are still here.

Hadrian's Wall

Who Invented Gunpowder?

The constituent ingredients are so commonplace and their combination so trouble-free that it seems amazing that gunpowder was not a much earlier invention. Given the long history of industrial activity in all human societies, the fact that it was invented as recently as the ninth century (and remained unknown in Western Europe for another 500 years) is hard to comprehend. But history is full of surprises, and the method for creating of one of the most deadly inventions in human history perhaps just appears obvious in hindsight.

The identity of the inventor of gunpowder is unknown. Unlike dynamite, we have no name to attach significant global prizes to. It is known that the Chinese were experimenting with some of the constituent elements of gunpowder as early as the first century B.C.E. *The Book of the Kinship of the Three* records experiments in combining sulfur and saltpeter under heat. The alchemist Wei Boyang was part of an imperially funded effort to develop substances capable of extending, hopefully indefinitely, human life. The imperial dynasty had sound political reasons to desire that the emperor attain that most godlike of conditions, eternal life.

Gunpowder retained its link with alchemy when it first appeared in Western Europe. The alchemist, seeking to transmute matter, often in pursuit of gold derived from base metals, was something of a shady character in medieval society, and such activities were sometimes associated with the satanic. As as result, the formulation of an explosive powder capable of great destruction was far from universally welcomed. The Church initially condemned gunpowder and its formulation as a dark art, with all that this implied for those who created and employed it.

It was not until the mid-ninth century C.E., during the reign of the Tang dynasty, that the breakthrough occurred. Whether deliberately or through the action of chance, charcoal was combined with sulfur and saltpeter in proportions that made it combustible. Called *huoyao*, the substance did not find immediate military applications. Instead, it was applied as a topical cure for skin ailments and even used to fumigate properties in order to cleanse them from insect pests. It was noted that the unfortunate effect of this second use was the occasional destruction of the dwellings.

FACT: *The word* **grenade** *comes from the French word for "pomegranate." This is believed to be because of the similarities in appearance.*

SUMMARY

Gunpowder was invented in China in the ninth century C.E. It was soon being used in weapons of war, and its later spread along the Silk Road in the thirteenth century brought this lethal technology to Europe.

For gunpowder to remain effective it had to be kept dry. Powder horns were used to store gunpowder for both personal weapons and artillery.

FACT: *The earliest picture of a gun in use in Western Europe is in a manuscript dating from 1326.*

A Weapon of War

In its military form, gunpowder created two classes of weapons. One was an object that detonated among the enemy, causing casualties principally through shrapnel wounds. These grenades were invented early in the military exploitation of gunpowder. The difficulties of manufacturing a reliable casing and projecting the grenade toward the enemy limited its development and use until the Industrial Revolution. It also appears that gunpowder as a means of impelling objects led to the creation of rudimentary forms of firearms using bamboo tubes from which arrows were projected.

It is difficult to believe, especially in the early stages of development, that gunpowder-based weapons were capable of making a decisive difference. Imperial China certainly had a strong incentive to develop the weapons. The wealth and prestige of China made it a tempting target for the Mongols. Subjected to constant incursions and regular waves of invasion, any weapon that offered an advantage would have been an attractive proposition. It may be that gunpowder weapons did not kill any more effectively than archers, but the psychological impact of the detonations may have been telling, both in undermining the morale of Mongol warriors and in boosting that of the Chinese. The sense of technological superiority may have been reassuring to men facing a surging Mongol horde.

FACT: *The Swedish scientist Alfred Nobel patented the nitroglycerine-based explosive dynamite in 1867. He later devoted his estate to founding a series of prestigious awards for new discoveries: the famous Nobel Prizes.*

The Move West

As a tightly organized and centralized society, the Chinese empire was able to retain the secret of gunpowder technology for a prolonged period. It was not until the thirteenth century that the invention began to spread along the trade artery of the Silk Road. Within 200 years of that point, it had changed the face of warfare in two dramatic ways. The age of the impregnable castle was brought to a close, undermining the ability of the nobility to assert their authority against the central authority of the monarch. Technological developments increasingly reduced the scale of gunpowder weapons, shifting them into the hands of the individual and thereby confirming the rise of the infantryman as a new class of soldier against whom the traditionally dominant knight was impotent.

<u>When</u> Was the Abacus Invented?

When you think of an abacus, you probably picture a simple calculating device, possibly a child's toy with rows of brightly colored sliding beads that is more for fun than practical use, but the abacus dates back several millennia and has taken many different forms through the ages and around the globe. It was vital to mathematical calculation and, what's more, it is still very much in use today.

There is evidence, in the form of an inscribed baboon bone found in the Congo, in West Africa, that humans had developed the ability to count, and possibly even carry out multiplication, some 20,000 years ago. The Sumerians and the Babylonians had a thorough grasp of all the basics of arithmetic—addition, subtraction, multiplication, and division—more than 4,000 years ago, and they used a simple set of columns to add and subtract, but not for more complicated operations.

The abacus developed from simple columns drawn in the sand, along which pebbles were moved (the word *abacus* may be linked to the Hebrew *abaq*, meaning dust), to being a grooved board with counters, and its use spread from Persia to the northern Mediterranean after the sixth century B.C.E. The Greeks made counting tables with counters running in slots on the surface, and the Romans adapted this to their number system. It is mainly from the Roman abacus that this tool developed into the counting table used in Europe. At the same time, it became an essential means of calculation in China and Japan, replacing a method of using counting rods. Here the abacus was normally made of a bamboo frame with a horizontal beam and vertical rods on which sliding beads were set. This remains the design we are most familiar with.

HEAVEN:
each worth 5

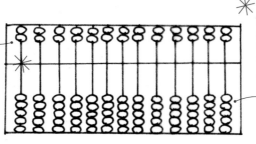

* The Chinese abacus has two beads in the top and five in the bottom on each row. The second bead in the top row is used to work in base 16, or a hexadecimal system, as we do when using pounds and ounces.

EARTH:
each worth 1

FACT: The Sumerian and Babylonian mathematical systems weren't based on the number ten, as ours is, but on the number sixty, which is why our minutes, hours, and the number of degrees in a circle are all divisible by sixty. The fact that the number sixty is divisible by many different numbers enabled them to make rapid progress in the science of mathematics.

FACT: *The Roman numeral system has a small set of symbols representing certain numbers. These are I (one), V (five), X (ten), L (fifty), C (one hundred), D (five hundred), and M (one thousand). A number is written down by breaking it up into these units and stringing the symbols together in descending order from left to right. It is read by adding them up. If a smaller number is placed to the left of a larger one, that means it is subtracted from the larger number. So DLVI means 500 + 50 + 5 + 1 = 556. DLIV is 554, because the I is subtracted from the V.*

Positional Value

Why was the abacus so popular for calculations? Why didn't people simply do their sums on paper? The answer is that many early numeral systems simply couldn't be used in that way because they didn't use what is called "positional notation." In the system we use today, if you see a three-figure digit written down you know that the right-hand digit refers to units (or ones), the middle one refers to tens, and the left refers to hundreds. You know this from their positions.

However, the Roman numeral system doesn't work like this. It's fine for writing down the answer, but it can't be used for carrying out arithmetic operations. The abacus, which does represent numbers in a positional numeral system, was needed to make calculations, and so it was used throughout Europe until the Roman numeral system was finally abandoned in the sixteenth century.

The Abacus Today

An experienced user can carry out a wide range of mathematical calculations very rapidly using an abacus, and for this reason it is still widely used by shopkeepers throughout China (where it is called a *suanpan*) and Japan (where it is called a *soroban*) and in Asian districts in the West. It was also commonly used until the 1990s throughout Russia, where it has now been replaced by electronic calculators. In the West it is still sometimes used to teach young children the basics of addition.

SUMMARY

The abacus, a device for carrying out mathematical calculations, has its origins in the Middle East in about 2000 B.C.E. Its use was developed by the Chinese, Japanese, Greeks, and Romans. It was widely used in Europe throughout the Middle Ages, and is still frequently employed in Japan and China, where its use is still taught in schools.

What *Is a Prime Number?*

If you think a number is a number is a number, you'll be surprised to learn that there are many different kinds. The basic set of numbers is the natural, or counting, numbers—the ones you'd use to count sheep, starting with one and continuing to infinity—but there are many other sets and subsets. The prime numbers are one of the subsets.

A prime number is a natural number that can be divided only by two other natural numbers—one and itself. In other words, it has just two "divisors." (The number one is not a prime number.) Examples of prime numbers are 3, 5, 7, 11, 13, 17, 19, 23, 29, 31.

The ancient Greeks, from Pythagoras (see pp. 84–85) onward, were keenly interested in the properties of numbers, believing them to offer the key to the secrets of the cosmos, and they studied prime numbers extensively. In the third century B.C.E., the Greek mathematician Euclid proved that there are infinitely many of these prime numbers, and about a century later another Greek devised a method for calculating primes: the "sieve of Eratosthenes."

The Search for Primes

Interest in prime numbers was revived in the seventeenth century, when Pierre de Fermat devised a way of finding the divisors of very large numbers. Fermat also showed that for a number n to be prime, it must be the case that $2n - 2$ is divisible by n; but this doesn't mean that all numbers for which this is true are primes. Indeed, there is no formula for finding all prime numbers. Another mathematician, the French monk Marin Mersenne, studied numbers of the form $2n - 1$, and showed that such numbers cannot be prime unless n is prime. These are known as Mersenne numbers, and he himself thought that any number for which n was greater than 257 would be composite; in other words, not a prime. But he was wrong, and many large primes take this form. These are called Mersenne primes.

Pierre de Fermat (1601–1665)
✳

QUOTE:

"And perhaps, posterity will thank me for having shown it that the ancients did not know everything." *Pierre de Fermat*

SUMMARY

A prime number is a natural number that can be divided only by one and by itself. It has no other divisors. Prime numbers are one example of numbers with strange characteristics that the ancient Greeks believed had magical powers. Primes have fascinated mathematicians through the ages, and continue to do so.

"Mathematicians have tried in vain to this day to discover some order in the sequence of prime numbers, and we have reason to believe that it is a mystery into which the human mind will never penetrate." Leonhard Euler

Computing Power

The computer age has seen a huge acceleration in the discovery of prime numbers. Before computers, the largest known Mersenne prime was thirty-nine digits long. By 2005, this had been increased to almost eight million digits, and the record prime is now $2^{43,112,609} - 1$, which is almost thirteen million digits long! This was discovered in August 2008 by the Great Internet Mersenne Prime Search or GIMPS, a computing project involving mathematicians and interested individuals around the globe. The Electronic Frontier Foundation awarded the finder, Edson Smith, a $100,000 prize for this first ten-million-digit prime.

Other Strange Numbers

The Greeks also investigated what they called "perfect numbers," which they believed had mystical powers. These are numbers whose divisors all add up to the number itself. For example, six is only divisible by one, two, and three, and when you add these together, they total six. Twenty-eight is another perfect number, being divisible by one, two, four, seven, and fourteen.

Taking this a step further, the Greeks also discovered "amicable numbers," pairs in which the divisors of one add up to the other and vice versa. The finders of amicable pairs include some well-known names. The first was Pythagoras, who discovered the pair 220 and 284. The divisors of 220 are 1, 2, 4, 5, 10, 11, 20, 22, 44, 55, and 110, which add up to 284. The divisors of 284 are 1, 2, 4, 71, and 142, which add up to 220. Fermat found the next pair (17,296 and 18,416), although it was probably discovered by the Moroccan mathematician Ibn al-Batta in the thirteenth century. Similarly, the seventeenth-century French philosopher and mathematician Rene Descartes found the pair 9,363,584 and 9,437,056, but it had been discovered a century earlier by the Iranian mathematician Muhammad Baqir Yazdi. The advent of the computer has boosted the number of known amicable pairs from fewer than 400 to several thousand.

FACT: At a time when only three amicable pairs were known, the mathematician Leonhard Euler devised a method for finding them, and in the mid-1700s he found almost 90 more. In 1866, a sixteen-year-old named Niccolò Paganini found an amicable pair that had been skipped by all the masters.

Where Does Zero Come From?

It's hard enough to believe that there is more than one kind of number, but how about more than one kind of zero? Without zero as a "place holder," we wouldn't be able to write down numbers that have units and hundreds but no tens, for example. And without another type of zero there could be no algebra or calculus.

These two uses—zero as a place holder and zero as a number in its own right—are quite distinct. More than 3,000 years ago the Babylonians had a place-value number system, based on sixty rather than ten, and for a thousand years they managed without a zero place holder, but the system relied on the reader working out from the context whether, in our notation, 34 meant 34, 304, or 340. After 400 B.C.E. a variety of zero place holders was used in Babylon, but the Greeks largely managed without, with the exception of their astronomers. Possibly because they used such a wide range of numbers, and couldn't rely on the context to provide enough clues, they started using 0 as a symbol of zero as a place holder. (It's important to note that in this capacity zero acts almost like punctuation, in the same way that an apostrophe can indicate a missing letter. It is not being used as a number.) The Romans used a numeral system that did not rely on positional notation and didn't adopt the Greek system, so the next chapter in the story of zero picks up in India.

QUOTE:

"When One made love to Zero, spheres embraced their arches and prime numbers caught their breath." **Raymond Queneau**

SUMMARY

The concept of zero as a number with its own properties arose in India, and was first written about in the seventh century by India's foremost mathematician, Brahmagupta (598–670 C.E.). The Indian base-ten system of numerals influenced Arabic scholars, and the Hindu-Arabic number system, which includes zero, is the system that is used today throughout the Western world.

India and Europe

In the seventh century, the Indian place-value system marked an empty place with a dot; this evolved into a circle, but zero also became a number in its own right. The brilliant Indian mathematician Brahmagupta (598–670 C.E.) made advances in astronomy and mathematics, and put forward rules for the use of zero as a number. He stated that the sum of zero and a negative number is negative; the sum of zero and a positive number is positive; and the sum of zero and zero is zero. A negative number subtracted from zero is positive; a positive number subtracted from zero is negative; zero subtracted from a negative number is negative; zero subtracted from a positive number is positive; and zero subtracted from zero is zero. Dividing by zero caused more problems, and it is now accepted that this has no meaning in ordinary arithmetic.

QUOTE:

"To those who ask what the infinitely small quantity in mathematics is, we answer that it is actually zero. Hence there are not so many mysteries hidden in this concept as there are usually believed to be." **Leonhard Euler**

Zero and negative numbers broadened the scope of mathematical calculation enormously, and the Indian advances made their way into both Islamic and Chinese math. The Hindu-Arabic number system, as it has become known, came to Europe via the Islamic world, and thanks largely to the Italian mathematician Fibonacci (see pp. 38–39), it is the base–ten positional system that we have today. It is from the Arabic word *sifr* that we get the word "zero," and the word "cipher" has the same origin.

New Kinds of Numbers

We have already met the natural or "counting" numbers, from one upward. The addition of zero creates a new set—the "whole" numbers, comprising zero, one, two, three, and so on. Indian mathematicians also developed the concept of negative numbers, and these, together with the whole numbers, constitute the set of "integers."

The next set is the set of rational numbers: those that can be expressed as a fraction made up of one integer divided by another (but not by zero!). This means that all integers, whole numbers, and natural numbers are rational (as any of them can be expressed as the integer divided by one). Expressed as a decimal, a rational number either terminates (such as 0.125, which is ⅛) or recurs (such as 0.3333333…, which is ⅓).

Irrational numbers don't include any of the numbers discussed so far. They are numbers that, when expressed as a decimal, do not terminate but do not repeat. The square root of two ($\sqrt{2}$) is an example of an irrational number.

FACT: *The Mayan people of Central America used a numeral system with base twenty (called a vigesimal system), and they used a form of zero as a place holder in the first century B.C.E. The practice may even have originated among the Olmec people several hundred years earlier.*

The Mayans may have used base 20 because it is the total of a person's fingers and toes, which would explain why the number 5 is a unit in its own right.

0   1   2   3   4   5   6   7   8   9

10   11   12   13   14   15   16   17   18   19   20

Who Was Fibonacci?

Leonardo of Pisa, later known as Fibonacci, was born in Italy in about 1170, and modern mathematics owes him a big debt. Undoubtedly an accomplished mathematician in his own right, he changed European mathematics by writing several books that introduced the Hindu-Arabic number system to the West. He is best known for telling the West about the weird and wonderful "Fibonacci numbers," a strange sequence first discovered in ancient India.

FACT: *Fibonacci died in 1250 in Pisa. There is a statue of him in the cemetery near the Leaning Tower of Pisa.*

Leonardo spent much of his early life in North Africa, where his father Guilielmo represented merchants from the Italian city of Pisa in the port of Béjaïa in Algeria. It was here the young boy met the Hindu-Arabic number system. This is the decimal ten-number (0 to 9) system that we use today, but at that time Europe was using the Roman number system. Leonardo soon realized that the Hindu-Arabic system was far better, as it made calculation much easier, and he traveled throughout the region, studying under Arabic mathematicians, before returning to Pisa, where he wrote several important books.

Restarting Mathematics

The most famous of these is *Liber Abaci* (*Book of Calculation*), which he wrote in 1202. In the first part of this book he explained the alternative number system and the way in which it worked using "place value." This simply means that the position of each digit in a number determines its value. As we all know, the right-hand number represents the units (or ones), the next is the tens, the next is the hundreds, and so on. This system made all arithmetic calculations simple to perform, unlike the Roman system that was in use in Europe during the Middle Ages, which only allowed the writing down of numbers. There was resistance to the idea of changing to a completely different number system, but Fibonacci's book was very persuasive (its second part included practical solutions for calculations in the marketplace), and when it was finally accepted it gave a kick-start to Western mathematics, which had ground to a halt.

Leonardo Fibonac (c. 1170-125

FACT: *Leonardo of Pisa was only given the name Fibonacci after his death. His father's nickname was Bonaccio, meaning "good-natured," and his son became known as "son of Bonaccio" or "filius Bonaccio" in Latin. This was abbreviated to Fibonacci.*

Fibonacci Numbers

In the third part of *Liber Abaci*, Leonardo revealed the rule for generating a sequence of numbers that has a strange and almost mystical quality, because this sequence is found to occur in many situations in the natural world. The sequence had been known in India for several hundred years, but it was Fibonacci who presented it to Europeans, and whose name has been given to it.

The rule could hardly be simpler: start with 1, and then add together the last two numbers to get the next. Well, when there's only 1 there's nothing to add to it, so we get 1 again. Add 1 plus 1, and you get 2. Add 1 plus 2 and you get 3. 2 plus 3 gives you 5, and so on. So what?

The sequence actually has some interesting consequences. For example, if you draw a series of squares with their sides corresponding to the numbers, adding the next square to the previous two, and then join up their corners, you get a logarithmically expanding spiral, a form that is found in the shells of creatures such as ammonites or nautiluses.

In the world of plants, many flowers have a number of petals that is in the Fibonacci sequence. Various species of daisy have thirteen, twenty-one, or thirty-four petals. Stranger still, the arrangement of seeds on a pine cone and florets on the head of a sunflower consists of two interlocking spirals rotating in opposite directions, and in each case the number of units in the two spirals is two consecutive Fibonacci numbers. The facets on a pineapple, for instance, form a spiral of eight in one direction and thirteen in the other. It has been suggested that they have evolved this way because, for mathematical reasons, it is the most efficient way of packing as large a number of elements as possible into a small space.

Finally, there's a relationship between the Fibonacci numbers and the "golden ratio." The golden ratio compares the ratio of two lengths. If the ratio of the shorter length to the longer one is the same as the ratio of the longer length to both lengths added together, you have the golden ratio. This ratio (approximately 1:1.6180339887) is roughly the ratio between any two sequential Fibonacci numbers, and the higher you go, the closer the approximation. The Fibonacci spiral is therefore almost a "golden spiral," in which the ratio between the radii of two adjacent quarter turns equals the "golden ratio."

Fibonacci was an Italian mathematician writing in the early thirteenth century. He was instrumental in introducing the Hindu-Arabic number system to Europe, and he also gave his name to a sequence of numbers that is found in nature.

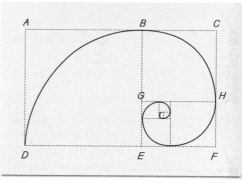

Both the Fibonacci sequence and the elegant form of the Fibonacci spiral, which is based on it, are found to occur naturally in some living organisms, such as in the seed heads of various plants and in some shellfish.

Why Is Pi Also a Number?

There is something about a circle that has drawn mathematicians to investigate its properties since ancient times. It has perfect symmetry, and because every point on the circumference is the same distance from its center, the circle has revolutionized civilization in the form of the wheel. Question: How far would you travel if the wheels on your vehicle had a diameter of one foot and they turned once? Answer: π feet.

Pi, or π, is the sixteenth letter of the Greek alphabet (the first two are alpha and beta, from which we take the word "alphabet"); but in 1707 a Welsh math teacher, William Jones, used it to denote a particular mathematical constant. He chose π because it is the first letter of the Greek word for "perimeter," and the constant is the ratio between the diameter of a circle (the distance across it through the center) and the circumference (the distance around the outside, or the perimeter). If you divide the circumference (let's call it c) of any circle, no matter what its size, by its diameter (d), you get π; i.e. ($\frac{c}{d} = \pi$).

Pi's Numerical Value

That $\frac{c}{d}$ is a constant has been known for almost 4,000 years. The Babylonians and ancient Egyptians knew that the value of this constant was a bit more than three, and mathematicians in India and Ancient Greece developed ever more sophisticated ways of calculating its value. Archimedes (287–212 B.C.E.) worked out the circumference of a circle by calculating the perimeters of a ninety-six-sided figure that enclosed the circle and one that fitted within it, and was able to say that the constant (it became known as Archimedes' constant) had a value between $\frac{223}{71}$ and $\frac{22}{7}$, giving an average of 3.1419.

FACT: *Some people regard memorizing π to an incredible number of decimal places as the ultimate challenge, and the world record has increased in leaps and bounds since the early 1970s, when it stood at 511 decimal places. In 1979, Japanese Hideaki Tomoyori was able to recount π to 40,000 decimal places by associating each group of ten digits with sounds and images that he used to recall the numbers. The current officially recognized record, held by Chinese student Lu Chao, is 67,890 digits, but much higher figures have been claimed.*

SUMMARY

As well as being a Greek letter, π is a mathematical constant defined as the ratio between the circumference and the diameter of a circle. However, π is not a rational number (see p. 37) and can potentially be refined to an infinite number of decimal places.

In the third century C.E., the Chinese mathematician Liu Hui honed it to 3.1416, and 200 years later his fellow countryman Zu Chongzhi refined it to 3.14159265. No one did any better for the next nine centuries.

So why was it proving so difficult to come up with a definitive answer for the ratio between the diameter and the circumference of a circle? The answer: there isn't one!

That's not rational!

One of π's peculiar qualities is that it is an irrational number, which means that it cannot be expressed as a fraction composed of two integers. As we have seen, π is the circumference of a circle divided by its diameter, so in that sense π is a fraction, but if the circumference is a whole number of units in length, then the diameter isn't. If the diameter is, the circumference isn't. It doesn't matter what size circle you use, or what units of length you choose, this is always true. If the diameter is 7, the circumference is about 22, but that's only a crude approximation.

The result of this is that when you express π as a decimal figure, you can go on adding decimal places until you're blue in the face, but you'll never get to the end. What's more, there is no pattern to the numbers. Pi has now been calculated to more than one trillion (that's 1,000,000,000,000) decimal places, and no repeating sequences have been detected.

Pi in Action

For most practical purposes, π to a few decimal places is good enough. It is commonly given as 3.14159, and it's a very useful constant. It relates the radius (which is half the diameter) not only to the circumference of a circle but also to the area of a circle and to the volume of a sphere. The three essential π formulas are:

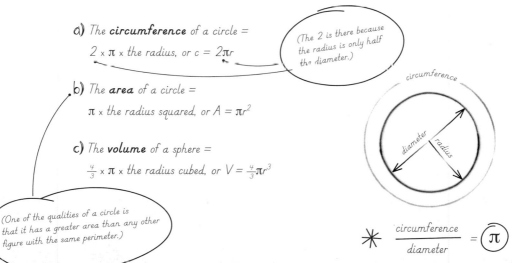

a) The **circumference** of a circle =
    2 × π × the radius, or $c = 2\pi r$

(The 2 is there because the radius is only half the diameter.)

b) The **area** of a circle =
    π × the radius squared, or $A = \pi r^2$

c) The **volume** of a sphere =
    $\frac{4}{3}$ × π × the radius cubed, or $V = \frac{4}{3}\pi r^3$

(One of the qualities of a circle is that it has a greater area than any other figure with the same perimeter.)

circumference

diameter   radius

$*$ $\dfrac{circumference}{diameter} = \pi$

What Is a Monotheistic Religion?

A short definition of monotheism is quite a simple one: it is the belief in a single deity; this is contrasted against polytheism—the belief in many deities. However, when we look more closely we will find that this simple definition has a profound impact on the way that monotheistic religions are practiced.

In polytheistic religions a number of gods are venerated, although there are many variations in their arrangement—for instance, one god may be considered greater than others. The practice of polytheism is often characterized by the petitioning of different deities, depending on the desired outcome; for example, believers may entreat one god to ensure a good harvest but invoke another to cure a sick relative. Monotheistic religions, on the other hand, focus on one god—the locus of all power.

That said, the boundaries between polytheism and monotheism are blurred at times; for example, trinitarianism—the Christian dogma of the threefold Godhead—maintains that God the Father, God the Son, and God the Holy Spirit are but three manifestations of the one supreme being.

New Kingdom, New Religion

It used to be taught that monotheism has its foundation in the first of the world religions that is rooted in the Old Testament: Judaism. However, this may not be the case. Although the records are sketchy, it seems that the first monotheistic religion actually began in ancient Egypt.

In the fourteenth century B.C.E., the pharaoh Akhenaten came to the throne, breaking with the long traditions of polytheism and introducing a monotheistic religion. His reign saw the gradual amalgamation of two gods in the Egyptian pantheon, Re and Amun. The cult of Amun-Re was extremely powerful and politically useful, but it had its dangers. The gods bestowed an immortal authority on earthly princes, but the priesthood also acquired power. It may be, therefore, that Akhenaten and his more famous wife, Nefertiti, were consolidating their political power as much as they were establishing a new religious order.

Akhenaten declared there to be one sole god, represented in the form of a sun disk with radiating shafts of light. In this form, the god Aten was visible to all and existed without rivals. A new city was built, new temples established, and a new priesthood with new rites and rituals formed.

The effort was, however, short-lived. Akhenaten's better-known son, Tutankhamen, was as much a polytheist as his grandfather Amenhotep III had been. The boy-king was revered for reinstating all the old gods, and under him much of his father's legacy was extirpated.

Pharaoh
Akhenaten

FACT: *Ancient Egyptian society recognized more than two thousand gods and goddesses. Many were the patrons of local cults and temples, but four were adopted nationally: Re, Amun, Ptah-Memphis, and Osiris.*

SUMMARY

On one level the definition of monotheism is straightforward: it is the belief in and worship of one god. However, monotheistic practice varies widely, from one religion to the next, and even between denominations. Nevertheless, the statement of belief in a single diety is a key part of montheistic faiths.

The cross is the principal symbol of Christianity, in remembrance of Christ's crucifixion.

The symbol for Judaism is the six-pointed Star of David.

Although its origins remain uncertain, the "star and crescent" is the most widely recognized symbol of Islam.

Abrahamic Faiths

The ancient world of the Middle East later became the cradle for the three monotheistic Abrahamic religions that retain prominence today: Judaism, Christianity, and Islam. The sacred books of these religions all state, in different ways, that there is but one god. For example, the Book of Isaiah—part of both Judaism's Tanakh and Christianity's Old Testament—includes the words "I am the Lord, and there is none else, there is no God beside me"; whereas Islam's Qu'ran instructs: "Say: He is Allah, the One and Only."

The affirmation of belief in a single god is vital to the practice of these faiths—a fact that is often reflected in the recitation of special prayers, such as Christianity's Nicene Creed, which states: "I believe in one God. . . ."

FACT: *Although Hinduism, the world's third-largest religion, has a large pantheon of gods, these are viewed by many Hindus as being different manifestations of one supreme being.*

43

Who Was Abraham?

It is amazing that Abraham is so well known by name yet his significance remains relatively unknown. From dimly remembered lessons at school, Abraham falls somewhere in a list that includes Moses, Adam, Joshua, David, and Jacob and has vague associations with psalms, prophesies, and deserts. Yet Abraham should stand front and center in any list of patriarchs. He did not have a promising start, but by the end of a very long life Abraham had secured his place in scripture.

Abraham is regarded by many as the founding figure of the three dominant monotheistic religions of the world today. His story can be found principally in the book of Genesis, which is common to the Jewish Torah and Christian Old Testament, although it is revisited in other places. The Muslim Koran also has regular references to the revered figure of Abraham. Through Hagar, his wife's servant, Abraham gained a son, Ishmael, who is considered the father of the Arab peoples. At a very advanced age, his wife Sarai (Sarah) gave birth to another son, Yitzhak (Isaac), the ancestor of the Jewish people. Yitzhak apparently means "laughter," which may have been joy or complete surprise for a couple who were a hundred years old and ninety years old, respectively.

***FACT:** Abraham in its Aramaic form means "father of nations."*

Ur, Abraham's birthplace, was located in ancient Sumer, in an area that is now part of modern-day Iraq. It was once a coastal settlement, although it is now inland. It is most famous for the ziggurat (a type of temple) erected to the moon goddess, Nanna.

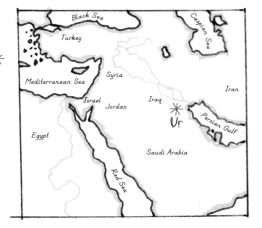

Abraham is at the heart of all three major monotheistic religions. In his offspring and in the concept of faith in one living God, Abraham represents the father of Christianity, Judaism, and Islam. His role and legacy are not without controversy, with his birthright still being hotly disputed by different believers, but his significance makes him a figure we should all be more aware of.

FACT: *The most famous of Abraham's ten tests was the commandment that he should sacrifice his son Isaac to God. Abraham was prevented from following this injunction by the timely intervention of an angel. This was good news for Isaac, but bad news for a nearby ram that was sacrificed in his place.*

The Smasher of Idols

The exact dates for the life of Abraham are uncertain, but he was probably born sometime around the year 1996 B.C.E. His birthplace was the city of Ur in modern-day Iraq. This may help to explain why he is referred to as a Hebrew (or Ivri), which may come from a root word meaning "to cross over," applying to the other side of the River Euphrates and thus to his birthplace. The details of Abraham's early life are more the subject of tradition than certainty. The thriving city of Ur was the site of much trade and many temples. It is told that Abraham's father cashed in on these two features, making a living as a producer and seller of idols.

It is traditionally believed that Abraham developed the idea that there was only one God and that polytheism was in error. He became increasingly uncomfortable with his father's trade and devotion to the gods. The story goes that, in his father's absence, Abraham smashed all of the idols in the shop except the largest. He placed the hammer that had inflicted the damage in the hands of that idol. When his furious father demanded to know the culprit, Abraham is supposed to have blamed the largest idol as the victor in a fight between the gods. Abraham's father, seeking to pin the blame on the real culprit, denied that the idols had any capacity for action, thereby blaming Abraham but also undermining the notion that they were worthy of worship.

The Chosen

As a consequence of the ten tests of faith God imposed on Abraham, he became a nomadic figure, wandering the Middle East. The tests were intended to establish the sincerity of Abraham's devotion, but it was not a one-way street. In accepting the tests of faith, Abraham entered into a contractual relationship with the deity. A covenant was formed that extended to all the Israelites. The notion of God's people—the chosen, the elect—had its origin in that initial relationship between God and Abraham.

FACT: *It is told that God promised Abraham descendants as numerous as the stars in the night sky. When you consider that Islam, Christianity, and Judaism have a combined three billion adherents, it would seem that the promise has been kept.*

When Was the Bible Written?

Ask most people to name the one book that has had the greatest religious, historical, cultural, social, political, and economic impact, and they will say the Bible. You do not have to be Jewish or Christian to acknowledge the role the Bible has played in the development of world culture in the past two millennia. The Bible, however, is not a single text. There are two main versions, Christian and Jewish (known as the Tanakh), each incorporating different books based on historical tradition. This makes determining when the Bible was written a matter of interpretation.

There is no single agreed text, or canon, of the Bible; there are as many versions as there are Jewish and Christian sects and denominations. For members of the Jewish faith, the Bible is known as the Tanakh. For Christian denominations, the Bible consists of the Old Testament (primarily the books of the Tanakh) and the New Testament, though the selection and ordering of the books of the New Testament varies with each denomination.

The Old Testament

The Jewish version of the Bible, the Tanakh, was written over an extended period and is divided into three sections: Teachings, Prophets, and Writings. Most of the Tanakh was written in ancient Hebrew, with several of the later books in ancient Aramaic. Sometime between the second and third centuries B.C.E., the Torah (the first five books of the Tanakh) was translated into Greek, and during the next century further biblical books were translated. This translation became known as the Septuagint and was widely used by Greek-speaking Jews. Between the ninth and the fifteenth centuries C.E., a group of Jewish scholars known as the Masoretes compared all existing Tanakhs in order to write a single standardized version, which is known as the Masoretic text.

FACT: *One of the most influential versions of the Bible was written in the reign of King James I of England and published in 1611.*

The Old Testament is the collection of books that were written before the life of Jesus but that are accepted by Christians as scripture. In general, it follows the Tanakh. However, it divides and orders the books differently, and varies from the Judaic text in interpretation and emphasis. Several Christian denominations incorporate additional books into their canons of the Old Testament. The Greek Septuagint was generally abandoned in favor of the Masoretic Text as the basis for translations of the Old Testament into Western languages from Martin Luther's Protestant Bible to the present day. In Eastern Christianity, however, translations based on the Septuagint still prevail. Some modern

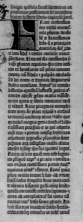

The Gutenberg Bible (an edition of the Vulgate Bible) marks the beginning of the age of the printing press in the mid-1450s.

Western translations make use of the Septuagint to clarify passages in the Masoretic text. A number of books that are part of the Greek Septuagint, but not found in the Tanakh, are accepted by Catholics but rejected by most Protestants as apocryphal.

The New Testament

The New Testament is a collection of twenty-seven books, divided into the four Gospels, the Acts of the Apostles, the Epistles, and the Apocalypse. Over the centuries, different regional versions were written, each with its own unique set of omissions and additions. The three main textual traditions of the Greek New Testament are the Alexandrian, the Byzantine, and the Western. There are also several ancient translations, the most important of which are written in Syriac Aramaic (the Peshitta and the Diatessaron Gospel), in the Ethiopian language of Ge'ez, and in Latin (the Vetus Latina and the Latin Vulgate).

A Work in Progress

The Bible has been written and rewritten many times. Each version has drawn on different preceding authorities, adding to the layers of variation. In the case of the Tanakh, the most significant phase of writing was its translation into common Greek, making the text accessible to a larger number of people in the ancient world. In the case of the Christian Bible, the formal adoption of the Christian faith as the official religion of the Roman Empire led to the writing of the text in a commonly agreed format. Since that time, versions have been produced in every language, even slang versions such as selected passages in London's Cockney rhyming slang.

FACT: In 382 C.E., Pope Damasus I commissioned Saint Jerome to write the definitive Latin version of the Bible. His edition, now know as the Latin Vulgate, remains an important source for modern Catholic translations of the Biblical text.

SUMMARY

There is no single date to which the writing of the Bible can be tied. As a collection of texts it has been written and revised for millennia. There have been attempts to achieve agreed versions, usually at religious or political turning points.

Where Is Mecca?

The location of Mecca can be interpreted in two interrelated ways. The first is the definition of Mecca's location in terms of physical geography. This is important because of the vast numbers of pilgrims who make their way to the city, giving it an economic vibrancy that its location would not otherwise allow. The second is the definition of Mecca's location in terms of religious significance—and it is this second definition that helps to explain why it is the site of holy pilgrimage.

The Physical City

The city of Mecca is the capital of the Hejaz region of Saudi Arabia. It is situated in a narrow valley where the neighboring mountains act as a defining feature to any construction. The current city covers approximately 450 square miles (1,165 square km), and its relative compactness has encouraged many of the structures to be more than three stories high, as space is at something of a premium. This only adds to the sense of a bustling and cosmopolitan city. Mecca is just over 900 feet (275 m) above sea level and nearly 45 miles (72.5 km) from the Red Sea. Water is a problem for two opposing reasons. The city relies on mountain springs to provide the chief source of drinking water, as the rainfall is erratic. However, when it rains, the crowded hills and narrow valley floor make the area prone to flooding, and a network of dams has been constructed to combat the threat.

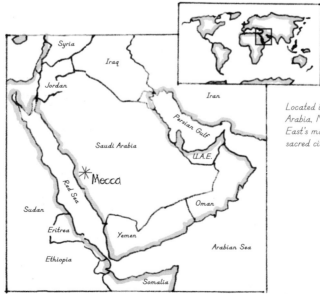

Located in the west of Saudi Arabia, Mecca is one of the Middle East's many holy sites, and the most sacred city in the Islamic world.

FACT: *The vast numbers of pilgrims who visit Mecca can lead to tragedy. In 2006, some 364 pilgrims were crushed to death in a stampede while making their way to the city. The worst incident in modern times occurred in 1990, when 1,426 pilgrims were crushed in tunnels leading to Mecca's most holy sites.*

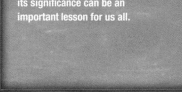

Mecca is in Saudi Arabia, but regardless of its geographical location, the city occupies a central place in Islam, one of the major religions of the world. Understanding and respecting the reasons behind its significance can be an important lesson for us all.

The geographical location of Mecca was determined initially by its role as a center of trade. There are records of the city from the period of the Old Testament, and legend attributes its foundation to the descendants of Abraham. This intersection of trade and culture encouraged the worship of a diverse range of gods by the Arabs of the region. Certainly, by the end of the sixth century it was a significant center, and It was at that time that the prophet Muhammad was born in the city. He proclaimed the Islamic faith in Mecca, and although he was forced to flee from the city, he later returned and captured it.

The Spiritual City

The central place of Mecca in the origin of the Islamic religion has given it a global significance for the more than one billion Muslims located throughout the globe. It is venerated as the most holy city in Islam. As such, daily worship is conducted facing the direction of Mecca, and to make a *hajj* (pilgrimage) there at least once in a lifetime is the duty of every able-bodied Muslim. This pilgrimage results, at peak periods, in the addition of two-and-a-half million inhabitants to a city with approximately one-and-a-half million permanent residents. The logistical implications for the Saudi authorities are enormous, but the economic opportunities of such an influx are also significant. Since the 1970s, oil wealth has greatly enhanced the infrastructure of Mecca, and this has helped in turn to boost the number of pilgrims.

At the heart of Mecca lies the Kaaba, the most sacred site in the Muslim world.

＊

FACT: *Mecca is also written as Makkah, or Makka al-Mukarrama. This can be literally translated as "honored Mecca."*

49

Why Does the Pope Live in the Vatican?

Today, the pope and the Vatican are so closely associated that the question of why they are linked is rarely asked. The eyes of the world turn to the Vatican when the new leader of the Roman Catholic Church is elected, and on those holy days when he addresses the vast crowds in St. Peter's Square. Surely this is how it has always been? Actually, no. The Vatican has not always been the home of the pope, and it has certainly not always been solely a location of spiritual significance.

The Vatican has played a part in the story of Christianity from the very earliest years. Having been drained and cleared, this unpromising area of the Roman capital was chosen by the emperor Caligula as the site for a new circus. Anxious to secure his influence, the emperor sought to please the populace of Rome with festivals, celebrations, and open bribery. A new and lavish circus was intended to win favor with the mob. As things turned out, Caligula was assassinated before it could be completed, but his successor, Nero, brought the project to a conclusion. One of the entertainments on offer was the execution of Christians. It is believed that Saint Peter was crucified, upside down, at the site, and the famous Basilica of St. Peter is believed by some to be constructed over the common grave where he was buried.

FACT: The name "Vatican" comes from the Latin **Mons Vaticanus** (Mount Vatican).

The famous dome of the Basilica of St. Peter lies beyond the Ponte Sant'Angelo.

FACT: Rome suffered from a very damaging fire in 64 C.E., during the reign of the emperor Nero. The incident prompted an even more vigorous persecution of Christians.

FACT: From 1207 to 1214, during the reign of King John, England suffered under a "papal interdict." This meant that no valid church services could occur there except baptisms and confessions.

The Christian Conversion

As the center of a powerful empire, the city of Rome had a natural attraction for the increasingly influential Christian faith. This relationship was cemented when the Emperor Constantine converted to Christianity in 312 C.E. As the Roman Empire in the West collapsed, the Roman Catholic Church remained a unifying institution, and the location of the Holy Father in Rome added the powerful luster of the ancient world. Popes sought to strengthen their position by acting as the validating authority of medieval rulers. They encouraged the notion of the divine right of monarchs, and as well as affirming their status, a pope could also undermine it by excommunicating a king or queen.

FACT: The papal palace at Avignon was declared to be a world heritage site in 1995.

Middle-Ages Crisis

During the Middle Ages, the close relationship between pontiffs and monarchs resulted in the Vatican ceasing to be the home of the popes. For seventy-two years, the central authority of the Roman Catholic Church was based in the south of France. Indeed, the French-born Pope Clement V never set foot within the Vatican. Elected in 1305, he determined to reside in Avignon, France, thereby aligning himself with the French king Philip IV against Holy Roman Emperor Henry VII. The following six popes all resided in Avignon, until Gregory XI returned in 1377. The authority of his successor was contested, causing a split that resulted in two popes, one in the Vatican and the other in Avignon.

The fusing of temporal and spiritual power lasted for 1,500 years until the seizure of Rome by King Victor Emanuel. He declared the city to be the capital of the new Italy in 1870, thereby ending the power of the pontiffs over portions of the Italian peninsula. Since the Middle Ages, the popes had controlled large areas of Italy as rulers in their own right. The disappearance of the Papal States on the peninsula left an unresolved question about the exact status of the Vatican. The Lateran Treaty, negotiated during Mussolini's dictatorship and signed in 1929, resolved the status of the Vatican as a city-state and cemented the concept of the Vatican as the home of the popes.

SUMMARY

Dominated by the famous dome of the Basilica of St. Peter—reputed by some to have been built over the common grave where Saint Peter was buried after his crucifixion—the Vatican draws on both the religious heritage and the cultural–political importance of Rome to provide a focal point for Catholicism.

Knowledge: *the ability to recall information*

1) Earth has existed for:
- **a.** 4,600 years
- **b.** 4.6 billion years
- **c.** 10,000 years
- **d.** 4.6 million years

2) Which of Earth's layers is liquid metal?
- **a.** The inner core
- **b.** The outer core
- **c.** The mantle
- **d.** The crust

3) How many ice ages has Earth experienced?
- **a.** 17
- **b.** 2
- **c.** 5
- **d.** 9

4) A 35,000-year-old ivory carving found in Germany depicts:
- **a.** A fur seal
- **b.** A snowman
- **c.** A moose
- **d.** A woolly mammoth

5) Which sciences did Alfred Wegener study?
- **a.** Astronomy
- **b.** Geology
- **c.** Meteorology
- **d.** All of these

6) What important theory did Alfred Wegener propose?
- **a.** Evolution
- **b.** Relativity
- **c.** Continental drift
- **d.** Quantum

7) What kind of tectonic plate boundary leads to the creation of oceanic ridges?
- **a.** Divergent
- **b.** Convergent subductive
- **c.** Convergent collision
- **d.** Transformational

8) The Himalayan mountains were created by:
- **a.** Molten rock being forced up through Earth's crust
- **b.** Sedimentary rock being deposited on the ocean floor
- **c.** Two tectonic plates colliding
- **d.** A volcanic explosion

9) What is the name of the active volcano located to the east of Java in Indonesia?
- **a.** Vesuvius
- **b.** Krakatoa
- **c.** Etna
- **d.** Mount Tambora

10) What name is given to the belt of seismic and volcanic activity around the Pacific?
- **a.** The Great Arc
- **b.** The Ring of Fire
- **c.** The Bermuda Triangle
- **d.** The Shake of Arabi

11) How many active volcanoes are there in Indonesia?
- **a.** 5
- **b.** 35
- **c.** 130
- **d.** 72

12) Large scattered boulders are called erratics. How did they get where they are?
- **a.** Carried by glaciers
- **b.** They are meteorites
- **c.** Volcanic activity
- **d.** Moved by stone-age builders

Understanding: *the ability to interpret information and make links between different aspects of it*

1) How was the Moon formed?

2) What are the factors that cause ice ages to occur and influence their progress?

3) What forces did Alfred Wegener suggest might be causing continental drift, and what was wrong with his explanation?

4) As new crust is created at certain boundaries between tectonic plates, where does the old crust go?

5) How is the Hawaiian island chain thought to have been formed?

6) Name the seven continents. Do these correspond to tectonic plates?

Knowledge: *the ability to recall information*

1) Which was the first civilization of the Fertile Crescent?
- **a.** The Egyptians
- **b.** The Sumerians
- **c.** The Romans
- **d.** The Byzantines

2) When were the first Mesopotamian Civilizations born?
- **a.** 200 C.E.
- **b.** 0
- **c.** 2000 B.C.E.
- **d.** 3500 B.C.E.

3) What does "Mesopotamia" translate as?
- **a.** Ancient land
- **b.** The highest point
- **c.** The land between rivers
- **d.** Civilized place

4) What year did Socrates poison himself?
- **a.** 399 B.C.E.
- **b.** 350 B.C.E.
- **c.** 300 C.E.
- **d.** 350 C.E.

5) How many people were in the jury that tried Socrates?
- **a.** 10
- **b.** 100
- **c.** 500
- **d.** 1000

6) What is the poison Socrates is thought to have taken?
- **a.** Arsenic
- **b.** Hemlock
- **c.** Yew berries
- **d.** Cyanide

7) What did Honorius and Arcadius do in 395 C.E. which potentially weakened the Roman Empire?
- **a.** Kill each other
- **b.** Split the empire in two
- **c.** Marry foreign princesses
- **d.** Abolish the Senate

8) What commodity was Egypt a vital source of in the Roman Empire?
- **a.** Fish
- **b.** Gold
- **c.** Bread
- **d.** Stone

9) During what century is gunpowder thought to have been invented in China?
- **a.** The 8th century C.E.
- **b.** The 13th century C.E.
- **c.** The 10th century C.E.
- **d.** The 15th century C.E.

10) During whose dynasty did this invention occur?
- **a.** The Xia Dynasty
- **b.** The Shang
- **c.** The Tang Dynasty
- **d.** The Qin Dynasty

11) In Neolithic times, clay tokens are thought to have been used for:
- **a.** Playing games
- **b.** Recording data
- **c.** Lighting fires
- **d.** Making buttons

12) What are hieroglyphics?
- **a.** A pictorial alphabet
- **b.** The material on which information was written
- **c.** The Egyptian god of writing
- **d.** A name for an ancient form of pencil

Understanding: *the ability to interpret information and make links between different aspects of it*

1) Why is it so hard to identify a single cradle of civilization?

2) Why was writing important?

3) Why has Socrates come to hold such a mythical status?

4) Why was the army an important force in the Roman Empire?

5) What was the link between alchemy and gunpowder?

6) When did the Roman Empire fall?

Knowledge: *the ability to recall information*

1) What number does the Roman numeral DCLXXIV represent?
 a. 674
 b. 434
 c. 1,626
 d. 176

2) When did the abacus fall out of use in China?
 a. 2,000 years ago
 b. 200 years ago
 c. 20 years ago
 d. It is still in use

3) The Electronic Frontier Foundation awarded a prize of $100,000 to the first person to find a prime number with more than:
 a. 100 digits
 b. 10,000 digits
 c. 1,000,000 digits
 d. 10,000,000 digits

4) The Babylonian number system was based on the number:
 a. 8
 b. 12
 c. 60
 d. 16

5) In what country was zero first used as a number in its own right?
 a. India
 b. Italy
 c. Arabia
 d. Germany

6) Which of the following had a number system based on the number 20?
 a. Ancient Egyptians
 b. Ancient Greeks
 c. Sumerians
 d. Mayans

7) Leonardo Fibonacci was born in the:
 a. 10th century
 b. 12th century
 c. 16th century
 d. 19th century

8) Which of the following is false?
 a. π = the area of a circle divided by the square of its radius
 b. π = the circumference of a circle divided by its diameter
 c. π = three-quarters of the volume of a sphere divided by the cube of its radius
 d. None of the above

9) Which of the following is true?
 a. π is a rational number
 b. π is a perfect number
 c. π is an irrational number
 d. π is a prime number

10) Fibonacci numbers are interesting because:
 a. They occur in the structure of some living things
 b. They describe the movement of the planets
 c. They are all prime numbers
 d. They are all divisible by 7

11) What is a "perfect number"?
 a. A number whose cube root is an integer
 b. A number whose divisors all add up to the number itself
 c. A number that is only divisible by 1 and itself
 d. A number that can be expressed as 2^n

12) What is meant by a "positional" number system?
 a. The position of a number determines its value
 b. Numbers can change position without changing their value
 c. The number defines the position of objects in space
 d. The system can only be used on an abacus

Understanding: *the ability to interpret information and make links between different aspects of it*

1) What is the definition of a prime number, and what are the first three such numbers?

2) How is the Fibonacci sequence of numbers generated, and what are the first eight numbers in the sequence?

3) What is the "golden ratio"?

4) Where did the decimal (10-figure) system that we use today come from, and how did it reach Europe?

5) What is the definition of an irrational number? Give an example of one. What happens when you express an irrational number as a decimal?

6) How did Leonard of Pisa come to be called Fibonacci?

Knowledge: *the ability to recall information*

1) Which of these world religions is not monotheistic?
- **a.** Islam
- **b.** Christianity
- **c.** Buddhism
- **d.** Judaism

2) Approximately how many gods were recognized in ancient Egyptian society?
- **a.** 1
- **b.** 10
- **c.** 200
- **d.** Over 2,000

3) What was the name of Abraham's youngest son?
- **a.** Isaac
- **b.** Ishmael
- **c.** Moses
- **d.** David

4) In which of these world religions was Abraham not a founding figure?
- **a.** Judaism
- **b.** Sikhism
- **c.** Christianity
- **d.** Islam

5) What is the Jewish version of the Bible called?
- **a.** The King James
- **b.** The Torah
- **c.** The Tanakh
- **d.** The Little Red Book

6) How many books are there in the New Testament?
- **a.** 27
- **b.** 4
- **c.** 25
- **d.** 13

7) Whom did the pope commission to write a definitive Latin version of the Bible in 382 C.E.?
- **a.** King James
- **b.** St. Peter
- **c.** St. John
- **d.** St. Jerome

8) How many copies of the Bible are there estimated to be in existence?
- **a.** 1 million
- **b.** 1 billion
- **c.** 2.5 billion
- **d.** 4 billion

9) In which country is Mecca located?
- **a.** Morocco
- **b.** Saudi Arabia
- **c.** Iran
- **d.** Iraq

10) Which commodity has helped Mecca's economic development since the 1970s?
- **a.** Oil
- **b.** Gold
- **c.** Diamonds
- **d.** Silicon

11) Over whose burial site is it believed that the famous Basilica in the Vatican is built?
- **a.** St. Peter
- **b.** St. Mark
- **c.** St. Luke
- **d.** Jesus Christ

12) During the Middle Ages, apart from Vatican City, where else did the authority of the papacy at times reside?
- **a.** Venice, Italy
- **b.** London, England
- **c.** Paris, France
- **d.** Avignon, France

Understanding: *the ability to interpret information and make links between different aspects of it*

1) Why are the boundaries between monotheism and polytheism sometimes blurred?

2) In what way does a monotheistic belief affect the practice of religious worship?

3) What is Abraham supposed to have done in his father's shop and what significance does this action have?

4) Why do historians find it so hard to say when the Bible was written?

5) What is the Prophet Muhammad's connection with Mecca?

6) Why was the papacy important to medieval kings?

55

Tuesday

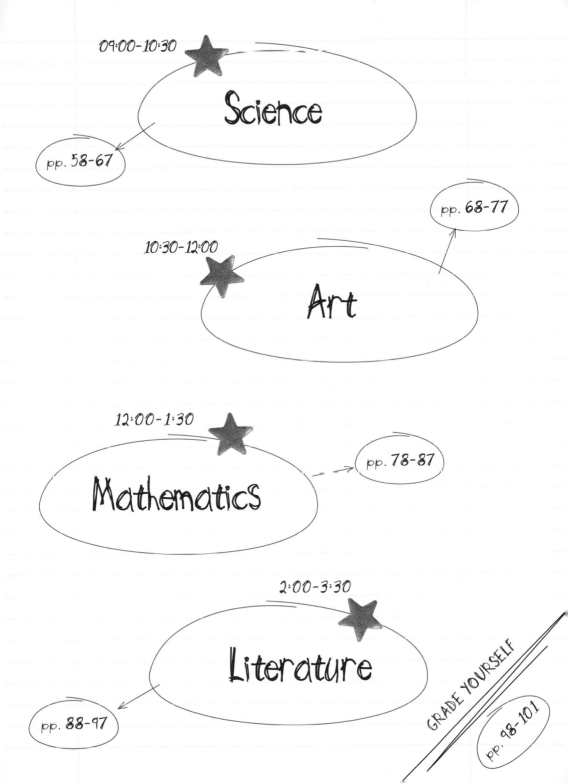

09:00-10:30

Science

pp. 58-67

pp. 68-77

10:30-12:00

Art

12:00-1:30

Mathematics

pp. 78-87

2:00-3:30

Literature

pp. 88-97

GRADE YOURSELF

pp. 98-101

When Was the Big Bang?

Being inquisitive creatures, we humans have posed questions about the origins of ourselves, of life, and of the universe since time immemorial, and we have come up with some very profound and very imaginative answers over the millennia. In the last 80 years, however, research in a range of scientific fields has provided a growing body of evidence that the universe began in a most dramatic and inexplicable way: the big bang.

Georges Lemaître
1894–1966

In the early twentieth century, the accepted scientific view of the universe was of relative stability, of spinning galaxies and orbiting planets, an unchanging cosmos operating according to Newton's laws. When Albert Einstein formulated his general theory of relativity, he introduced a mathematical constant into his equations to maintain this static description of the universe, but Georges Lemaître, a Roman Catholic priest and astronomer, showed in 1927 that Einstein's equations predicted an expanding universe. Lemaître was the first to suggest that the universe came into existence at a single point, which he referred to as the "primeval atom." His ideas explained the "red shift" in the light received from distant galaxies, which had been discovered by the American astronomer V. M. Slipher. This change in the wavelength of light shows that the galaxies are moving away from us.

Hubble, Hoyle, and the Big Bang

By studying both the speed at which galaxies are moving away from us and their distances from us, the American astronomer Edwin Hubble showed that the two were directly proportional. A galaxy that is twice as far away from us as another is moving away at twice the speed. Now known as Hubble's Law, this confirmed that the universe is expanding, and led to the conclusion that everything was born, as Lemaître had suggested, from an infinitely small point.

Some cosmologists, including the British astronomer Sir Fred Hoyle, rejected this idea and clung to the concept of a "steady-state" universe. It is ironic that it was Hoyle who first coined the term "big bang" to describe the hypothesis that he dismissed.

FACT: *It is tempting to imagine the big bang as an exploding bomb, with its contents being blasted out from a central point, and, when we hear that all galaxies are receding from us, to think we must be at that central point. But that's not how it is. The fact is that everything is moving away from everything else. It is space itself that is expanding.*

"We are stardust; billion-year-old carbon."

Joni Mitchell, "Woodstock" (from *Ladies of the Canyon*, 1970)

SUMMARY

The universe came into existence as a "singularity" about 13.7 billion years ago, in an event that has been characterized as the big bang. In the first fractions of a second, the universe expanded rapidly, and the forces and particles of physics were created. That expansion still continues.

Further Confirmation

Just as an explosion leaves a hot spot, surely the cosmic big bang would leave some trace of its occurrence? In 1965, scientists at Bell Laboratories who were studying radio interference discovered what has become known as CMBR—Cosmic Microwave Background Radiation—an "afterglow" of the big bang that is found throughout the observable universe. Within a few years, two British mathematicians and physicists, Stephen Hawking and Roger Penrose, showed that a "singularity" from which the universe could have been born was consistent with Einstein's general theory of relativity, and the big bang hypothesis was fully accepted as scientific theory.

So What Actually Happened?

According to the theory, a little more than 13.7 billion years ago there was nothing anywhere. There wasn't even a *somewhere* for anything to be. Then there was a singularity, an infinitely dense something that contained everything.

Scientists remain a little vague about what happened in the first ten-thousand-trillionth of a second, but the rest of that first second was extremely busy. The new high-energy, high-temperature, high-pressure universe expanded rapidly, and elementary particles and antiparticles came into existence. In a storm of creation and collision, particles came to outweigh antiparticles by a tiny proportion, which explains why there is more matter than antimatter in the universe. After about one picosecond (0.000000000001 of a second), the four fundamental physical forces—gravity, electromagnetism, and the strong and weak nuclear forces—had settled down to their present values, as had the parameters of the elementary particles. After about one millionth of a second, neutrons and protons were formed, and by the end of the first second, electrons were in existence.

It took thousands of years for these particles to begin to form the atoms of the elements, and billions of years for material to start to clump together to form the galaxies, stars, and planets that populate the universe. It took billions more for life to appear on this planet, to evolve, and to start working out what happened in the beginning.

Named after Edwin Hubble, the Hubble Space Telescope has been orbiting Earth since 1990.

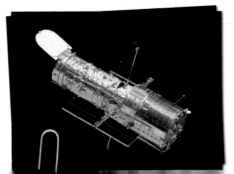

Who Was Albert Einstein?

Hear the name Einstein and the image that springs to mind is that of the archetypal mad scientist: flowing white hair, wild eyes, and a frighteningly powerful intellect. But who was he, what did he do, and why did he become so famous?

Albert Einstein's life features three prominent locations—Germany, Switzerland, and the United States—but his achievements have universal significance. He was born in 1879 into a lower-middle-class family, his father a small businessman with a patchy record of success. At school, Einstein was regarded as difficult and not particularly promising by some of his teachers (so there is hope for us all).

* Albert Einstein 1879–1955

FACT: *In his lifetime, Einstein was a citizen of Germany, Switzerland, and the United States. From 1896 to 1901 he was technically stateless, not having citizenship of any country.*

His breakthrough year came in 1905. In that year, he obtained his doctorate from the University of Zurich and wrote four groundbreaking papers. The most famous of these was "On the Electrodynamics of Moving Bodies," which set out Einstein's "special theory of relativity." This contained the famous equation $E = mc^2$, which defines the relationship between energy (E), mass (m), and the speed of light (c). It also proposed that space and time are relative; in other words, how we measure them depends on our position relative to other observers. Einstein was awarded the 1921 Nobel Prize in Physics (although the award was announced in late 1922) "for his services to Theoretical Physics, and especially for his discovery of the law of the photoelectric effect."

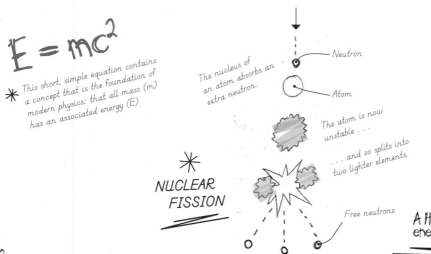

$$E = mc^2$$

* This short, simple equation contains a concept that is the foundation of modern physics: that all mass (m) has an associated energy (E)

The nucleus of an atom absorbs an extra neutron.

— Neutron

— Atom

The atom is now unstable . . .

. . . and so splits into two lighter elements.

* **NUCLEAR FISSION**

Free neutrons

A HUGE amount of energy is released.

FACT: *Before his cremation, Einstein's brain was removed for preservation, without the permission of his family. It disappeared within a few years and was rediscovered in 1978, divided into sections and preserved in alcohol inside two jars.*

Einstein's work had two important consequences. First, it sounded the death knell of the long-standing, but by the early twentieth century quite shaky, Newtonian view of the universe. Second, it provided the theoretical foundation for nuclear fission—the splitting of the atom. The first may not seem relevant to your everyday life, but the second affects us all very directly indeed.

Splitting the Atom

As a Jew and a declared pacifist, Albert Einstein was an ideal target for the growing Nazi Party of the early 1930s. When Hitler came to power in 1933, Einstein left the country, taking up a post in the United States. He was never to return to the land of his birth. In the States, Einstein achieved celebrity status; he was instantly recognizable and famous for theories that few could grasp.

When World War II broke out, Einstein and another scientist, Leó Szilárd, wrote to President Franklin D. Roosevelt, urging him to fund research into the military application of nuclear fission. The letter hinted at Germany's awareness of the destructive potential of radioactive elements. It also proposed that any weapon would probably be too heavy for air transport but might be delivered onboard a ship. The Manhattan Project, the program that resulted in the development of the first atomic bombs, was established in 1942.

Einstein later regretted promoting the development of nuclear weapons, and he played no direct role in the project. His opposition to nuclear weapons, devotion to Zionism, support of civil rights, and criticism of capitalism led to many years of FBI surveillance. From 1945 to 1950, the director of the FBI, J. Edgar Hoover, encouraged attempts to discredit Einstein and link him with Communism. Einstein died in 1955, but he remains an iconic figure today. His legacy is greater than the sum of his theories; and, in 1999, *Time* magazine declared Einstein to be the "person of the century."

SUMMARY

Einstein's theories changed our understanding of the universe in which we live. A victim of persecution, he believed passionately in the value of learning. He was and remains the popular conception of the scientific genius.

QUOTE:

"Great spirits have always found violent opposition from mediocrities. The latter cannot understand it when a man does not thoughtlessly submit to hereditary prejudices, but honestly and courageously uses his intelligence." Albert Einstein

What Is Light?

From at least the fifth century B.C.E., light was generally believed to be made up of tiny invisible particles, and this theory explained much of its behavior. From the sixteenth century on, scientists were able to show that light also travels in the form of waves. In the twentieth century it was found that although light has the properties of both particles and waves, it is more than either.

The great physicist Isaac Newton backed the particle, or "corpuscular," theory of light and showed how it accounted for reflection. It was less easy to explain refraction through a lens or why a prism splits white light into the colors of the rainbow, but his influential view held sway despite the fact that several scientists, including René Descartes, Robert Hooke, and Christiaan Huygens, had made convincing cases for a wave theory. In 1801, light's wavelike properties were demonstrated by the English physicist Thomas Young. His two-slit experiment showed that two sources of light produce an interference pattern similar to that created by two sets of waves on water—something that particles could not do.

The particles create two lines on the screen.

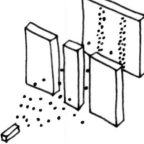

Particles are being fired at the slits.

Is light a wave?

If light were made up of particles, shining a beam through two slits would produce two bright lines like this. In fact, a series of lines is produced by the two sets of waves interacting.

Electromagnetic Waves

Later in the nineteenth century, the Scottish physicist James Clerk Maxwell, working on the broad areas of electricity and magnetism, developed the electromagnetic theory. He showed not only that electrical and magnetic fields travel in the form of waves at the speed of light but that light itself is a form of electromagnetic radiation, being just the visible part of a spectrum that extends from short-wavelength radiation, such as X-rays and gamma rays, through ultraviolet radiation and visible light, to infrared radiation, microwaves, and radio waves.

QUOTE: *"Since Maxwell's time, physical reality has been thought of as represented by continuous fields, and not capable of any mechanical interpretation. This change in the conception of reality is the most profound and the most fruitful that physics has experienced since the time of Newton." Albert Einstein (1879-1955)*

FACT: *As long ago as the seventh century, Indian Buddhist philosophers developed the idea that matter consisted of particles that were themselves composed of light and energy, a concept that could be interpreted as foreshadowing quantum theory. The Iraqi scholar Alhazen, writing in the eleventh century, stated that light was composed of particles of which the only quality is that of energy.*

We have evolved to see only this "visible spectrum," but some animals can detect other parts. Bees, for example, can detect ultraviolet light. The colors that we see correspond to different wavelengths in the visible spectrum, red light having the longest wavelength and violet having the shortest. A prism splits a narrow beam of white light into the colors of the rainbow because the light changes speed when it passes from one medium to another. (Note that the speed of light is a constant only in a vacuum.) The light is therefore bent as it passes from the air into the glass, and again as it leaves the glass. The degree of this "refraction" depends on the angle at which the light strikes the prism, the "refractive indices" of the air and the prism, and the wavelength of the light. The shorter the wavelength, the greater the bending, and the more the colors fan out.

When white light passes through a prism, the different wavelengths are refracted by different amounts, and this splits up the light into its constituent wavelengths.

The Particle Returns

The story doesn't end here. Maxwell's breakthrough could not explain certain anomalies. For example, in the case of the photoelectric effect, in which light striking a metal surface knocks off electrons and causes an electric current to flow, it was found that the energy of the electrons was not proportional to the intensity of the light but to its frequency, and that there was a frequency below which no current flowed. If the energy was in the form of a wave, it should increase with intensity and there would be no cutoff point. It was Einstein who suggested that light energy exists as discrete packets (photons) and that their energy is proportional to the frequency. The energy in low-frequency photons was insufficient to dislodge the electrons. He was later proved correct and received the Nobel Prize for this work, which contributed significantly to quantum theory. It is now known that light and all other forms of electromagnetic radiation consist of photons of energy that exhibit "wave–particle duality"—they have the properties of both particles and waves.

SUMMARY — Light is composed of elementary particles—called photons, packets, or quanta—of energy that make up all forms of electromagnetic radiation. Photons have no mass and no charge, but they have energy and momentum. They are governed by quantum mechanics and show properties of both waves and particles.

Where Is the Limit of the Universe?

What is absolutely known for certain about the limit of the universe is precisely nothing, but the question is a very old one, and modern physics, astronomy, cosmology, and mathematics are making it possible to investigate a range of fascinating theories in ever more detail. Some of the possibilities are truly mind-boggling.

Taking it as given that the big bang theory of the universe is broadly correct, the universe is expanding. Searching for images to help us visualize what is happening, scientists have come up with the example of an inflating balloon, but the analogy is problematic. A balloon has a limit that separates the air inside from the air outside, but there is nothing outside the universe. That doesn't mean that there is nothing in that realm beyond our universe. It means that the phrase "beyond our universe" is meaningless. The idea of a limit, in the sense of a boundary, supposes that there is an outside and an inside to be separated, but there is no outside, so there can be no boundary.

A Limited Extent

Nonetheless, it is reasonable to ask how far this expanding universe has expanded. We know that the universe has existed for 13.7 billion years, and we know that the fastest anything can travel is the speed of light. The distance that light travels in a year is called a light-year, so it might be reasonable to suppose that the maximum radius of the universe is 13.7 billion years . . . but no. There are two things wrong with that calculation. First, there is no central point from which the radius of the universe can be measured, because the big bang was not like a bomb going off at a point in space. And second, as we learned when discussing space and time, matter is not moving through space in this expanding universe—space itself is expanding, and it can do so at a speed that moves galaxies apart faster than the speed of light. The latest estimate for the distance across the universe is 156 billion light-years!

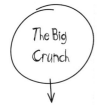

The Big Crunch

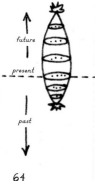

Recollapsing universe

future

present

past

The Shape of Things to Come

As the universe expands, it does so in opposition to the attractive force of gravity. It was therefore thought that the expansion must gradually slow down and that eventually gravity would take the upper hand, the universe would contract, and everything would condense into a "big crunch," returning to a singularity. It might then go bang again, in a scenario that has been called "big bounce," although the chances that all the chips would fall the same way—that all the particles and forces would be identical to those in this universe—would be infinitely small. However, that was before it was discovered that the rate of expansion is increasing . . . which brings us to dark matter and dark energy.

FACT: *Einstein recognized that if gravity bends light, celestial bodies could act as lenses, magnifying more distant objects. This phenomenon is now being used to locate dense masses of dark matter, as these act as lenses in places where no matter can be seen.*

SUMMARY

The concept of a boundary to the universe is meaningless, as there is nothing outside the universe, but the width of the expanding universe could be as much as 156 billion light-years. The universe isn't infinite . . . yet.

The faint arcs of light are the distorted images of galaxies that lie beyond the central yellow cluster. This effect is known as "gravitational lensing."

QUOTE:

"There is a theory which states that if ever for any reason anyone discovers what exactly the universe is for and why it is here it will instantly disappear and be replaced by something even more bizarre and inexplicable. There is another that states that this has already happened." Douglas Adams (1952–2001).

Hitchhiker's Guide to the Galaxy

The Dark Component

Imagine that not all matter is what we know as matter. Imagine that there's another kind, the presence of which can only be inferred from unexplained gravitational effects. Well, it seems that this may the case. This hypothetical invisible material has been called dark matter, and there may even be far more of it than there is ordinary matter. What's more, space may be filled with a corresponding dark energy that is evenly spread throughout the universe. This would explain why the universe's expansion is accelerating rather than slowing—it is being powered by dark energy.

How Does It End?

If the dark energy hypothesis is correct, the universe will continue to expand at an ever faster rate. The outcome thought most likely is that the universe becomes ever colder, a scenario that has been described as the "big freeze."

If dark energy exerts an even greater force, a "big rip" could occur, in which the universe expands so fast that the forces holding matter together are overcome, ripping all particles apart from each other and distributing matter evenly throughout the universe. But don't panic, the universe is expected to last at least one hundred billion years.

The Big Freeze

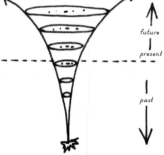

Accelerating universe

future
present
past

<u>Why</u> Are Time and Space the Same Thing?

Everything in the universe came into existence with the big bang. Everything. Not just the matter and energy of which the universe is composed and the physical laws that govern their behavior, but time and space as well. In Albert Einstein's special and general theories of relativity, space and time can be treated as aspects of a single continuum called space-time, and Einstein demonstrated that both space and time can be altered at very high speeds and by gravity.

At the heart of Einstein's work is the speed of light. We've already looked at what light is, but here we are interested in Einstein's discovery that in a vacuum light always travels at the same speed, regardless of the observer. The implications of this are enormous. We are used to the idea that time and space are constants, and that the speed of an object—its movement through space over a period of time—is relative to the observer. If I am in a car traveling at 100 mph and I fire a rifle forward that projects the bullet at 500 mph, the bullet will travel at 500 mph relative to me, but at 600 mph relative to a stationary observer. Einstein said that's not how it works for light, and many experimental and theoretical physicists have since shown that he was right.

Hermann Minkowski
(1864–1909)
✴

QUOTE:

"Space by itself, and time by itself, are doomed to fade away into mere shadows, and only a kind of union of the two will preserve an independent reality."

Hermann Minkowski (1864–1909)

FACT: *It was the German mathematician Hermann Minkowski, a former teacher of Albert Einstein, who showed in 1908 that a concept of four-dimensional space-time, combining time with the three spatial dimensions, was in keeping with Einstein's theories. In Minkowski space-time, an object has four coordinates that define its position spatially and temporally.*

SUMMARY

Space and time can be considered as aspects of a combined space-time continuum. The idea was put forward by Hermann Minkowski, but is implicit in Einstein's theories of relativity.

Time and Space Dilation

Imagine two rockets traveling through space side by side
at a speed approaching the speed of light. An astronaut in
one rocket flashes a pulse of light to an astronaut in the
other rocket. Both of them see it travel the distance
between the rockets in a straight line. However, in the
time it took the light to cross the gap, the fast-mov-
ing rockets have traveled a significant distance, so
to an observer in a nearby space station the
light has traveled a longer, diagonal distance.
The speed at which the light was traveling
is constant, so for the pulse to have
traveled further for the outside observer,
more time must have passed for the
observer than for the astronauts. Time itself
slows as one approaches the speed of light or, to
put it another way, the faster an object moves through
space, the more slowly it moves through time. This has been demonstrated
by flying highly accurate atomic clocks around the world at high speed and
showing that they register the passage of less time than clocks on the ground.

The spatial dimensions of an object are also relative to its speed, and the
faster something travels, the smaller it becomes in the direction of motion.
If it were possible for an object to travel at the speed of light, it would shrink
to nothing, which is why the speed of light is an absolute speed limit.

Einstein also showed that intense gravitational fields warp the fabric of time
and space, slowing the passage of time and causing light to bend.

The Fabric of Space-Time

We have seen that, according to Hubble's Law, a galaxy that is twice as far
away from us as another is moving away from us twice as fast. If this is true,
then surely there must be a distance at which galaxies are moving away from
us faster than the speed of light. But isn't this contrary to Einstein's theory?
In fact, this is not a contradiction. It is the space-time fabric itself that is
expanding, and this expansion can take place at a rate that increases the
distance between us and another galaxy faster than the speed of light. Of
course, such galaxies are beyond the observable "horizon," because light
from them will never reach us.

QUOTE:

"Space is to place as eternity is to time."

Joseph Joubert (1754-1824)

<u>Where</u> Are the Oldest Cave Paintings?

In 1994, three explorers cleared some rocks at the back of a cave in the Ardèche Valley of southern France. In doing so, they opened a passage to a cave system nearly 1,200 feet (365 m) long. Here they discovered intricate and complex painted designs, watched over by the skull of a bear many times larger than any modern species, placed with care on a rock. The cave is known as the Chauvet Cave after Jean-Marie Chauvet, one of the three explorers, and it holds the oldest known cave paintings in the world.

The south of France is today associated with harsh winters, but benevolent and hot summers. When the cave paintings were created, circumstances were very different. The region was principally peopled by small groups of early humans, who traveled in bands and sustained themselves through a combination of hunting and gathering. Their world was colder than ours is today, gripped in an ice age that created the conditions for vast forests of birches and pines. In those forests roamed animals now long extinct, such as mammoths, cave lions, aurochs (the ancestor of domestic cattle), and bears. Life was harsh and short. In such precarious times it seems incredible that time and effort should have been invested in the creation of this early art, a fact that serves to underline the importance and vitality of these ancient images.

Hidden Secrets

The caves were mostly formed by water erosion. This gives them a twisting and sinuous feeling. At times they broaden to as much as 150 feet (45 m) wide. There are stalagmites and the walls glisten with moisture; this is a place of darkness and secrets. It is a place in which it is not difficult to imagine sacred rites and initiations, efforts to placate the harsh natural world and seek comfort in its formidable strength.

Dating the Chauvet cave paintings is contentious. The possible range is between 30,000 and 28,000 B.C.E. There then appears to have been an interlude of just under 1,500 years in which the cave was not used. It appears that not much, if any, artwork was added during the second phase of use, but it did leave us with another touching glimpse of early human life: the footprint of a child believed to have been approximately eleven years old.

FACT: *Bears are known to have occupied the cave at different periods. There are remnants of bones and skulls, as well as marks in the walls gouged by their claws. Some of the indentations in the cave floor may have been created by generations of bears hibernating in the caves.*

Subjects and Techniques

The paintings show tremendous sophistication. They include representations of many different animals, caught in different aspects and full of vitality and movement. The cave artists prepared the rock surface on which they worked. They used different colors (mainly red and black) and employed shading. In some cases, the figures have been given additional emphasis by being engraved in the rock wall. The artists also used techniques such as blowing the paint and using their hands as stencils. Such diversity may indicate that the practice of cave painting had been in existence for a considerable period before the Chauvet record. The thought has been voiced that techniques such as those evident in the cave indicate a steady development and interaction between bands across generations, although this is only speculation.

The representations of animals do not follow an easily discerned pattern. In terms of color, they can be divided in two: in one part the images are principally red; in the other they are mainly black. Four species—lions, mammoths, cave bears, and rhinoceroses—account for the majority of the images. The art reveals close observation of the animals; they are often shown in careful detail. Their representation may have linked the human occupants of the cave with the strength, power, and grace of the animals. It is possible that they were an important part of some religious rite.

An Unlikely Survivor

These are the oldest cave paintings discovered to date, but there may be others awaiting discovery. Australian aborigines have an ancient history, and their rock art is striking and complex. However, it is rarely concealed in caves, so erosion quickly obliterates evidence of its existence. The Chauvet Cave itself demonstrates how unlikely the survival of paintings over thirty millennia is. The paint barely clings to the damp walls, which themselves show evidence of animal occupation. From the second phase of human occupation there are the carbon smudges of torch marks. Further erosion, flooding, or roof collapse could have forever destroyed this most ancient of art.

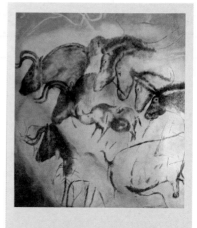

Chauvet Cave, France

* Horses, cattle, and rhinoceroses from Chauvet Cave, showing the close observation and great skill of the unknown artists.

SUMMARY

The oldest known cave paintings are in the Chauvet Cave in the Ardèche Valley of southern France. They are thought to date from between 30,000 and 28,000 B.C.E.

<u>**What**</u> *Is the Bayeux Tapestry?*

The Bayeux tapestry is four things in one: it is an historical record of dubious reliability; it is an art treasure of global importance that has been imperiled on several occasions; it is an example of early medieval propaganda; and, lastly, it is a central icon in a regional tourist industry. All that in 230 feet (70 m) of embroidery!

The "tapestry" is technically an embroidery, but the name has stuck. It was commissioned by Bishop Odo, a leading member of the Norman aristocracy, and claims to show events leading up to, and during, the Norman conquest of England in 1066. At a little more than 230 feet (70 m) long and 20 inches (50 cm) wide, it represents a considerable resource for historians.

The Events Behind the Tapestry

King Harold came to the English throne in 1066, his claim disputed by two other candidates: Harald Hardrada claimed the throne because kings of Norway had held it before, and William, Duke of Normandy, claimed the throne as a relative of the former king and because he said that Harold Godwinson had pledged his loyalty when staying as his guest. King Harold successfully overwhelmed a Scandinavian invasion, but was then defeated by the Normans at the battle of Hastings.

FACT: *King Harold is infamously shown being slain by an arrow in the eye. It is more likely that Norman horsemen cut him down when the Saxon shield wall crumbled.*

✳ *Someone is shown being shot in the eye, and the inscription reads* **Harold rex interfectus est** *("King Harold is Killed").*

QUOTE:

"History is written by the victors." Winston Churchill (1874–1965), British Prime Minister 1940–1945 and 1951–1955

FACT: *The Bayeux tapestry is not a single length of cloth. In fact, it consists of eight pieces, and it may have had more in its past.*

SUMMARY

Actually a long, thin work of embroidery, the Bayeux tapestry is a record of the Norman Conquest of England in 1066. However, the fact that it was commissioned by a member of the Norman nobility means it may not be wholly accurate.

As an historical record the tapestry has some interest for historians. Weapons technology, military activity, and tactics are all shown in the story. For example, we know that William constructed the first motte-and-bailey castle in England shortly after the initial invasion, and the tapestry identifies Hastings as the location. We cannot, however, be sure that the designer of the tapestry witnessed the crucial battle. The key facts are present, but there is no indication of who actually created it. The tapestry gives historians some insight into features of ordinary day-to-day life, too. It shows dogs, horses, and ships, and the borders include pictures of mythical creatures. But the tapestry today may tell only part of the original story. It is possible that at least one panel, the final one, is missing. Just how it was supposed to end is unknown.

Why Not the Hastings Tapestry?

For 700 years after the battle of Hastings, the tapestry was of no real interest to the English. Instead, it was hung in the cathedral at Bayeux, France, where the inventory indicates that it remained for hundreds of years. Then, during the French Revolution, the area around Bayeux rose in revolt and the tapestry found a new life. But it was not a glamorous one—the panels were used as cloth coverings for carts! The intervention of a local man, who offered an alternative supply of cloth, saved the tapestry. A similar fate almost occurred two years later in 1794, this time to make decorations during a public holiday. Since then, a local fine-arts council has existed to protect and preserve this treasure. It has had to hide the relic from invading German forces three times.

Winston Churchill once stated that "History is written by the victors," and that is precisely how the Bayeux tapestry should be considered. The man who commissioned it was the half-brother of a victorious king. The story that it tells was a neat piece of pro-Norman propaganda. King Harold is shown as a doomed man. Even his death carries the inference of divine intervention. But the tapestry's propaganda role didn't end there. In 1803, the Emperor Napoleon seized the tapestry and had it taken to Paris. At the time, Britain was at war with France. Contemplating a very expensive invasion of the British Isles, it was useful for Napoleon to remind his country that this had been successfully done before.

Hastings

Bayeux

When *Was the Renaissance?*

The Renaissance is usually given as the period from the fourteenth to the seventeenth centuries, when Western European culture, science, and arts were reborn from the stagnant era of the Middle Ages. Of course, the idea of a specific period of rebirth sounds good, and is nice and neat, but that doesn't necessarily make it right.

To anyone actually living between the fourteenth and seventeenth centuries in Western Europe, the term "Renaissance" would have meant absolutely nothing. This was a period of significant change, but with no single point of origin. The transformation of Western Europe was multicentered and the nature of the changes was multifaceted. It wasn't even considered to be a homogeneous period, let alone one that you could put a name to.

Italian Origins

The city-states of Italy are commonly cited as the birthplace of the Renaissance. In these thriving and competitive urban areas, trade produced vast wealth for powerful family clans. These families, such as the Borgias and Medicis, wanted to assert their authority and status in the form of art and learning. In doing so, they provided a market for a culture that had previously scarcely existed. Before the Renaissance, the Roman Catholic Church was the single most influential arbiter of culture. Then the focus had been primarily on religious themes, and although the noble families of Renaissance Italy certainly didn't reject the faith (there was too much power and money there to ignore), they also looked to classical antiquity to enhance their standing in society.

In addition to providing wealth and patrons, the expansion of trade encouraged innovation. Three inventions in particular broke previously secure boundaries of knowledge. The telescope enabled astronomers such as Galileo to look into the heavens, while the microscope allowed scientists to observe previously undiscovered microbes. These ideas and many more were recorded and distributed using the third innovation: the moveable-type printing press. This single piece of technology effectively broke both the religious and secular authorities' control over learning.

Galileo Galilei
1564–1642

*

*FACT: Jacob Burckhardt (1818–1897) was a Swiss historian. Famous for his book **The Civilization of the Renaissance in Italy**, he was the first to apply the term "Renaissance" to the time and place with which it is now associated.*

A New World Takes Shape

It is at this point—with the intersection of new technology, new wealth, and new ideas—that we start to recognize the modern Western world. Christianity split under the strain, leading to the founding of Protestantism. Humanism and the values of the Enlightenment also sprang from this time. Political reform and the growth of modern democracy have their roots in this revolutionary period.

The term "Renaissance" literally means "rebirth," but to many it would have been difficult to define what was being reborn. The Roman Catholic Church drew on the teachings of classical antiquity throughout the Middle Ages. Those elements that remained after the collapse of the Western Roman Empire were treasured and taught in European universities. Arab translations of the classics were hungrily sought after. In the field of medicine, the works of Hippocrates and Galen were held to be the pinnacle of human understanding. However, during the period that we call the Middle Ages, the exploratory and experimental methodologies of the classical period were applied with a new energy, and revealed that some of the assumed facts of antiquity were wrong.

Copernicus showed that the Sun did not revolve around Earth; da Vinci demonstrated that a human fetus was not the same as a dog's; Martin Luther argued that the Church was not the arbiter of a person's relationship with God. New ideas and their sometimes unintended and unexpected consequences litter the period. It is a sense of reborn enquiry that perhaps best defines the Renaissance.

Reevaluating the Facts

The terms "Renaissance" and "Middle Ages" have recently become controversial. Some historians defend the idea of a definable rebirth, whereas some acknowledge the terms as shorthand for periods that are less clearly defined. Others argue that the concepts are invalid, preferring the term "Early Modern" to Renaissance. These critics argue that the Middle Ages were far from stagnant, and the breakthroughs of the Renaissance are therefore reinterpreted as the products of a long period of development following the collapse of the Western Roman Empire.

Even though the term "Renaissance" was coined long after the era, it does represent some definable themes. Rational enquiry, based on classical principles, led to challenging discoveries that were facilitated and enhanced by new technologies. The consequences were fundamental changes in art, culture, trade, and politics. As a result, it is possible to argue that the Renaissance laid the foundation for much that the modern world takes for granted.

FACT: Copernicus published De Revolutionibus Orbium Coelestium in 1543. He made it clear in the introduction that he did not challenge the conception of Earth's position at the center of the universe, but was simply using the idea that it wasn't as a more accurate aid to plotting the passage of the planets and stars. One of the best get-out clauses in history?

<u>**Who**</u> *Painted the* Mona Lisa?

There is no doubt about this one, right? Everyone knows his name: Leonardo da Vinci. But who was he? We all recognize the sketched self-portrait of the elderly man, looking like an Old Testament prophet, and we know that he painted that famous one-sided smile, but who he actually was is less well understood.

Born in 1452, Leonardo di ser Piero da Vinci lived until 1519. During that time his name became a byword for genius. Coming from a modest background, he appears to have shown early promise. Contemporary accounts refer to his good looks, grace, charm, and intelligence. He received a thorough education in the city of Florence and became an accomplished musician as well as demonstrating a talent for art. He completed his apprenticeship as a painter in 1478, but Leonardo's career far exceeded any early expectations.

*
Leonardo da Vinci
1452–1519

Finding a Patron

Duke Ludovico Sforza of Milan received an extraordinary letter from the young Leonardo. In the letter, Leonardo boasted of his knowledge and aspirations in a wide range of fields. He wrote that he had devised a plan to build portable bridges and construct armored vehicles. He stated that his talents included an understanding of the forging of bombards and cannons. And he made it clear that sculpture and painting were well within his grasp. The letter worked. The Duke was intrigued and went on to appoint Leonardo to serve as an engineer and architect. He continued to pour forth a prolific stream of drawings and ideas for some truly revolutionary concepts.

One of the hallmarks of Leonardo's early work appears to have been the infrequency with which it was completed. His first commission as a master painter in 1478 was never finished. Two other commissions in 1481 remained incomplete, nor was his *Battle of Anghiari* in the great hall of the Palazzo Vecchio brought to completion. Even when a work was completed, it was often following a long preparatory period. It him took two years to complete the *Last Supper* at the Monastery of Santa Maria delle Grazie in Milan.

FACT: *Napoleon took the portrait from the Louvre and kept it as a decorative addition to his bedroom.*

SUMMARY

Leonardo da Vinci was a true polymath, a Renaissance man. His works encompassed a wide range of fields and demonstrated that he had many gifts and talents. He was endlessly inventive, keeping notes on subjects as diverse as human anatomy and the principles of a machine gun—all written in mirror writing. The enduring popularity of the *Mona Lisa* remains a testament to his genius.

FACT: *Modern X-rays have revealed three previous versions of the* ***Mona Lisa*** *beneath the one that is known to the world today. Even that famous image does not really reflect its original glory, as many of the colors have faded and its protective coat of varnish has yellowed with age.*

A History of the Portrait

In 1502, Leonardo da Vinci had a change of patron. He returned to Florence for the second time to work for Duke Cesare Borgia of Romagna. It was at this time that he painted the *Mona Lisa*. The painting took two years to create and was never given to its rightful owner, the person who commissioned the work. Instead, da Vinci kept the painting with him until his death. That fact alone has helped give the portrait an air of further mystery in the eyes of many.

Between 1506 and 1519, Leonardo lived in Milan, Florence, Rome, and the town of Cloux, in France, where he died. He benefited from the patronage of two kings of France, Louis XII and Francis I, as well as Pope Leo X. It was Francis I who purchased the *Mona Lisa* after the death of Leonardo. During the French Revolution, it was taken from royal ownership and hung in the Louvre. It is now displayed in a bullet-proof and climate-controlled transparent box that is opened just once a year.

That Mysterious Smile

The *Mona Lisa* is considered to be one of the most enigmatic portraits ever created. It is most likely to be of Lisa Gherardini, the wife of a Florentine silk merchant. In the painting Leonardo demonstrated his mastery of two particular techniques. He created a hazy, subtle effect through the use of gently graduated colors—a technique called *sfumato*—and the modulation of light in order to establish contrast, called *chiaroscuro*. These techniques enhanced the ambiguity of the sitter's one-sided smile.

The reasons for that particular expression are unknown. There is some speculation that it simply reflects a contemporary fashion for women to smile in that manner. Others have suggested that it was a family trait. One doctor has even proposed that it was evidence that she suffered from "bruxism," the habit of grinding the teeth while asleep. Maybe she was just tense and bored with the two-year wait!

<u>Why</u> *Were the Impressionists Initially Unpopular?*

It is hard for us to appreciate the extent to which the painters who became collectively known as the Impressionists challenged the conventions of their time. Reactions to their first exhibition were extreme, with critics declaring their absolute disgust with the art on display. The very term "Impressionist" was intended as an insult, implying that these pieces were on a par with unfinished sketches.

The Paris of the 1870s was at the heart of the art world. The dominant force in determining whether or not a work constituted art was the Paris Salon, which presented an annual exhibition that could make or break the fortunes of an aspiring artist. For the Salon, good art meant realism imparted by close attention to detail, intricacy of composition, and a narrative that had its roots in the classical tradition. It might almost be described as art that aspired to photographic realism. In 1874, a group of artists who had not achieved success at the Salon mounted their own exhibition. Among those artists were some who became known as "Impressionists"; but the exhibition was not well received.

The Leading Lights

The names of the leading Impressionists—such as Degas, Cezanne, Gauguin, and Pissarro—have become familiar even to people who have no particular interest in art. Among them, Pissarro is sometimes described as the "father of Impressionism." Of all the Impressionists, he was the only one to show work at all eight exhibitions, and he was widely considered to be at the forefront of the development of Impressionist technique. What made Pissarro's work initially so unpopular tells us a great deal about why the movement was condemned. He painted rural and urban scenes, showing the ordinary and commonplace with seemingly little regard for formal composition. There was certainly no attempt to reference the work to themes of antiquity. In Pissarro's paintings, ordinary people were shown in cafés and bars. Renoir also showed scenes of ease and relaxation, such as the luminous *Luncheon of the Boating Party*.

Claude Monet 1840-1926

FACT: *The use of the word "Impressionist" by critics was inspired by Claude Monet's painting* **Impression, Sunrise**.

To their contemporaries, the Impressionists were sacrificing the dignity of art. *Impression, Sunrise* took Claude Monet just forty minutes to paint. Like other Impressionists, he was anxious to capture a momentary quality of light and movement. The development of paint that was available in tubes freed the artist from the studio. In one painting by Monet of his wife, Camille, some of the sand from the beach at Trouville is visible in the paint, such was the immediacy of his work. These were virtually snapshots, seemingly informal and unstudied, created in great haste. The early responses to this approach were shock and revulsion. It was only a decade later that critics began to consider and value the philosophy behind the movement.

Into the Mainstream

In condemning the Impressionists, one art critic, Ernest Chesneau, wrote that "it is a foregone conclusion that the public will declare itself in favor of the conventional work at the expense of the work of innovation." This clearly illustrates the main reason for the initial unpopularity of the movement. In their efforts to capture the quality of light and movement at a particular moment in time, they created a new realism. Colors were mixed and intense; for example, Renoir contrasted cobalt-blue water against an orange boat in *La Yole (The Skiff)*. The same location or object could be revisited repeatedly and never appear the same; Monet painted the Cathedral of Rouen over and over in 1892, never copying himself. The challenge to convention was initially too much, but tastes change. The Impressionists were absorbed into the mainstream during the lifetime of Pissarro. What had been unacceptable, described as lunacy at the outset, became the new convention for later generations of artists to break.

 FACT: *Claude Monet's masterpiece* **Nymphéas** *sold at auction for more than $30 m (around £18.5 m) at Sotheby's, London, in 2007.*

SUMMARY

What was unconventional and shocking about the Impressionists—the way that they challenged the prevailing traditions; the speed and casualness with which they painted—has now become part of what many people consider to be good art.

Why Does $1 + 1 = 2$?

Such a seemingly simple equation actually reveals a surprising amount about our system of mathematics. It touches upon the development of mathematics itself, the symbols that we use, and even the philosophy of logic.

Today we think of mathematics as being a universal language, but that hasn't always been the case. Let's start at the beginning, or at least close to it. The four basic operations of arithmetic—addition and subtraction, multiplication and division—were being practiced by the Sumerians of Mesopotamia, in what is now Iraq, as early as the third millennium B.C.E., but since that time various civilizations have developed their own different number systems and ways of calculating. The Babylonians developed cuneiform, or wedge-shaped, numerals. In their system there were only two symbols, one for units and one for tens, from which all digits were formed, and these were used in a place-value system that indicated by the position of the symbols whether they referred to units, 60s, 60^2s (3,600s), or 60^3s (216,000s), much as our base-ten system does for units and powers of ten. These divisions of sixty are still found in the units that we use for time and for the divisions of a circle.

Their numbers were inscribed on soft clay tablets using a sharpened reed, and the tablets were then baked hard. Several hundred have survived, and they show that the Babylonians used reference tables for multiplication and other calculations.

Numbers and Symbols

Many different systems developed in different civilizations; but it was in India that the simpler, more efficient place-value base-ten system we use today had its genesis. This ingeniously simple system, together with its numerals (see opposite), was taken up in the ninth century by Arab and Persian mathematicians and, largely thanks to Fibonacci, was brought to Europe in the early thirteenth century.

The story, however, doesn't end there. To facilitate its use, the system of numerals was augmented by symbols for mathematical operations and relations. At first these varied from one scholar to the next, but as certain key works gained influence, so notation

> **QUOTE:**
> "There are only 10 kinds of people: those who understand binary and those who don't." Anon.

Our modern understanding of the equation $1 + 1 = 2$ relies upon the European inheritance of Hindu-Arabic numerals, as well as the subsequent development and dissemination of mathematical symbols. It also relies on the use of a number base greater than two; in other words, not binary, in which the symbol for two is 10.

| 1 | 2 | 3 | 4 | 5 | 6 | 7 | 8 | 9 | 0 | *c. 969 C.E.* |

*

Even Indian–Arabic numerals from over a thousand years ago bear great similarity to those we use today.

became more settled. It is thought that the first use of + (an abbreviation of the Latin *et*, meaning "and") was in *Algorismus proportionum*, a mid-fourteenth-century work by the French polymath Nicole d'Oresme; whereas Robert Recorde was the first to use the modern symbol for equality, = (chosen because it shows two lines of equal length), in 1557.

An Exception to the Rule

As we have learned, not all civilizations used a base-ten number system, but the majority have done so. Base ten seems a natural choice, simply because we have ten fingers that we can use for counting. Indeed, the word for number and for finger are the same in several languages (for example, the English word "digit").

However, another number system in wide use today has just two digits: 0 and 1. The base-two, or binary, system is the one on which computers operate. Information is stored and manipulated in the form of strings of binary digits, abbreviated to "bits." A string of eight bits, which can provide 256 different combinations, is called a byte, and file sizes are given in these units.

When a number is written in base ten, a unit in any column has ten times the value of a unit in the column to the right of it; but in base two, the column value is twice that of the column to the right of it. For example, 47 would be written as "101111." This means that two is actually written as "10" (whereas ten is written as "1010"). In this system, 1 + 1 = 10.

QUOTE:

"The numbers may be said to rule the whole world of quantity, and the four rules of arithmetic may be regarded as the complete equipment of the mathematician."
James Clerk Maxwell (1831–1879)

FACT: *Moving away from the mathematical symbols involved, we intuitively understand the concept of "one plus one equals two." However, it was only in the early twentieth century that British philosophers Alfred North Whitehead and Bertrand Russell offered a logical proof for this in their* **Principia Mathematica***, a work that sought to lay the foundations of mathematical truths. Their proof provides a strange juxtaposition between the series of logical notations, impenetrable to the uninitiated, and its incongruously simple conclusion: "From this proposition it will follow, when arithmetical addition has been defined, that 1 + 1 = 2."*

When does $4(x + 3)^2 + 5 = \sqrt{9}(2 + 6 + 7 + 8)$?

The word "algebra" comes from an Arabic root (in this case meaning "reunion"), but this method of mathematical calculation dates back further, to the Babylonians. They developed methods of determining the values of unknown numbers, and algebra remains a fundamental part of mathematics today.

Al-Khwarizmi

*

"al-jabra"

Their method was developed in the second millennium b.c.e., and relied on tables of squares and geometrical figures to solve linear equations (in which there is an unknown variable of the first power: x) and quadratic equations (in which the variable is squared: $x2$). In the first millennium b.c.e., the Egyptians, and later the Greeks, Chinese, and Indians, extended these methods. The Greek mathematician Diophantus, who lived in Alexandria in the third century c.e., developed more sophisticated methods of problem solving, and later Muslim scholars took these further. At the forefront was the Persian mathematician Al-Khwarizmi, who wrote the book from which the word "al-jabra" was taken and in which he introduced the method of canceling "like terms" on opposite sides of an equation, which is still used. Al-Khwarizmi's development of symbolic notation (the x's and y's we use today) to replace geometric methods freed algebra from the physical world and opened the possibility of solving general, rather than particular, algebraic problems.

Into Europe

As in the cases of astronomy, alchemy, physics, chemistry, and other aspects of mathematics, algebra came to Europe from the Islamic world, but it wasn't until the seventeenth century that further progress was made. Independently of each other, Gottfried Leibniz in Germany, Isaac Newton in England, and Seki Kowa in Japan all extended the power of algebra, and made developments that were crucial to the progress of the physical sciences. Leibniz's work laid the foundations for a form of algebra, developed further by George Boole in the mid-1800s and now called Boolean algebra, that is fundamental to computing. The nineteenth century also saw the evolution of more abstract and complex forms of algebra.

FACT: *The order in which operations are carried out on an algebraic equation can have a major effect on the outcome. The correct order of operations is remembered using the acronym PEDMAS (or BEDMAS, or BODMAS, depending on where you live). Anything inside parentheses (or brackets) is dealt with first, then exponentials (anything to a power, such as squared or cubed, also called "orders"), then division, multiplication, addition, and subtraction.*

FACT: *The elements used in algebra are called terms. A term can be a constant (such as an integer, a fraction, or pi), the product of a number and a variable (such as 3x), or the product of two or more variables (such as xy, x^3). An expression is one or more terms (such as $x^2 + 3y - 5$); whereas an equation is two expressions linked by an equality or inequality sign (such as $x^2 + 3y - 5 = 17 - 9$).*

Algebra in Action

To look at a worked example of a linear algebraic equation, we'll turn to a Greek book of riddles written in the fifth century C.E. in which it is said that something approaching the following was found on Diophantus' tombstone: "Diophantus was a boy for the sixth part of his life; after a further twelfth, he had a beard; after a seventh, Diophantus was married. Five years later a son was born, but the boy died when he was half his father's age, and Diophantus died four years later. How old was Diophantus when he died?"

Taking Diophantus' lifespan to be x, we can write down the information in the form of this equation:

$$x = \frac{x}{6} + \frac{x}{12} + \frac{x}{7} + 5 + \frac{x}{2} + 4$$

To get all the x's on one side, we subtract $\frac{x}{6}$, $\frac{x}{12}$, $\frac{x}{7}$, and $\frac{x}{2}$ from both sides, which gives us:

$$x - \frac{x}{6} + \frac{x}{12} + \frac{x}{7} + 5 + \frac{x}{2} = 9$$

In order to subtract the fractions, they all need to have the same divisor (the number in the bottom half of the fraction), so we need a common denominator (a number into which all the divisors will divide). 6, 12, 7, and 2 all divide into 84. 84 divided by 6 is 14, so $\frac{x}{6}$ is $\frac{14x}{84}$, and we do the same for all the fractions to get:

$$\frac{84x}{84} - \frac{14x}{84} - \frac{7x}{84} - \frac{12x}{84} - \frac{42x}{84} = 9$$

Subtracting the numerators (the top numbers) gives:

$$\frac{9x}{84} = 9$$

After multiplying both sides by 84 we have $9x = 756$; then, to find x all we need do is divide both sides by 9. Diophantus was eighty-four when he died.

SUMMARY

To answer the original question: $4(x+3)^2 + 5 = \sqrt{9(2+6+7+8)}$ when $x=1$. The techniques of algebra allow us to solve problems such as this without recourse to using lines, areas, and circles as the Greeks did, and these techniques can be applied to very abstract problems that are not necessarily grounded in the physical world but exist in the realm of pure mathematics.

What Is Calculus?

Just as algebra takes arithmetic to a higher level, calculus ramps the calculating power up another notch. Calculus is the study of change, in the sense of the changing curve of a graph, and the two main types are integral calculus and differential calculus. Calculus is used widely throughout the sciences and in economics to solve problems that can't be solved using algebra.

The ancient Egyptians and Greeks developed methods for calculating volumes and areas by essentially dividing them into very thin slices that could then be added together, foreshadowing the basics of integral calculus. A papyrus from about 1820 B.C.E. shows a calculation of the internal volume of a truncated pyramid, and between the fifth and third centuries B.C.E. the Greek mathematicians Antiphon, Eudoxus, and Archimedes refined what has become known as the method of exhaustion. In Archimedes' hands, this consisted of calculating the area of a geometric shape by working out the area of successive polygons with ever more sides that fit within it. He was able to calculate the areas and volumes of various geometric shapes and forms and was the first to do so. The method, which was developed further by the Chinese mathematicians Liu Hui and Zu Chongzhi in the third and fifth centuries C.E., introduces the idea of a "limit," which is central to calculus. Archimedes also found a method of determining the angle of a line that is tangential to a curve, a task for which differential calculus is now used.

FACT: *The word "calculus" is Latin for a small pebble used for counting, as in early forms of the abacus. The word "calculate" comes from same root.*

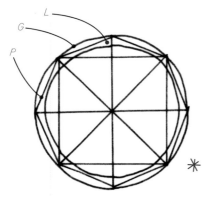

By working out the area of polygons with ever more sides that fit within the circle, it is possible to get closer and closer to the exact area.

SUMMARY

Calculus is an advanced form of mathematical calculation that allows one to work with the very large and the very small. The two main branches of calculus are integral calculus, which gives you the area under a curve, and differential calculus, which allows you to measure the slope of a curve at any point.

FACT: *Calculus is the study of the infinitely small and the infinitely large, integration being the addition of infinitely small rectangles, and differentiation being the division of two infinitely small numbers.*

True Calculus

In the last lesson we learned that Gottfried Leibniz and Isaac Newton contributed to the development of algebra. They were also responsible for the "discovery" of calculus as we know it today. In 1665, an outbreak of the plague led to the closure of Cambridge University, where Newton was a student. He returned to his family home in the country, and in a two-year period he made an astounding number of discoveries in the fields of astronomy, physics, optics, and mathematics, including the discovery of differential and integral calculus, but on these subjects he decided not to publish his findings. Leibniz made his calculus discoveries a few years later, but was quick to publish and therefore received the acclaim. It was Leibniz who introduced notation such as "dy/dx" and the integral symbol, $\int$. A bitter quarrel broke out between the two men, each accusing the other of plagiarism. As in the case of algebra, their breakthroughs were made independently, but the question of who should take the greater credit still rumbles on.

The Swiss mathematician Leonhard Euler (1707–1783) was another influential figure in the development of calculus. Euler worked on many different aspects of pure and applied mathematics and was one of the most prolific writers on the subject, publishing more than 800 papers, despite going blind in 1766. Most of his contributions to calculus were in the branches of calculus of variations and differential equations.

Calculus in action

We won't try to deal here with how calculus is performed, but to give an indication of its use, let's take a graph that shows the changing speed of a car over time. The horizontal (x) axis represents time, and the vertical (y) axis represents velocity. Integral calculus allows us to calculate the area of the graph under the curve at a particular time. The shaded area on this graph tells us the distance that has been covered at time a. Differential calculus enables us to determine the angle of a line tangential to the curve at a particular point (for example, point b on this graph). This tells us the rate of change of v with respect to t (or $\frac{\partial v}{\partial t}$), which is the acceleration of the car at that moment.

Graph of velocity against time

The angle of this line tells us the rate of acceleration at point **b**.

The area under the curve tells us the distance covered by time **a**.

<u>Who</u> Was Pythagoras?

Pythagoras was a Greek philosopher and mathematician who lived in the sixth century B.C.E. Referred to as the "father of numbers," he is best known for proving the geometric theorem that bears his name: Pythagoras's theorem or the Pythagorean theorem. But his influence on mathematics goes way beyond this; he saw numbers as the key to understanding the universe, rather than just a means of recording business transactions.

＊

In this detail from Raphael's sixteenth-century painting of the School of Athens, Pythagoras is shown teaching his students.

Unfortunately, Pythagoras left no written records, and many of the tales attributed to his life, especially those concerning his mathematical discoveries, may owe more to legend than fact. He was born on the Greek island of Samos around 570 B.C.E., the son of Mnesarchus and Pythais. As a young man he left Samos for the island of Lesbos, where he studied with the philosopher and mathematician Thales of Miletus and his student Anaximander, an astronomer and philosopher. Impressed with the young man's abilities, Thales encouraged him to visit Egypt. Pythagoras traveled there in around 547 B.C.E. and studied under the Egyptian priests for some twenty years. It is probable that Pythagoras first encountered the theorem that now bears his name during this time. He returned to Samos, where he established a school, but then moved to Croton in southern Italy, where he founded a secret ascetic community. His students, both men and women, were known as Pythagoreans. They led a monastic life: they ate a vegetarian diet, personal possessions were forbidden, and they observed a rule of silence. Their studies included astronomy, mathematics, music, philosophy, and religion.

Pythagoras's Theorem

Although it is unlikely that he was the first to propose the theorem that bears his name, later writers attribute to Pythagoras its first systematic proof. The theorem goes as follows: "The square of the hypotenuse of a right triangle is equal to the sum of the squares of the lengths of each of the other two sides."

> **QUOTE:**
>
> *"Number is the ruler of forms and ideas and the cause of gods and demons." Attributed to Pythagoras by Iamblichus of Chalcis.*

＊ *If a triangle has sides of lengths a, b, and c, and the angle ab is 90° (a right angle), then Pythagoras's theorem tells us that $c^2 = a^2 + b^2$.*

"The so-called Pythagoreans, who were the first to take up mathematics, not only advanced this subject, but saturated with it, they fancied that the principles of mathematics were the principles of all things." **Aristotle,** Metaphysics I-5, c. 350 B.C.E.

Pythagoras (c. 570–475 B.C.E.) was a Greek philosopher and mathematician who studied geometry and mathematics in Ionia and Egypt and founded a scholarly community in southern Italy. He is credited with a theorem that describes the ratios of the sides of a right-angled triangle, and he and his followers raised the profile of mathematics as a philosophical, even religious, discipline.

Let's consider a triangle with sides a and b meeting at 90°: a right angle. The third side, c, is the long side, the hypotenuse. The theorem states that the length of the hypotenuse multiplied by itself is equal to the sum of the lengths of each of the other two sides multiplied by themselves, or $c^2 = a^2 + b^2$. To appreciate this visually, we can draw three squares: with its side on c, another at a, and another at b. According to the theorem, the area of square c is the same as that of square a plus square b. The classic example is a square that has sides of 3, 4, and 5 units: $3^2 + 4^2 = 5^2$, or 9 + 16 = 25. Any triangle that has those proportions is must be a right-angled triangle.

A Mathematical Philosophy

Much that has been attributed to Pythagoras over the centuries may really have been achieved by his followers. Nevertheless, he set mathematics at the heart of his philosophy, believing that numbers held the key to understanding the cosmos and that the universe functioned on the basis of predictable patterns, rhythms, and cycles. At a time when natural phenomena were explained by reference to the gods, he took a more rational approach, probably influenced by his former teacher, Thales. Pythagoras is said to have determined the relationships of the intervals between musical notes and to have believed that the movements of the Sun, Moon, and planets were governed by the same laws of harmony: the "music of the spheres."

The Pythagoreans influenced subsequent mathematicians and philosophers, including Euclid and Plato. Their emphasis on numbers is seen in the work of the Islamic alchemists, and most modern physicists would agree that measurement and mathematics are the keys to understanding the universe.

FACT: *A believer in reincarnation, Pythagoras advocated vegetarianism as he believed that souls transmigrated between animals and humans in a process of purification. His followers were only permitted to eat meat that had first been ritually sacrificed to the gods. He himself was said (centuries later) to have sacrificed oxen in honor of "his" theorem.*

Where Was the Metric System Invented?

Despite attempts by various civilizations to use different number bases for counting, the base-ten system has long been the standard around the globe, perhaps because we still like to count on our fingers. But when it comes to weights and measures, complete inconsistency was the rule until relatively recently. Why did it take so long, and where did sanity first creep in?

✳

The logo of the Bureau Inter-national des Poids et Mesures, the guardian of the metric system.

Take the U.S. and British Imperial units of length. There are 1,760 yards in a mile, 3 feet in a yard, 12 inches in a foot, and the inch can be divided by 2, 4, 8, 16, 32, 64, or 1,000! And every other kind of measurement, including area and weight, has its own traditional collection of idiosyncratic units, all adding up to a very complex system that's hard to use.

The situation in seventeenth-century Europe was further complicated by the fact that trading nations frequently used different units or different definitions of the same units. In the late 1600s, a French clergyman and astronomer, Gabriel Mouton, suggested a metric system—one that uses powers of ten—based on a unit of length equivalent to one minute of arc (one-sixtieth of one degree) of a great circle of Earth; and another French astronomer, Jean Picard, proposed a similar system based on the length of a pendulum that swung every second. However, nothing changed for more than a century, and it took a revolution for something to happen.

Going Metric

The French Revolution began in 1789, and the National Assembly of France made weights and measures a priority, asking the French Academy of Sciences to come up with a coherent and scientific system. They returned to Gabriel Mouton's idea of basing the unit of length on a portion of Earth's circumference, deriving units for volume and mass from this, and dividing and multiplying these by powers of ten. In this way, calculations could be made by simply moving a decimal point.

FACT: *After 1799, the meter was redefined several times, based on the wavelengths of particular parts of the light spectrum; then, in 1983, it was given the definition that we have today. This is "the length of the path traveled by light in vacuum during a time interval of $1/299,792,458$ of a second." This, of course, requires a definition of the second, which is now based on the radiation properties of a cesium atom.*

QUOTE:

"The current effort toward national metrication is based on the conclusion that industrial and commercial productivity, mathematics and science education, and the competitiveness of American products and services in world markets, will be enhanced by completing the change to the metric system of units. Failure to complete the change will increasingly handicap the Nation's industry and economy."

U.S. National Institute for Standards and Technology, 2002

The idea was accepted, and the system went ahead. The fundamental unit was called the meter—from the Greek word for "measure"—and it was defined as one ten-millionth (0.0000001) of the distance from the north pole to the equator along the meridian that passes through Paris and Barcelona. The unit of mass, the gram, was defined as the mass of one cubic centimeter (a cube with sides a hundredth of a meter in length) of water at its temperature of maximum density. The unit of fluid volume, the liter, was defined as the volume of a cube having sides a tenth of a meter long.

Setting Standards

In 1799, the "meter of the archive"—a platinum bar with parallel ends—was created, and the meter was defined as the length of this bar at a particular temperature (metal expands and contracts with changes of temperature). The use of the newly adopted "metric" system was slow to spread at first, but in the nineteenth century, when there were rapid developments in science and engineering, its usefulness became clear, and seventeen countries signed up to the "treaty of the meter" in 1875. Each received a set of metric standards so it could implement the system

By the 1960s, most countries had adopted or were adopting the metric system. Today only a handful of nations use pre-metric units. The United States is the only industrialized country not to have "gone metric." Even here, with the need for international communication and agreement, the metric system is widely used in science, engineering, and medicine.

INTERNATIONAL SYSTEM

The seven base units of the *Système International d'Unités*, or SI for short, were established in 1960, and they are:

- the meter (m), for length
- the kilogram (kg), for mass
- the second (s), for time
- the ampere (A), for electric current
- the kelvin (K), for thermodynamic temperature
- the mole (mol), for amount of substance
- the candela (cd), for luminous intensity.

SUMMARY

The metric system of weights and measures was invented in France in the eighteenth century. It is now used in almost every country and in all scientific fields as it is easy to use in calculations, it is based on unchanging physical constants, and it relates all units within it to each other.

When Were the Norse Sagas Created?

The Norse sagas conjure up strong images of bloodthirsty tales told in longhouses by heavily bearded Vikings, accompanied by large quantities of alcohol and the occasional brawl. *The Vikings* (1958), starring Kirk Douglas, seems to be the epitome of the Norse saga, but few of us could take more than a guess about when all this happened, let alone why.

From the collapse of the Western Roman Empire in the fifth century C.E. until the early centuries of the second millennium, the world witnessed a dramatic migration of Germanic and Norse peoples. Scandinavia's harsh environment forced communities to mix small-scale agriculture, fishing, trade, and piracy in order to survive. The opportunities offered by expansion into the heartlands of Europe and across the Atlantic were sufficiently attractive to draw succeeding generations ever farther outward.

We tend to associate Vikings with plunder and pillage, but this is an unfortunate caricature. Much expansion was based on trade and the establishment of new colonies as far apart as Iceland, Greenland, Ireland, northern France, Russia, and the Black Sea coast. The longship proved to be a very adaptable craft, capable of epic voyages—even as far as North America—as well as withstanding being hauled overland as the Vikings pushed their way into Russia. Hoards of coins from all over the Old World have been discovered in Scandinavia, demonstrating the massive extent of their trading network.

Style and Content

The sagas are set during this period of expansion and consolidation. They probably originate from the early tenth century as formal, structured accounts. It is believed that the main body of sagas was formed between the mid-tenth and mid-eleventh centuries, coinciding with some of the greatest phases of expansion. This era is sometimes described as the "age of sagas."

The word *saga* means "to say" or "to tell." The Scandinavian and Germanic peoples valued the oral tradition of recounting epic tales in formal and informal settings, so they were not written down for several hundred years. This means that categorizing the sagas and identifying their origins can be very

FACT: Some historians believe that the trigger for Viking expansion came around 800 C.E., when the climate of the Northern Hemisphere warmed sufficiently to cause the pack ice to withdraw, thereby increasing the potential sailing range of the longships.

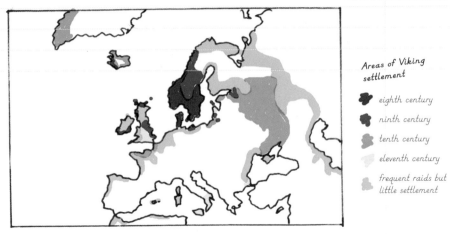

Areas of Viking settlement

eighth century

ninth century

tenth century

eleventh century

frequent raids but little settlement

difficult. Some can be attributed to particular poets; for example, the Icelandic poet Egill Skallagrimsson (910–990) is believed to be the author of *Revenge Denied*, and *Orb of the World* can be attributed to Snorri Sturluson (1179–1241). Other sagas, however, have no clear origin.

The sagas are perhaps more conveniently divided into historical and fictional tales, although even here there is confusion, with historical figures sometimes being given divine ancestors. Perhaps the most clear-cut distinction is that sagas can be related to three aspects of Nordic life: rulers, families, and heroes.

Stylistically, the sagas dwell on three themes. As narratives they all have a preoccupation with the notion of fate. This applies to both pagan- and Christian-era tales. Facing and overcoming adversity is the second, regularly occurring theme, and, related to that, the qualities of character give the stories an enduring humanity. The fact that they are engaging and entertaining has enabled the Norse sagas to have an impact long after their creation. They influenced the English saga tradition, of which the most famous example is *Beowulf*. The heroic narrative also plays a strong part in the epic qualities of Hollywood Westerns. The *Ring Cycle* operas of Wagner (of which "The Ride of the Valkyries" is perhaps the most widely known piece, having been used in the score for *Apocalypse Now*) dwell on the central characters of Norse mythology. Most famously of all, J. R. R. Tolkien was inspired by the Norse sagas to create the Middle-earth stories now known and loved around the globe.

FACT: J. R. R. Tolkien, author of *The Lord of the Rings*, drew inspiration from the sagas. The term "Middle-earth" can be found in the Norse tradition, and the name Gandalf has its origin in the **Edda** saga.

SUMMARY

Even if the authorship of many of the sagas is uncertain, we do know that they were intimately linked with the great period of Norse expansion that commenced in the mid–tenth century. The mythic qualities of the sagas are in some respects enhanced by the fact that their exact origins are shrouded in the mists of time.

<u>Why</u> Don't All Poems Rhyme?

Even if we don't all know what a poem should be, we do have some expectations; for example, we expect a poem to make some sense to us. Samuel Taylor Coleridge argued that poetry was "the best words in the best order." We expect it to be different from prose, and the key distinction for many people is that poetry should rhyme—but that is not always so.

As writing evolved in human society, it was driven by three fundamental requirements. The process of trade needed a record of purchases and sales, of commitments to be fulfilled at a given time and place. The demands of government were that place, rank, rule, and obligation were acknowledged and observed. The aspirations of religion, however, were different; spiritual belief required something less prosaic. Perhaps it was in this field that poetry had its origins. Certainly, poetry can be found in some of the earliest religious texts, such as the Old Testament and the Sanskrit Vedas. Where emotion and language intersect, we find poetry.

The Advantage of Rhyme

For many people, prose, the lyrics of a song, and a poem have indistinct boundaries. In distinguishing poetry from prose, though, there is often an expectation that poetry will contain some form of rhyme. A rhyme sequence can be pleasing to the ear: we find pleasure in the structure that it creates, as it helps to give a form that can enhance the message of the work. The rhyme can also serve to make the poem memorable, and it would have been useful within societies where an oral tradition valued the recounting of epic stories in the form of poems. The epic poem has a vibrant

Gustav Doré's illustration of Satan's fall, in **Paradise Lost***.*

✳

QUOTE:

"The first sort by their own suggestions fell,
Self-tempted, self-depraved: man falls deceived
By the other first: man therefore shall find grace,
The other none."

John Milton, *Paradise Lost*

QUOTE:

"Poetry is the spontaneous overflow of powerful feelings."

William Wordsworth (1770–1850), English poet

tradition and wonderful examples that are popular to the present day, such as *The Odyssey*, *The Iliad*, *The Rime of the Ancient Mariner*, and *Paradise Lost*. A rhyming structure can lead the reader through the poem, developing and expanding the imagery that it employs. The structure can be simple, such as in a four-line verse where the rhyme xyxy is known as cross-rhyme, and xyyx is sometimes referred to as an envelope-rhyme (whereas xxyy is just a couple of couplets). However, the structure can be more complicated—such as xyzxyz, which represents a six-line verse in which the first line rhymes with the fourth, the second with the fifth, and the third with the sixth. There is also the nine-line Balassi verse structure, which rhymes yyxzzxaaz. At that point, it might become difficult to recognize the rhyming sequence without close scrutiny—so sometimes a poem might not appear to rhyme, even though it does!

Poetry without Rhyme

When poems do not rhyme it can be for a range of reasons, of which some are practical and others are esoteric. The most common practical reason is the difficulty of translating poetry from one language into another. The dilemma is whether to translate directly or in a manner that hopes to express the original essence at the cost of altering the text. Even when no translation is required, the fact that rhyming relies on identical pronunciation means that different intonations of speech and accents can destroy the intended rhyme.

Sometimes poets deliberately break conventions and expectations such as rhyming structures. They may seek to challenge complacent preconceptions in the reader. In free-form poetry, the rhyme is abandoned altogether, leading some to deny that it is poetry at all, in the same way that some critics argue that some contemporary art does not deserve the name. The most common form of non-rhyming poetry is blank verse. This relies on rhythm rather than rhyme to create a recognizable structure in the poetry. Probably the best-known example of this is the iambic pentameter of Shakespearean plays. The advantage of relying on rhythm rather than rhyme is the degree of flexibility that it allows the poet.

QUOTE:

"Water, water, everywhere,
And all the boards did shrink;
Water, water, everywhere,
Nor any drop to drink."

Samuel Taylor Coleridge (1772–1834),

The Rime of the Ancient Mariner

SUMMARY

Opening any compilation of popular poetry reveals that most poems have some form of rhyming structure. This is a testament to the enduring success of the rhyme as part of poetic expression—it also helps to explain why we are often surprised when a poem doesn't rhyme.

Who Was Shakespeare?

Academic investigation and public fascination has provided us with a wealth of information about the works of Shakespeare. But what do we know about the man himself? Much of the information we have is supposition, and hard facts about who William Shakespeare really was are surprisingly hard to come by.

William Shakespeare
(1564–1616)

The town records that detail aspects of his family history reveal Shakespeare the youth. We know that his father, John Shakespeare, had married Mary Arden, and that they set up home in the town of Stratford-upon-Avon in the county of Warwickshire. The baptismal records inform us that William Shakespeare was baptized on April 26, 1564. John was successful in his trade as a glove maker and wool dealer. He acquired some prominence in the town and served on its council. From this it is sometimes deduced that William may have received a formal education, at least until his early teens, at Stratford's grammar school. Here his education would have included a thorough grounding in the classics.

The second clear piece of evidence we have—his marriage certificate— places Shakespeare as a young man. At the age of eighteen, he was married to Anne Hathaway. She was twenty-six at the time, an age difference that points to an unconventional or at least adventurous outlook. Seven months after the wedding, we discover a baptismal certificate for Susanna, the oldest of his three children. Shakespeare was husband and father no younger than many of his contemporaries, but how he sustained his family is unknown. There is some speculation that he worked as some type of schoolmaster. There is also a suggestion that he lived dangerously, following the pursuits of a poacher. Those who hold to that view say that it explains his sudden appearance in London in 1586, perhaps avoiding some punishment for poaching.

QUOTE:

" . . . an upstart crow, beautified with our feathers, that with his Tiger's heart wrapped in a player's hide, supposes he is as well able to bombast out a blank verse as the best of you." *Robert Greene (1558–1592), dramatist, on Shakespeare*

FACT: *The authorship of Shakespeare's body of work has been called into question by those who believe that some or all of the plays were actually written by another hand. The most famous candidate is perhaps Christopher "Kit" Marlowe, who some believe faked his own death, but continued to write under the name of Shakespeare; other notable alternatives put forward have included Francis Bacon and Edward de Vere, the seventeenth Earl of Oxford.*

FACT: *Shakespeare's patron, the Earl of Southampton, was a favorite at the court of Queen Elizabeth I. He later fell from grace and died from a fever while battling the Spanish in the United Provinces (Holland) in 1624.*

The name of William Shakespeare is world-renowned and will probably remain so long into the future. As a poet and playwright he is widely acknowledged as a genius, and his works are much loved. But this is one aspect of the man. To consider who he really was, we must remember the youth, the husband and father, the gentleman, and the entrepreneur—although astonishingly few concrete facts about his life have survived the centuries.

The London Playwright

Shakespeare was certainly an actor and playwright by 1592. It is then that we have a documented criticism of the young star by another dramatist, Robert Greene. His dramas at this stage are often rooted in the stories of English history, and the fact that two of them were dedicated to the Earl of Southampton demonstrates that he had already acquired a powerful patron.

We know that William Shakespeare became coproprietor of a new theatrical company, the Lord Chamberlain's Men, in 1594. This became the King's Men in 1603 thanks to the patronage of the newly crowned King James I. These facts help us to appreciate the influence and success that Shakespeare attained in his lifetime. We also know that he was industrious, writing and producing at least two plays a year. The patronage of the rich and powerful did not in itself confer social standing, but the rank of gentleman did. John Shakespeare had been granted the right to bear a coat-of-arms in 1596. When John died in 1601, William Shakespeare inherited the arms and the social standing of a gentleman, despite being in a profession that usually lacked status.

Deeds and other legal documentation then give us an insight into Shakespeare as a wealthy and successful man. In 1597 he purchased a large house in Stratford, New Place. The property portfolio grew with other purchases in the town, culminating in the acquisition of more than one hundred acres of land in 1602. As well as being successful in the arts, Shakespeare was clearly a shrewd investor. By 1611 he had acquired sufficient wealth to retire in comfort. His will, written in the same year, bequeaths most of his estate to his oldest daughter, who had married well to a doctor.

The final record of Shakespeare the man dates from 1616, and shows that he was buried at Holy Trinity Church, Stratford, on April 25. The first published collection of his complete works—the so-called First Folio—appeared in 1623. Over half of its contents had never before been published, and—as one final mystery—because some of the plays were interpolated from working drafts, we will never know how accurately the First Folio records Shakespeare's original words.

Where Does Haiku Come From?

Just like a haiku itself, this question seems simple, but it has hidden complexities. It can be answered in three senses. The first is literal: where, geographically, does haiku come from? The second is stylistic: where in literary terms does haiku come from? Finally, and most esoterically, there is the question of where philosophically haiku comes from. Following so far? All three are interlinked, but considering them in these three senses improves the clarity of our understanding.

Geographic Origins

The geographical issue is the easiest to deal with, and also the best-known. Haiku originates in Japan. The form emerged in the seventeenth century and shows evidence of the influence of a Chinese poetic tradition. One of the acknowledged early masters of haiku was Matsuo Bashō (1644–1694). Since his lifetime, haiku has spread to become a global form of poetry, and there are many organizations, study groups, and periodicals devoted to the writing, performance, and promotion of haiku.

QUOTE:

"Gray hairs being plucked,
and from below my pillow
a cricket singing."

Matsuo Bashō (1644–1694), Japanese poet

* *The masters of haiku were, and still are, highly respected in Japan. Foremost among them was Matsuo Bashō.*

SUMMARY

From its Japanese roots, haiku has become an international art form. Haiku can be found in many languages and can express a wide range of cultural perspectives. Although it has been over three hundred years since the birth of haiku, it remains stylistically tied to its origins. Try writing haiku for yourself. It can be dangerously addictive.

QUOTE:

"the simple writing
of seventeen syllables
doth not haiku make"

Gerald England, "Not a Haiku,"

from *The Art of Haiku* (1990)

Stylistic Origins

Some accounts attribute the poetic style of haiku to light verse, while others suggest that it has more courtly antecedents. The style comes from a desire to be expressive within a refined and carefully regulated structure. It looks easy to write a haiku, but it is actually really tough. The structure appears to be simple. A traditional haiku has three lines with a set number of syllables in each line—usually five in the first and third lines and seven syllables in the second line. So far, so good, but there is a problem, which is that the Japanese language has much shorter syllable sounds than languages like English. Whether you choose to stick with the 5–7–5 rule or shorten it to 2–3–2 when writing in English, it is best to remember the often-quoted Gerald England who wrote the haiku shown above.

So haiku appears to be simple in structure, but that simplicity is what makes them so tricky. You have to be so economical and try to compress so much meaning into the few words that you have at your disposal.

Philosophical Origins

Philosophically, haiku comes from the Zen Buddhist tradition of Japanese society. When expressing the feeling of Zen, it is believed to be important to create a sense of stillness and aloneness. This is called *sabi*. It can make a haiku feel wistful and, frankly, a bit depressing. Another important aspect to Zen is locating the poem in nature, especially the seasons of the natural world. If a haiku deals with human nature and does not make a seasonal reference, it is called a *senryu*. Most haiku do include a word that links the poem to a season. This can be a direct reference or it can be indirect, by referring to an activity or occurrence associated with a particular season. For example, the cricket is always linked to summer.

FACT: Bashō is traditionally believed to have created the word "haiku" from two words used to mean "funny" or "light" poetry, "hokku" and "haikai." Haiku is traditionally untitled, and a master of the art of haiku is called a haijin.

What Is a Stanza?

As a writing form, poetry is difficult to define precisely. It frequently attempts to break rules and challenge conventions. However, the stanza as one structural device does have some reasonably consistent rules. Now, just what is a stanza again?

It might help to jog your memory if we say that stanzas are more often called "verses." A poet usually employs stanzas in a consistent manner within a poem. Thus, the poem might have stanzas that are all seven lines long with the same regular rhythm, or "meter." In Italian, the word *stanza* literally means "stopping place." Stanzas are an opportunity to introduce a break, sometimes at the end of a sentence, the completion of a distinct thought, or the introduction of a different action. Beyond that point, the definition begins to break down. There is no requirement to have a set number of words or lines, nor is there any necessity to introduce a given number of stanzas. It is all rather vague!

Perhaps the most convenient way of giving definition to stanzas is to consider the number of lines included in each one. This does not mean that they necessarily have to rhyme. Nor does it mean that there has to be a particular meter. Once again, it's rather vague!

FACT: *Chaucer lived from around 1343 to 1400. A prolific author, he is most famous for* **The Canterbury Tales**, *a sequence of stories told by different pilgrims traveling as a band to the shrine of St. Thomas Becket.*

Types of Stanzas

A two-line stanza is called a "couplet," and perhaps the most famous exponent of this form was Geoffrey Chaucer. Couplets provide a neat, rhythmic quality that can act as a device to create a sense of contrast when used in extended works of poetry.

A three-line stanza is sometimes called a "tercet." If all three lines rhyme, the tercet stanza is defined as a "triplet." Haiku, a form of poetry that originated in Japan (see pp. 94–95), demands the use of the tercet form. This is often accompanied by a given number of syllables in each line, usually 5–7–5, in order to create a very spare style. The following example is of a traditional haiku by the poet Matsuo Bashō: "No one travels / Along this way but I, / This autumn evening." The four-line stanza is called a "quatrain." This can be formed by joining two couplets within a single verse. A good example of quatrain-

QUOTE:

"The caravan of life shall always pass
Beware that is fresh as sweet young grass
Let's not worry about what tomorrow will amass
Fill my cup again, this night will pass, alas."
Omar Khayyám (1048–1123), Rubaiyat of Omar Khayyám

Edward Lear, the artist and nonsense poet, corrects a stranger who thought his name was merely a pseudonym by showing him the label inside his hat.

structured poetry is the *Rubaiyat*, written by Omar Khayyám (see quote). The *Rubaiyat* was written in Farsi, creating a difficulty for translators: Would it be better to translate literally, and lose the essence of the quatrain, or retain the form but sacrifice the exact expressions of Khayyám?

The five-line stanza is perhaps most often employed in the limerick. It is believed that the term "limerick" comes from bawdy songs sung in the public houses of Limerick in Ireland. This form of poetry deliberately attempts to be irreverent and humorous. One of the most famous writers of limericks was Edward Lear, who described them as "nonsense verses."

This manner of defining a stanza can go on and on—for example, some nine-line stanzas are called "Spenserian" because of Edmund Spenser's use of them in the *Faerie Queene*. He employed a specific form of rhyme sequence in each stanza to such acclaim that his name now defines it.

QUOTE:

"There was an Old Person whose habits,
Induced him to feed upon rabbits;
When he'd eaten eighteen,
He turned perfectly green,
Upon which he relinquished those habits."

Edward Lear (1812–1888), artist, author, and poet

SUMMARY

A stanza is essentially a verse that is employed to provide a break in a poem; however, it can take a huge variety of forms, which are most commonly defined by the number of lines it contains.

FACT: Omar Khayyám lived in Persia at some point between the mid–eleventh and twelfth centuries. He contributed to astrology, astronomy, mathematics, and philosophy, but is best known for his poetry.

Knowledge: *the ability to recall information*

1) Who first coined the term "Big Bang" in reference to the origin of the universe?
- **a.** Georges Lemaître
- **b.** Fred Hoyle
- **c.** V. M. Slipher
- **d.** Edwin Hubble

2) Approximately how long ago did the Big Bang occur?
- **a.** 14 billion years
- **b.** 10 billion years
- **c.** 4 billion years
- **d.** 4 million years

3) In what year did the Hubble Space Telescope start to operate?
- **a.** 1989
- **b.** 1990
- **c.** 1889
- **d.** 2001

4) In Einstein's famous equation $E = mc^2$, what does c stand for?
- **a.** The gravitational constant
- **b.** The circumference of the universe
- **c.** The speed of light
- **d.** Electrical current

5) What was the name of the program that developed the first atomic bombs?
- **a.** The Big One
- **b.** Los Alamos
- **c.** Project X
- **d.** The Manhattan Project

6) Light displays the properties of:
- **a.** A beam of particles
- **b.** A set of waves
- **c.** Both particles and waves
- **d.** Neither particles nor waves

7) Photons possess:
- **a.** Energy and momentum
- **b.** Energy and charge
- **c.** Mass and momentum
- **d.** Mass and charge

8) Which great physicist backed the particle, or "corpuscular," theory of light?
- **a.** Isaac Newton
- **b.** Albert Einstein
- **c.** Fred Hoyle
- **d.** Albert Newton

9) If dark energy is extremely powerful, which of these best describes the fate of the universe?
- **a.** Big Bounce
- **b.** Big Crunch
- **c.** Big Rip
- **d.** Big Freeze

10) What exists beyond the limits of our universe?
- **a.** Other universes
- **b.** Empty space
- **c.** Antispace
- **d.** The question is meaningless

11) According to Einstein, gravity:
- **a.** Slows light
- **b.** Bends light
- **c.** Speeds up light
- **d.** Reduces light

12) How much longer do scientists believe the universe will last?
- **a.** 1 billion years
- **b.** 100,000 years
- **c.** 100 billion years
- **d.** 100 million years

Understanding: *the ability to interpret information and make links between different aspects of it*

1) What are the four fundamental physical forces, and approximately how soon after the Big Bang did they come to have their present values?

2) Was Albert Einstein in favor of the United States developing nuclear weapons, or was he opposed to it?

3) Why does a prism split light into various colors?

4) If nothing can travel faster than the speed of light, how can galaxies be moving apart at a greater speed than that?

Knowledge: *the ability to recall information*

1) What is the estimated age of the Chauvet Cave paintings?
- **a.** 200,000–100,000 B.C.E.
- **b.** 30,000–28,000 B.C.E.
- **c.** 20,000–15,000 B.C.E.
- **d.** 15,000–5,000 B.C.E.

2) Which colors were mainly used in the cave paintings found in the Chauvet Cave?
- **a.** Blue and green
- **b.** Black and white
- **c.** Pink and orange
- **d.** Red and black

3) In what year was the Chauvet Cave discovered?
- **a.** 1980
- **b.** 1984
- **c.** 1990
- **d.** 1994

4) Who is believed to have commissioned the Bayeux Tapestry?
- **a.** William, Duke of Normandy
- **b.** Harold Godwinson
- **c.** Bishop Odo
- **d.** Harald Hardrada

5) How long is what remains of the Bayeux Tapestry?
- **a.** 10 m
- **b.** 50 m
- **c.** 70 m
- **d.** 100 m

6) What does the word "Renaissance" mean?
- **a.** Ancient
- **b.** Italian
- **c.** Rebirth
- **d.** Restored

7) Which of these was not an important Renaissance invention?
- **a.** The printing press
- **b.** The microscope
- **c.** The telescope
- **d.** The photographic camera

8) Which of these thinkers was not a Renaissance man?
- **a.** Martin Luther
- **b.** Leonardo da Vinci
- **c.** John Stuart Mill
- **d.** Copernicus

9) In which year was Leonardo da Vinci born?
- **a.** 1452
- **b.** 1400
- **c.** 1492
- **d.** 1450

10) Who is the *Mona Lisa* believed to be a portrait of?
- **a.** The Queen of France
- **b.** The Queen of England
- **c.** Leonardo da Vinci's wife
- **d.** The wife of a Florentine silk merchant

11) Who is sometimes called "the Father of Impressionism"?
- **a.** Degas
- **b.** Monet
- **c.** Pissarro
- **d.** Gauguin

12) Where did the name "Impressionist" come from?
- **a.** A Shakespeare play
- **b.** A Monet painting
- **c.** The Latin word for "unfinished"
- **d.** The French word for "rubbish"

Understanding: *the ability to interpret information and make links between different aspects of it*

1) Why are the Chauvet Cave paintings predominantly of animals?

2) How accurate is the Bayeux Tapestry's account of the Battle of Hastings?

3) Why was the Bayeux Tapestry used in the French Revolution and during the Napoleonic wars?

4) Why can using the term "Renaissance" be misleading?

5) Why has the *Mona Lisa*'s smile proved so inscrutable?

6) What were the impressionists hoping to achieve in their paintings?

Knowledge: *the ability to recall information*

1) Which of these binary expressions represents the decimal number 22?
- **a.** 1111
- **b.** 1010
- **c.** 11111
- **d.** 10110

2) What is the origin of the word "calculate"?
- **a.** A Hebrew word for "dust"
- **b.** A Greek word for "headache"
- **c.** A Latin word for "pebble"
- **d.** An Egyptian word for "taxes"

3) Which two mathematicians quarreled over which of them had first discovered calculus?
- **a.** Leonhard Euler and René Descartes
- **b.** Gottfried Leibniz and Isaac Newton
- **c.** Liu Hui and Zu Chongzhi
- **d.** Eudoxus and Archimedes

4) What kind of triangle does Pythagoras's theorem relate to?
- **a.** An equilateral triangle
- **b.** An isosceles triangle
- **c.** An oblique triangle
- **d.** A right-angled triangle

5) In what language does the word *algebra* have its roots?
- **a.** Arabic
- **b.** Hindi
- **c.** Italian
- **d.** German

6) On what island was the philosopher and mathematician Pythagoras born?
- **a.** The Italian island of Sicily
- **b.** The Greek island of Samos
- **c.** The French island of Corsica
- **d.** The Spanish island of Ibiza

7) What is the fundamental unit of the metric system?
- **a.** The gram
- **b.** The kilogram
- **c.** The meter
- **d.** The liter

8) The metric system came into existence as a result of the:
- **a.** Cuban Revolution
- **b.** Hundred Years War
- **c.** Industrial Revolution
- **d.** French Revolution

9) Which of these countries has not yet adopted the metric system?
- **a.** Mexico
- **b.** The United States
- **c.** Australia
- **d.** Canada

10) There are two types of calculus—integral calculus and:
- **a.** Disintegrating calculus
- **b.** Divisional calculus
- **c.** Differential calculus
- **d.** Divergent calculus

11) The 18th-century mathematician Leonhard Euler was:
- **a.** French
- **b.** German
- **c.** Swedish
- **d.** Swiss

12) On what material did the Babylonians record their mathematical calculations?
- **a.** Paper
- **b.** Clay
- **c.** Rock
- **d.** Slate

Understanding: *the ability to interpret information and make links between different aspects of it*

1) What are the four basic operations of arithmetic, and how long have they been in use?

2) It is important to carry out the operations on an algebraic equation in the right order. What is that order and how can it be memorized?

3) State Pythagoras's theorem.

4) Name the seven base units of the International System of Units, and state what properties they are used to measure.

Knowledge: *the ability to recall information*

1) When was the "age of sagas"?
- **a.** 4–5th centuries C.E.
- **b.** Mid 7th–mid 8th centuries C.E.
- **c.** Mid 10th–mid 11th centuries C.E.
- **d.** 12th–13th centuries C.E.

2) What does the word "saga" mean?
- **a.** To say
- **b.** Story
- **c.** To act
- **d.** Song

3) Who said poetry was "the best words in the best order?"
- **a.** William Wordsworth
- **b.** William Shakespeare
- **c.** Percy Shelley
- **d.** Samuel Coleridge

4) Which of these is not an epic poem?
- **a.** *The Odyssey*
- **b.** *The Iliad*
- **c.** *Paradise Lost*
- **d.** *Daffodils*

5) When was William Shakespeare born?
- **a.** April 26, 1564
- **b.** April 26, 1595
- **c.** November 5, 1550
- **d.** December 1, 1500

6) What was the name of Shakespeare's wife?
- **a.** Susanna Greene
- **b.** Mary Arden
- **c.** Anne Hathaway
- **d.** Lady Macbeth

7) Where is Shakespeare buried?
- **a.** The City of London
- **b.** Stratford
- **c.** Oxford
- **d.** Cambridge

8) Where did Haiku originate?
- **a.** Japan
- **b.** China
- **c.** France
- **d.** England

9) Who is generally attributed with having created the word *Haiku*?
- **a.** Gerald England
- **b.** Robert Greene
- **c.** Matsuo Bashō
- **d.** Christopher Marlowe

10) What is the traditional syllable requirement for haiku?
- **a.** 5-7-5
- **b.** 3-5-3
- **c.** 2-3-2
- **d.** 7-5-7

11) What does the Italian word "stanza" literally mean in English?
- **a.** Fast
- **b.** Verse
- **c.** Stopping place
- **d.** Couplet

12) What type of poetry was Edward Lear famous for?
- **a.** Sonnets
- **b.** Epic poems
- **c.** Haiku
- **d.** Limericks

Understanding: *the ability to interpret information and make links between different aspects of it*

1) Why did the Vikings seek land overseas?

2) What was the legacy of the Norse Sagas?

3) Why can translating a poem be problematic?

4) Why can't we be sure that the Shakespeare plays we know today accurately reflect the originals?

5) What is the link between haiku and the natural world?

6) Why is it so difficult to write haiku?

7) Why is it so hard to define "stanza"?

Wednesday

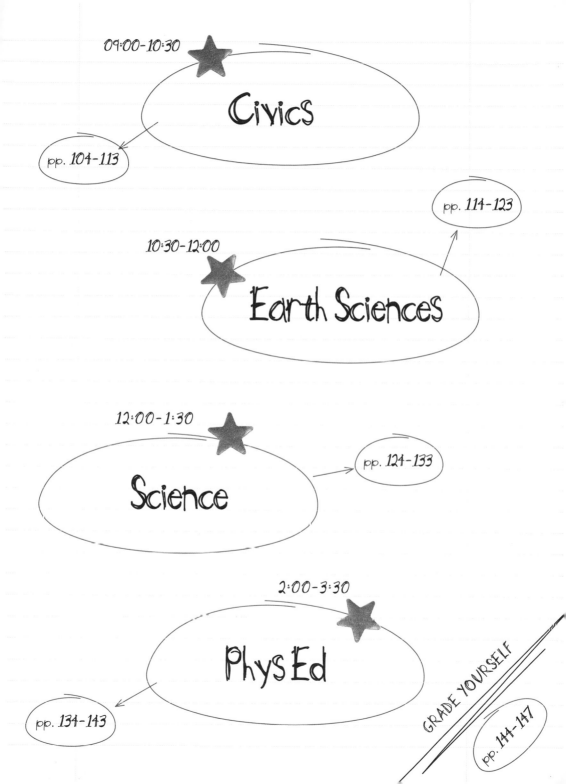

09:00-10:30

Civics

pp. 104-113

pp. 114-123

10:30-12:00

Earth Sciences

12:00-1:30

Science

pp. 124-133

2:00-3:30

Phys Ed

pp. 134-143

GRADE YOURSELF

pp. 144-147

What *Is a Constitution?*

Surely that should be "What is *the* Constitution?" . . . right? Well, not quite. The concept of a constitution can be traced all the way back to ancient Greece. In his *Politics*, Aristotle considered 150 different constitutions, mostly from Greek city-states, and attempted to discern their defining features. He arrived at the conclusion that they were rules for governance, and that remains the case today.

When most people think about a constitution, they imagine a venerable piece of paper, drafted by thoughtful and noble statesmen. In other words, they imagine the Constitution of the United States of America. This document is the oldest continuously applied constitution in the world, and it has been a model for many other constitutions, especially for countries that emerged from the crumbling empires of the twentieth century. The U.S. Constitution was drawn up by the Constitutional Convention of 1787. It is a remarkably short document—the main text is just eight thousand words. It is also limited in its intentions. The U.S. Constitution is principally a document intended to define, and thereby restrict, the powers of the three branches of government: executive, legislative, and judicial. Its other main consideration is the mechanism for its own amendment.

FACT: *Britain's "Glorious Revolution" of 1688 saw the Roman Catholic King James II ousted from his throne by a staunchly Protestant Parliament. He was accused of acting contrary to the "fundamental constitution of the kingdom." His successors, William and Mary, signed a Bill of Rights, which forms a key part of a de facto constitution.*

Philadelphia was the location of the U.S. Constitutional Convention in 1787.

QUOTE:
"A constitution is the arrangement of magistracies in a state."

Aristotle (384–322 B.C.E.), Greek philosopher

A constitution can take many forms. The term can also be applied to more than nation states. Nongovernmental organizations and other branches of civic society create and operate according to their own constitutions. In all cases, the intention of the constitution is to define a set of rules to govern by. That doesn't mean it's fair or reasonable—it just means that you have been told.

Revolution vs. Evolution

The U.S. Constitution was the product of revolutionary change. Faced with the overthrow of the old order, an opportunity existed to create a new framework. In 1787, the statesmen who created the Constitution showed remarkable restraint in their ambitions.

In contrast to constitutions of revolutionary origin, Britain's form of constitution is the product of evolution. Sometimes (misleadingly) called an unwritten constitution, it is not a single document; it is the accumulation of law and precedent. It was in British history that the word "constitution" was first employed in its modern sense, regarding the powers of the state and the rights of individuals. This form is supported by those who argue that the legislature should be supreme. In Britain, no Parliament may bind its successor. It is also argued that such a constitution provides flexibility in the face of changing circumstances. Its critics argue that it creates unhelpful, even harmful, ambiguities that can allow the executive to act with little restraint.

Although Britain does not possess a single written constitution, the most famous piece of legislation in its history, the Magna Carta ("Great Charter") dating from 1215, has been influential in the development of constitutional law.

Breaking the Rules

A constitution carries no guarantee of being upheld. Dictatorships past and present have produced some of the most impressive constitutions without any intention of putting them into practice. The various constitutions of the USSR promised many freedoms, including those of the media and speech, which were then repressed. In 1976, Pol Pot used a new constitution for Cambodia as an open declaration of all the things, such as "reactionary religion," that the people of that country would be forcibly "freed" from. As a rule, if the constitution provides for lots of liberties but no mechanisms for redress, it is a sure sign that it isn't worth the paper it's written on. For Adolph Hitler, the entire issue was redundant—he didn't abolish the constitution of the Weimar Republic when he took power, he just ignored it.

<u>**Who**</u> Was George Washington?

Most famous for being the first president of the United States of America, George Washington was also a gentleman farmer, a successful military leader, and an astute politician. His influence during his lifetime was considerable, and his legacy has had a profound impact on the development of a world superpower.

FACT: *George Washington is the only president of the United States to have been elected by 100 percent of the available votes.*

George Washington was first elected president of the United States of America in 1789. His inauguration was held on April 30 in New York City. It was a turbulent time in geopolitics, and the young nation that Washington was to lead had a difficult course ahead of it. George Washington went on to serve as president for a second term. On the first occasion Washington had been unanimously elected by a convention representing the twelve states of the union. Their unanimity reflected their faith in Washington and their need for leadership at a difficult time. Such agreement was absent when Washington was reelected in 1792. Divisions had developed in the politics of the new country. By 1797 Washington had retired from public life, refusing to stand for a third term.

FACT: *By refusing to serve a third term George Washington began the precedent that a president serve no more than two successive terms. This was later enshrined in the 22nd Amendment to the Constitution.*

President George Washington focused on laying the foundations for the effective administration of the country. He was a good delegator and selected able lieutenants to serve in his cabinet, including two who were to go on to become presidents in their own right, John Adams and Thomas Jefferson. Washington put a great deal of effort into establishing the City of Washington in the Territory of Columbia (later called the District of Columbia, hence D.C.) as the seat of federal government. When protests about excise duties on distilled spirits threatened to grow into a wider rebellion (the Whiskey Rebellion) he took decisive action, summoning a militia army and quickly asserting control.

As a politician Washington was careful to avoid being identified too closely with one group or another. He did not belong to a political party and argued that the existence of political parties was potentially dangerous, causing division and fostering loyalties that might conflict with the national interest. He kept ceremony to a minimum and at first refused to accept payment for being president. He changed his mind

FACT: *George Washington introduced the term "Mr. President" in preference to titles that had a more imperial or royal sound.*

FACT: *Aged just sixteen, George Washington had contributed to the survey of the Shenandoah region under Lord Fairfax.*

when it became clear that leaving the post unpaid would increase the likelihood that the presidency would only be accessible to a wealthy man.

Washington was disappointed in his hope that party politics could be avoided. The two superpowers of the era, Britain and France, were locked in a Continental war and a global imperial struggle. The effects of that struggle and other differences resulted in the gradual formation of a two-party system with the pro-British Federalist Party ranged against pro-French Democratic-Republican Party. Washington was inclined toward the Federalists, but his main belief was that the destiny of America would be shaped by expansion westward.

* George Washington
(1732–1799)

Arms and Agriculture

The overthrow of British power was largely due to the military leadership of Washington as commander-in-chief of the Continental Army. Facing the military might of Britain, and with the colonists divided among themselves, Washington quickly developed a strategy of avoiding full-scale engagements, saying, "We should on all Occasions avoid a general action." Instead, Washington was careful to exploit the terrain and the long supply lines that left the British vulnerable to surprise attacks and skirmishing. The conflict was to last for six years. With the aid of his French allies, Washington was able to force British capitulation at Yorktown in 1781, effectively ending the war, although a peace treaty was a long time in coming.

George Washington was also a gentleman farmer from a Virginia planter family. An advantageous marriage to a wealthy widow, Martha Custis, had given him the opportunity to develop an extensive estate at Mount Vernon. Before the revolution he had been a very successful planter and, when Washington retired, he returned to Mount Vernon. Retirement to his beloved estate and a return to the manners and society of plantation life was a long-held ambition. Sadly, it was not to be long-lived. On December 14, 1799, George Washington died. He had been retired for less than three years.

Principally George Washington was the political and military leader who laid the foundations for the extraordinary development of the United States of America. He failed to prevent the development of party politics and the entanglement of the country with European quarrels. However, he succeeded in establishing the principles and practices that have made the office of president revered.

Where Is the World's Oldest Capital City?

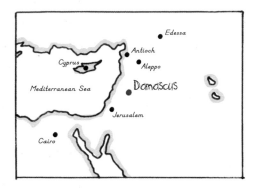

There are plenty of old cities in the world. Of these, many have served as capitals for different nations at different times. However, only one urban center can claim continuous habitation for 1,700 years while retaining its role as capital city. That place is the Syrian capital of Damascus, and its story is one of great turmoil.

The city of Damascus is located on the fringes of the Syrian Desert. A focal point in the Middle East, its location has been both the strength and weakness of Damascus throughout its history. It has enabled the city to look out to the wider world, but has also allowed the wider world to threaten and invade at several points in the city's history. Each successive wave of invasion has changed the nature of the city, leaving another sedimentary layer in its complex past.

Ancient Invaders

The first mention of Damascus in recorded history was an invasion. In the fifteenth century B.C.E., the city was conquered by Pharaoh Thutmosis III. At this period in its history Damascus formed the core of a sort of extended city-state. Like many other cities in the Middle East, it exploited an agricultural hinterland and benefited from a network of trading routes. The Old Testament records the city as being the capital of an Aramean kingdom, and it participated in different conflicts with neighboring states. Damascus was successful and prosperous, developing a state powerful enough to withstand the influence of the much more substantial Assyrian Empire on its borders. The downfall of Damascus came at the hands of the Babylonians in 732 B.C.E., but it recovered and was an attractive prize for the whirlwind conquests of Alexander the Great's Macedonian armies in 333 B.C.E.

FACT: The first Allied troops to enter Damascus upon its "liberation" from Ottoman rule were the forces of the Arab Revolt, under the leadership of Emir Faisal. The principal British officer in their ranks was T. E. Lawrence, better known as Lawrence of Arabia. He recounted his adventures in his book, **The Seven Pillars of Wisdom**.

T. E. Lawrence, a key figure in the 1918 liberation of Damascus, was reputed to suffer from motion sickness when riding a camel.

FACT: *The Umayyad Dynasty ruled from 661 to 750 C.E. During that time it established and held sway over a great caliphate that stretched from Spain in the west to India in the east.*

SUMMARY

The world's oldest capital city is Damascus, located in modern-day Syria. Over the years it has formed an important part of many states and empires, and its location means that it continues to play a crucial role in the politics of the Middle East.

For the next 250 years, Damascus was the subject of Greek and Egyptian control, until the Roman conquest made it part of the province of Syria. The city prospered but changed as Christianity spread across the empire. When the Roman world divided, Damascus remained part of the Christian Byzantine Empire (the continuation of the Eastern Roman Empire). Through this time the city had been threatened first by the Persian Empire, then by the new religion of Islam during the time of the Byzantines. In 634 C.E. the city fell to Arab forces, beginning a shift to an Islamic culture.

Islamic Rule

In the late seventh century, Damascus occupied a significant location in the Umayyad Caliphate. Able to trade towards the Mediterranean in the west, the Arabian Peninsula to the south, and India in the east, the city was a focal point for commerce and culture. Until the capital of this vast empire moved to Baghdad in 750 C.E., Damascus enjoyed a golden age, attracting scholars, theologians, scientists, and traders from across the empire. The decline precipitated by the shift in political power toward Baghdad was exacerbated by successive conflicts, which included a siege during the Crusades and an invasion by the Mongol hordes.

From 1516 to 1918 Damascus was part of the Ottoman Empire, but as Ottoman rule collapsed toward the end of World War I, the city was taken by the Allies. A Syrian National Congress was formed and for a time it seemed that Syria would gain independence, with Damascus as its capital; but it was not to be. In 1920, France took control under the jurisdiction of the League of Nations (the forerunner of the United Nations). This sparked a revolt in Syria that rumbled on until the country eventually achieved independence in 1946.

Since the mid-twentieth century Damascus has served as the capital of Syria. It has developed an industrial base and grown rapidly. Once more its location lends it great significance, as the government of Syria seeks to develop influence in the Middle East. The story of the oldest capital city in the world goes on.

When Was the United Nations Formed?

The simple answer is October 24, 1945; but that only tells a fraction of the story. There are four alternative ways to look at the origins of the United Nations. One way refers to the sequence of global institutions that have been established in modern times; two ways are linked with the darkest days of World War II; and the fourth way considers the birth of the United Nations as part of the postwar world.

History is littered with alliances. They are usually formed to promote a common cause or to defend against an outside threat. Some have been based on trade and mutual economic interest, others have been formed for the purpose of common defense; for example, the Triple Entente of Great Britain, Russia, and France was intended to provide security in the face of a perceived threat from Germany at the outset of the twentieth century. Alliances have always existed—and probably always will—where nations find a mutual benefit in cooperation.

✳
The blue of the UN flag's background, and the olive branches that surround the world—both symbolize peace.

The First International Bodies

As the impact of the Industrial Revolution became truly global in the mid-nineteenth century, new organizations began to emerge that were not alliances in the classic sense, but were pan-national bodies of a new kind. These were intended to promote global accord through negotiation. The earliest examples of this were the International Telegraph Union (1865) and the Universal Postal Union (1874), which were created to bring harmony to a global communications network. It could even be argued that the United Nations was formed at this time, because both of these bodies still exist today, as agencies of the UN.

The League of Nations

In August 1941, a British warship, HMS *Prince of Wales*, sailed in secret to the coast of Newfoundland. There the ship was host to a meeting between the Prime Minister of Great Britain, Winston Churchill, and the President of the United States, Franklin D. Roosevelt. This meeting could be cited as the point at which the United Nations was formed. For Britain and her allies, these were the darkest and most despairing days of the war. The United States had not yet joined the war, but at that meeting the two leaders considered the shape of the postwar world. Both men had lived through World War I and the challenges that emerged from it. The treaty process that concluded that war had

FACT: The Atlantic Charter (1942) had four ambitions: to promote democratic government, to encourage free trade, to support a fair distribution of prosperity, and to facilitate arms reduction.

FACT: *The Hanseatic League existed from the thirteenth to the fifteenth centuries. At its height, 150 trading towns and cities in northern Europe were part of the League. It dominated trade on the Baltic and North Atlantic coasts. The name comes from "hanse," a word of German origin meaning "association."*

SUMMARY

The United Nations does have a definite birthday, but when it was formed is more debatable. This is because it didn't spring out of thin air. Rather, it was the product of a long development. In this sense, you could be right if you said that the United Nations as a concept was formed long before its official establishment in 1945.

given rise to the League of Nations (1919). Both Churchill and Roosevelt approved of the concept of the League, which had finally collapsed with the outbreak of World War II. It had aimed to preserve international peace through collective action, and to promote international cooperation in a range of social and economic areas. These basic aims became the inspiration for the deliberations on that British warship at a pivotal moment in the global conflict.

Just a few months later, on January 1, 1942, Roosevelt first publicly coined the term "United Nations." It was used in the Declaration of the United Nations, which committed the Allied nations to the struggle against the Axis powers led by Japan and Germany. Many view this as the point at which the United Nations was formed in principle. The document drew on the points outlined in their earlier meeting by Churchill and Roosevelt, and was known as the Atlantic Charter. It was an attempt to distinguish the intentions of the Allies from the intentions of the Axis countries and to give hope that a better world would emerge from such a terrible conflict.

The UN Charter

Although, as we have seen, there are a number of dates that could be considered suitable alternatives, the birthday of the United Nations is actually celebrated on October 24. The reason is that it was on this date that China, France, Great Britain, the USSR, the United States, and forty-six other nations ratified the United Nations Charter in 1945. Fifty countries had contributed to the conference in San Francisco that drew up the Charter. It was based on earlier meetings at Dumbarton Oaks, Washington D.C., involving the "big five" powers. The structure that it created reflected the balance of power that existed when World War II ended—a structure that many developing nations argue is now outdated and in need of reform.

FACT: *The League of Nations involved fifty-seven countries at its peak. It was created in an attempt to prevent another conflict as terrible as World War I. The United States never joined, and other countries, such as Germany, Japan, Italy, and the USSR, were only temporarily members. Its credibility was destroyed by its failure to prevent or adequately sanction the Japanese massacre at Shanghai in 1932 and Italy's invasion of Ethiopia in 1935.*

Why Did Karl Marx Write Das Kapital?

Everyone has heard of Karl Marx, right? The name of Marx is inextricably linked to communism through the term "Marxism," although the word itself represents a form of political theory that is not necessarily synonymous with the later forms taken by communist nations. Connected to that is the idea that *Das Kapital* somehow sums Marx up. It's big, formidable, and, beyond a few key phrases, unintelligible. So why did he write it?

In February 1848, Karl Marx and his friend Friedrich Engels published *Manifest der Kommunistischen Partei* (*The Manifesto of the Communist Party*), more commonly known as simply *The Communist Manifesto*. A short, pamphlet-sized document, it formed the inspiration for the communist movement. Written in 1847, its appearance on the world stage was extremely timely, as 1848 saw the old powers of Europe rocked by a wave of uprisings and revolutions. This may have inspired Marx to feel that the tide of history was running in his favor and that capitalism was doomed. But the manifesto lacked depth and critical analysis. Something weightier was required to secure the new ideology.

What followed was the work of thirty years, resulting in three volumes, two of which were published posthumously. Actually, the majority of the writing was completed in the 1860s, but Marx worked and reworked it for the rest of his life. It may be that he felt his analysis to be incomplete, or he may have simply been distracted by being actively involved in the early growth of international communism. Whichever it was, the resulting text is known by many, read by some—and understood by few.

SUMMARY

If Marx hoped that *Das Kapital* would be the spark for a revolutionary explosion in his lifetime, he was disappointed. He wanted the volumes to be the intellectual cornerstone of communism, illustrating the "laws of motion" in capitalism so that it could be understood and attacked. In this he was successful. *Das Kapital* has acted as the rationale for an interpretation of history and for the analysis of economics. Most of all, though, it went on to inspire movements in Russia, South America, Southeast Asia, and China that helped to shape the twentieth century.

QUOTE:

"[Capitalists] mutilate the laborer into a fragment of a man, degrade him to the level of an appendage of a machine, destroy every remnant of charm in his work and turn it into hated toil."

Karl Marx (1818-1883), Das Kapital

FACT: *Although Karl Marx lived in poverty, his co-author Friedrich Engels did not. He actually owned a mill in Manchester, England.*

> "From each according to his ability, to each according to his needs."
>
> *Karl Marx in his 1875 Critique of the Gotha Program*

Workers Unite

Das Kapital is a fusion of history, politics, and economics—Marx placed a central importance on economics, as he believed that it was the driving force for the other two facets. He was motivated to write the three volumes because he wanted to enable everyone to understand his analysis of capitalism. He believed that it was a doomed stage in the development of human society. It encouraged the vast production and accumulation of commodities, not to enrich those who produced and purchased them, but for the benefit of those who owned the means to produce them. Competition between these capitalists would steadily increase their power and reduce their number, while placing an ever-increasing burden on the workers. Eventually the workers would reconcile their shallow differences in a revolution intended to throw off the oppression of the capitalists. In the final part of *Das Kapital*, Marx set out to explain how the revolution would occur and what would follow it.

At the time he was writing *Das Kapital*, Marx may have been motivated by the sense that a crisis in capitalism was coming to a head. International communism had steadily grown since he had been elected to the International Workingmen's Association (also known as the First International) in 1864. Everyday life in his adopted home of Britain provided plenty of evidence that the powers of industry, assisted by the government, were happy to smash organized labor and squeeze every drop from those who worked and lived in appalling conditions. In 1871, the Paris Commune relit the flame of revolution in Europe for two heady months. Revolution felt imminent, and Marx argued that it was most likely to occur where capitalism was most advanced. But it wasn't to be.

Later communists, such as Lenin, believed that an active communist party could expedite the moment of revolution, rather than waiting for the point when the workers would have become "disciplined, united, and organized by the very mechanism of the process of capitalist production."

FACT: *The Paris Commune was formed when the citizens of Paris, France, rebelled and took over the city. It was crushed by government troops at the cost of over 30,000 lives.*

Why Do Animals Migrate?

If you have ever wondered why certain animals are only seen at a particular time of year, the answer in most cases is that they have been elsewhere the rest of the time. All over the world, animals are moving with the seasons; but why is it worth their while to expend all this energy to travel, sometimes for thousands of miles twice a year?

The example of migration that commonly springs to the mind of people in northern latitudes is that of birds such as swallows, swans, ducks, geese, and—in North America—hummingbirds. Many bird species spend their winters in relatively warm regions such as the Mediterranean, North Africa, or Central America, and their northerly flight is a sign that summer is coming. But close to the Equator temperatures don't vary significantly throughout the year, so why do they head north at all? After all, there are many costs. Birds are good at using air currents, but the long journey still takes a lot of energy. The chances of being eaten by predatory birds are also high, and when the travelers congregate at stopovers they can spread disease and parasites to each other. All of these problems, however, are outweighed by the increased hours of daylight in the north during summer, producing a much greater food supply and more time in which to feed, which enables the birds to breed and feed their young more successfully. As the summer ends and their offspring gain strength, the birds head south again to a winter of warm weather and a steady food supply.

FACT: *Until the nineteenth century, it was unclear why many European birds disappeared for the winter, and there were many theories, including the possibility that they spent the cold months on the Moon! In 1822, scientists were given a helpful clue when a white stork in Germany was found to have a central African arrow through its neck. Since then, more than twenty examples of "arrow storks," or Pfeilstorchen, have been found.*

Migration Relay

Several kinds of insects, including butterflies, moths, beetles, and dragonflies, migrate over considerable distances. The North American monarch butterfly makes a spectacular flight from Canada and the northern United States all the way to the southern states and Mexico, but its lifespan is less than one year, so the same individuals never return. Instead, the overwintering monarchs mate in early spring then migrate north until they find milkweed. Here they lay their eggs, which hatch into caterpillars that feed on the milkweed (taking up the poison that the plant contains). After two weeks as a caterpillar and two more as a pupa, the mature (now poisonous) butterfly takes up the journey, and it is this, or even the next, generation that reaches the northern zone.

*
Monarch
butterfly

FACT: *Some sea creatures undertake a daily migration vertically! Zooplankton (microscopic animals) and fish find their food in the upper layers of the ocean, but that's also where the predators are, so they feed near the surface at night and descend to the safety of the deep in the daytime. On the other hand, phytoplankton (microscopic plants), find nutrients in the deeper, cooler waters of the ocean at night, but come to the surface for the daylight that they also need.*

SUMMARY

Migration is the seasonal movement of animals from one location to another. The principal reasons for this movement are to find suitable habitats in which to breed, more food for themselves or for their newborn young, and protection from extremes of weather, especially low temperatures. Migrations can take place over many thousands of miles, and creatures such as swallows and whales have amazing powers of navigation that ensure they end up in the right place.

Whereas in the case of birds there is evidence that the adults teach the migration route to their young, the monarch clearly inherits a genetic navigation program, as it manages to find its way back south to overwinter.

One-Way Ticket

Many species of fish also migrate. Those that spend most of their lives in saltwater and move into freshwater to breed, such as salmon, are known as "anadromous," but for some species there is no return. Whereas Atlantic salmon come back year upon year to breed in the river in which they were born, the six species of Pacific salmon (pink, chum, coho, sockeye, chinook, and cherry—which is found only in the western Pacific) all die after spawning. Their bodies form an essential part of the food chain, nourishing not only their young but also other fish species, bears, and the forests into which the bears carry the carcasses.

FACT: *Humpback whales hold the migration record. They have been found to migrate from their feeding grounds in the Antarctic to Costa Rica, ten degrees north of the equator, a distance of more than 5,000 miles (8,000 km). The cold Antarctic Ocean is rich in the tiny shrimplike krill on which the 40-metric-ton whales feed, but they need warmer water for breeding.*

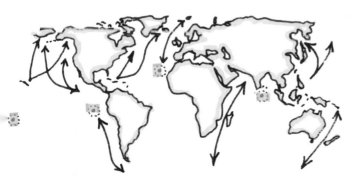

Breeding grounds for humpback whales

Who Found the Source of the Nile?

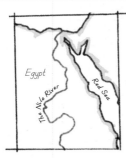

Although there is still argument about whether the Nile or the Amazon is the world's longest river, there is no doubt that the River Nile occupies a special place in our imaginations as one of the cradles of civilization. The source of the water that is the lifeblood of Egypt had been a puzzle since ancient times, a puzzle that has been solved only relatively recently, and that has proved to have several answers.

The ancient Egyptian civilization began around 5,000 years ago in the northeast corner of the African continent. It was to last for almost 3,000 years, falling to the Persians in 343 B.C.E. The rich Egyptian culture developed a writing system, astounding feats of architecture and construction, mining, far-flung trade, a complex religious life, and an army that carried its rule into surrounding territories. The wealth on which all this was founded came from agriculture, made possible by the Nile's annual floods, which deposited fertile silt, and its year-round use for irrigation as it flowed northward through the desert.

Twin Rivers

The Nile has two main tributaries—the Blue Nile and the longer White Nile—that come together in Khartoum, in northern Sudan, to form the single river that flows through Egypt. Both the Greeks and the Romans explored the rivers, and in the third century B.C.E. it was known that the Blue Nile had its origins in the highlands of Ethiopia; but the source of the White Nile, named for the pale silt it carries, remained a mystery, largely because of the vast and impenetrable wetlands of the Sudd, in southern Sudan, through which it flows.

In 1770, the Scottish traveler James Bruce visited a small swamp in the mountains of Ethiopia from which a stream flowed into Lake Tana, out of which the Blue Nile flows, and he claimed to be the first European to have done so. However, the presence of a small chapel at the site should have given him a clue—a Jesuit missionary named Pedro Páez had been there more than 150 years earlier and had written an account of the place, which is indeed the source of the Blue Nile.

In 1858, the British explorer John Hanning Speke discovered the vast lake that he named Victoria. He claimed, correctly, that the White Nile flowed from this lake and that the lake is effectively the source. Several small rivers flow into Lake Victoria, and the source of the longest of these was located in 2006.

FACT: *In 1864 a debate was arranged in which Speke and Burton were to present their conflicting cases. On the day of the debate, Burton was on stage preparing to speak when he was informed that Speke had died the previous evening. He had been climbing over a wall on his uncle's estate, on his way to shoot partridges with his cousin, when his shotgun went off, killing him. There was talk of suicide, but it was probably an accident.*

* *John Hanning Speke (1827–1864)*

The Great White Brother

The source of the White Nile remained a mystery for much longer. Not until the nineteenth century did the hunt begin in earnest, in a wave of Victorian exploration spurred on by such romantic figures as Dr. David Livingstone. It was the British explorer John Hanning Speke (1827–1864) who, in 1858, gazed upon the vast waters of the lake that he named Victoria and claimed that he had found the source of the Nile. His companion on the trip was the larger-than-life Richard Francis Burton (1821–1890), but he was too ill to visit the lake. Burton felt that Speke had too little evidence for the claim, and disputed it when Speke made his announcement in London. In 1862, Speke returned to Africa and found the point at which a large river flowed out of the lake, which he named Ripon Falls; he felt that this confirmed his claim, but didn't explore downstream to find out whether the river actually was the Nile. Burton continued to deny Speke's claim, but when the Welsh explorer Henry Morton Stanley (1841–1904) returned in 1877 from an expedition to Lake Victoria he confirmed that Speke had been right—the White Nile does indeed flow from Lake Victoria.

The Source of the Source

But where does the water come from that feeds Lake Victoria? In March 2006, Neil McGrigor from England and New Zealanders Cam McCleay and Garth MacIntyre traveled deep into the heart of the Nyungwe rainforest in northern Rwanda to what they believe is the true source of the Nile, 66 miles (106 km) west of Lake Victoria. Their colleague Steve Willis died on the journey, shot when the group was attacked by Ugandan rebels between Lake Victoria and Lake Albert.

FACT: *David Livingstone (1813–1873), the first European to see the mighty Victoria Falls on the Zambesi River, spent the last years of his life suffering extreme hardships and disease in an unsuccessful attempt to find the "true" source of the Nile, which he correctly believed lay beyond Lake Victoria.*

Where Is the Great Barrier Reef?

The location of the Great Barrier Reef is no secret. It is Earth's largest living structure, and it can even be seen from space. Consisting of hundreds of coral reefs and islands, this natural wonder lies off the coast of Queensland and stretches along Australia's northeastern tip and the waters of Papua New Guinea, a distance of more than 1,200 miles (2,000 km). What makes it remarkable is the enormous diversity of life that it supports.

The Great Barrier Reef isn't one structure, but consists of some 3,000 underwater reefs and about 900 islands, all made up of the skeletons of billions upon billions of small creatures, called coral polyps, that have accumulated over more than 6,000 years. Coral polyps are small, sea anemonelike animals that generally grow in warm, shallow seas. Each polyp is only a few tenths of an inch in diameter, having a tubular body with tentacles around the mouth at the upper end. These tentacles have stinging cells to capture plankton and even small fish. Coral polyps live in colonies that can be up to five feet (1.5 m) in diameter.

The many different species of coral fall into two types. Soft-bodied coral have a skeleton made of protein and can exist in cooler, deeper water. The hard-bodied coral produce a shell of calcium carbonate, and as successive generations build upon the skeletons of their deceased ancestors they create distinctive and beautiful coral forms. Coral colonies can grow at a rate of up to one inch (2.5 cm) per year. Over hundreds and thousands of years these accumulate to form reefs.

FACT: *The colonies of the various hard coral species grow into distinctive shapes that give many of them their names, such as brain, staghorn, pillar, rock, and star coral. There are some 500 reef-building coral in the world, and 350 of these are found on the Great Barrier Reef.*

FACT: *Hard-bodied coral have a symbiotic relationship (one in which both parties benefit) with algae called zooxanthellae. These live within the polyp, using the waste material and carbon dioxide that the polyp releases, and carrying out photosynthesis. The polyp gains up to 90 percent of its nutrients from the photosynthesis and uses surplus energy to form its hard skeleton. Hard coral are only found in water less than 200 feet (60 m) deep, because the zooxanthellae need sunlight.*

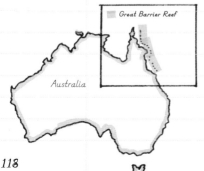

Great Barrier Reef

Australia

FACT: *Several species that live on the reefs are highly poisonous. The tentacles of the pale blue box jellyfish can inflict a sting that causes such excruciating pain that swimmers have been known to go into shock and drown before they can reach help. The sting of the tiny irukandji jellyfish produces intense muscle pain and nausea, and can be fatal; the lion fish, stone fish, and stingray all have venomous spines.*

The Great Barrier Reef is a string of coral reefs and islands some 1,200 miles (2,000 km) long. It lies off the northeast coast of Australia. The coral reef ecosystem supports an enormous diversity of marine life, but it is highly sensitive to environmental factors such as pollution and climate change.

The Reef Ecosystem

The intricate nooks and crannies of the coral reef offer shelter and food, in the form of plankton, sponges, marine worms, and algae, to an amazing variety of marine species. These include sharks, whales, dolphins, dugongs, sea snakes, octopus, some 1,500 species of fish (many of which are extremely colorful), and 4,000 species of mollusks, including the giant clam.

The Great Barrier Reef is one of the world's most important marine ecosystems, and it is very healthy but also extremely fragile. Hard coral is especially sensitive to changes in the ocean temperature, and there have already been incidents of "bleaching" when warm ocean currents have caused the algae, on which the coral polyps depend, to die. A report by the World Wildlife Fund for Nature has warned that the Great Barrier Reef could lose 95 percent of its living coral in the next 40 years if ocean temperatures increase by 2°F (1.5°C) as a result of global climate change, which has been predicted.

Tourism

The beauty of the Great Barrier Reef has drawn tourists since the 1890s, and permanent resorts were built in the 1930s at Green Island and Heron Island. Tourism is now the largest commercial activity in the Great Barrier Reef Marine Park, with about 1.6 million visitors each year. Through tourism, many people learn about this key World Heritage area, but large numbers of people and boats can do considerable harm, and the various authorities work hard to reduce their impact and protect the reef's integrity.

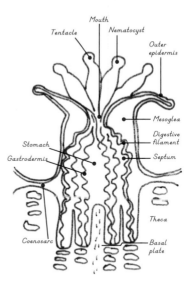

* *The mouth of each coral polyp is surrounded by a ring of tentacles that capture food such as small floating animals or even fish.*

What *Is the Driest Place on Earth?*

Water is always on the move. Evaporating from the surfaces of oceans, lakes, and rivers, water rises into the atmosphere, forming clouds that are driven along by air currents. When clouds rise over high land or meet colder air, the water vapor condenses to form droplets that fall as rain, hail, or snow, returning to the cycle, but there are places where this rarely happens. Two regions vie for the title of the driest place on Earth, and they couldn't be more different.

FACT: *The word "desert" comes from the Latin for "an abandoned place." At one time it was used to refer to any sparsely populated area, but now it is used only to mean an arid region.*

The driest parts of the planet are generally called deserts, defined as regions receiving an average of less than 10 inches (25 cm) of precipitation per year or losing more moisture than they receive. When we hear the word "desert" we think of a handful of locations, such as Arizona, the Sahara in North Africa, and the Australian interior, but deserts, surprisingly, constitute almost one-third of Earth's land surface.

In desert regions there is very little humidity in the atmosphere to block or retain the Sun's heat, so the temperature tends to fluctuate widely, from extremely hot in the daytime to very cold at night. These harsh conditions limit the range of plants and animals to those that can survive with very little water and can make the most of any that falls.

What Creates Deserts?

If an area receives little rain, it is because the air currents moving over it contain very little moisture. There are four main reasons why this happens:

1) Winds along the tropics of Cancer and Capricorn are dry because they are composed of air that has been heated at the Equator, has risen, and has flowed north and south. As it does so it cools, sinks, and loses its moisture as rain, so it is dry by the time it reaches the tropics. The Sahara Desert exists for this reason.

2) The interior parts of large continents may simply be too far from the ocean, which is the source of most moisture, and rain clouds just never reach them. The Gobi Desert that straddles the border of China and Mongolia is an example of this. It is the largest desert in Asia.

3) Where a cold ocean current runs along a coastline, it cools the air above it, causing rain to fall before the air reaches the coast and producing desert conditions.

4) Air cools as it rises, so when air passes over a mountain range the moisture in it falls as rain on the upwind slopes. The downwind side of the mountain is said to be in a "rain shadow" and there will be little precipitation there. An area that lies between two mountain ranges may receive almost no moisture at all, and this is the case in Death Valley, on the border of California and Nevada.

World Deserts

Unlike polar ice caps, deserts are found at all latitudes, which reflects the fact that they exist for many reasons

Dry and Hot

The driest place on Earth has a bumper pack of causes. Lying just a few degrees south of the Tropic of Capricorn, trapped between the Andes mountains to the east and the Chilean Coast Range to the west, with the cold Humboldt ocean current running along the coast, the Atacama Desert has plenty of reasons to be dry. This region of Chile, on the west coast of South America, is the driest hot desert in the world, and there is evidence that during the four centuries up until 1971 it received no significant rainfall at all. That's dry!

Dry and Cold

Not all deserts are hot, and indeed the second contender for the title of driest place is in Antarctica! The McMurdo Dry Valleys are a series of bare, rocky valleys close to the Antarctic coast. The almost complete lack of humidity is due to the very low temperatures (an annual average of −16°F, −26.7°C) and fierce winds of up to 200 miles per hour (320 kph) that remove any moisture. These winds, called "katabatic" winds, sweep downward, pulled by the force of gravity, and they are bone-dry. It is thought that there has been no precipitation in the valleys for more than two million years.

FACT: The extreme temperatures and lack of moisture in the McMurdo Dry Valleys are thought to be close to the conditions on Mars, and for this reason the valleys have been used for training astronauts and getting a feel for what travel to the red planet might mean.

FACT: The Sahara is the world's largest hot desert, stretching across Africa from the Atlantic in the west to the Red Sea in the east and covering an area of 3.5 million square miles (9 million square km). Despite the difficulties of crossing this inhospitable terrain, trans-Saharan trade flourished in the Middle Ages, as merchants and their camel caravans brought gold and slaves north from countries such as Ghana and Mali and traded salt from the northern desert.

SUMMARY

There are a great many very dry places on Earth, but the two most extreme examples are the Atacama Desert in Chile and the McMurdo Dry Valleys in Antarctica.

When Was the Grand Canyon Formed?

Named as one of the seven "natural wonders of the world," the Grand Canyon in Arizona is the largest gorge on the planet—277 miles (446 km) long as the Colorado River flows, and an average of 10 miles (16 km) across and a mile (1.6 km) deep. It is a major tourist attraction, visited by more than five million people every year, but it's particularly fascinating for geologists, because the story of the Grand Canyon's formation is a brief history of the planet itself.

John Wesley Powell led the first team to travel down the canyon by boat. ✳

The Grand Canyon carves its way across the northwestern corner of the state of Arizona, from Utah to Nevada. ✳

United States of America

✳ The Grand Canyon

Gazing across the canyon, the most noticeable feature of the rock is its striped appearance. These are the layers that have been laid down over hundreds of millions of years, and the erosion of the rock by the Colorado River has revealed the story of the rock beneath. The farther down the canyon wall you go, the further you go back in time, and at the bottom of the gorge the rock is estimated to be 1.7 billion—or 1,700,000,000—years old. That is one-third of the age of Earth itself. At that time, there was a huge mountain range here, possibly higher than the Rocky Mountains are now, pushed up by the colliding tectonic plates (see pp. 16–17) that caused the land to buckle. Over millions of years, this mountain range was eroded to form a vast flat plateau, and then the story starts to become colorful.

The colored bands that make up the walls of the Grand Canyon show the layers of rock that were laid down over almost two billion years.

FACT: *The Grand Canyon contains more than ninety different kinds of rock. The dramatic colors that are seen in the rocks are caused by the presence of minerals, especially iron, which gives the red color. Mining in the canyon began in the nineteenth century, mainly for copper and silver, and during the 1950s there was a boom in uranium mining as a result of the Cold War.*

SUMMARY

The Grand Canyon was formed about five million years ago by the Colorado River cutting its way down through layers of rock that had been laid down over a period of about a billion years. The walls of the canyon provide a detailed history of the geology of this area.

Laying It Down

The multicolored layers of rock that stripe the canyon walls are mainly sedimentary, meaning that they were deposited underwater. Earth's climate has varied considerably over the eons, and the sea level has changed as the ice caps melted and refroze. Successive layers of rock tell us that the whole of this area has been repeatedly submerged and exposed as the waters have risen and fallen, leaving layers of sandstone (made from sand deposited when this was a coastal area), shale (made of mud left by the receding water), and limestone (made of the skeletons of tiny marine organisms). There have also been periods of volcanic activity that left seams of hardened lava called basalt. It is possible to date the layers by means of radiometric dating and by looking in detail at the fossil record. The first layer was deposited about 1.7 billion years ago, and contains fossilized algae that show the area was on the coast at that time. For a billion years the layers continued to be laid down, and the top layer—containing fossils of marine creatures that show that it was seabed—is about 250 million years old. Anything laid down after that has since been eroded.

FACT: *The first successful journey through the canyon by boat was made in 1869 by Major John Wesley Powell and a team of nine men. Their journey took three months, over the course of which they mapped the canyon and named many of its famous landmarks.*

And the Canyon?

Between 100 million and 65 million years ago, the tectonic movement caused the land to the east to buckle and rise, forming the Rocky Mountains. Rain and meltwater flowed westward, and the Colorado River formed. There are several theories about the life of the river and various changes of course that may have taken place, but it is generally agreed that until about five million years ago the land here gradually rose as the result of movements of Earth's crust, and the river began to flow along the course that it takes today. Since then the force of the water, coupled with the rocks and boulders that the river carries, has eroded away the relatively soft sedimentary rock, steadily carving down through the many layers of rock to form the Grand Canyon.

What Is Alchemy?

The combining, changing, and purifying of matter has been a preoccupation throughout human history. Alchemy, with its heady mix of mysticism and science, was an important part of the path that led to modern chemistry.

Alchemy as practiced in Medieval Europe was a search for knowledge and transformation not only of the material world but also of the self, a quest for the purification of the individual and the attainment of immortality. The great goals of the alchemist were the transmutation of base metal into gold, the formula for the universal panacea or elixir of life that would cure all ills and confer immortality, and the discovery of the universal solvent that would dissolve all things (which would have made storage a bit of a problem).

Alchemists gave elements symbols, some being those of the planets that "ruled" them. These were used well into the eighteenth century.

A Brief History

The history of the word "alchemy" mirrors that of the discipline itself. Its origin is probably the Greek word *kimia*, which means "transformation" but may also refer to ancient Egypt, the land of Khem. For the Egyptians, alchemy was linked to Thoth, the ibis-headed god of magic and science.

The Greeks identified their god Hermes with Thoth, and under their rule alchemy flourished in Alexandria, blending the Egyptian tradition with the Greek interest in astrology, numbers, and geometric forms, and developing the concept of the four elements: earth, fire, air, and water. A fifth element of *ether* was added later.

The Romans adopted alchemy from the Greeks, and developed the cult of Hermeticism. Many alchemical writings are attributed to Hermes "Trismegistus" (meaning "thrice great," one of the titles of Thoth), but most of these were destroyed in Alexandria in 292 C.E. on the orders of the Roman emperor Diocletian.

FACT: *Sir Isaac Newton actually spent more time, and wrote more works, on alchemical studies than he did on the groundbreaking scientific work for which he is famous. On the other hand, his seventeenth-century contemporary, Robert Boyle, who wrote a book entitled* **The Sceptical Chymist**, *rejected alchemy entirely and placed chemistry on the purely scientific footing that it has today.*

Isaac Newton 1643–1727

FACT: *The philosopher's stone, one of the many medieval and mythical motifs recycled by J. K. Rowling in the Harry Potter books, was central to both Islamic and European alchemy. It was thought that this material, if it could be found, would act as an intermediary in the transmutation of base metal into gold.*

Islamic Science

After the fall of the Roman Empire, the seat of alchemy moved to the Islamic world, where it became known as *al-kimiya* (much Egyptian, Greek, and Roman literature survived only in Arabic translations). The mystical aspects of alchemy endured, but by the eighth century the metaphorical language and complex symbols used to communicate, or sometimes obscure, its "truths" had given way to a more scientific approach. Persian-born Jabir ibn Hayyan introduced the idea of laboratory experiments, writing down his methods and observations. He wrote many treatises, and his writings profoundly influenced European alchemists. He has been called "the father of chemistry."

Into Europe

Islamic science came to Europe through Spain in the tenth century; and, by the thirteenth, alchemists such as Roger Bacon were making their mark. He and others combined alchemy with Christian philosophy, seeing experience and observation as the route to true knowledge. Many alchemists were members of the clergy, and alchemy was seen as a branch of theology; but the Church eventually turned its back on alchemy as it became increasingly viewed as magic and sorcery.

It was the Swiss physician, botanist, and alchemist Paracelsus who, in the sixteenth century, harnessed alchemy with medicine. He believed in the Hermetic concept of the human body as a microcosm of the universe, and that the two must be in harmony for the body to be healthy. He proposed that illness was caused by outside agents and prescribed chemicals and minerals to deal with these.

In the course of the next hundred years, alchemy gave way to much more rigorous scientific methods, and its intangible goals and principles were discarded in favor of observable data and repeatable experiments. Alchemy eventually lost all academic credibility and was relegated to the realm of superstition and charlatanism.

SUMMARY Alchemy as both a mystical philosophy and a practical art had its origins in ancient Egypt. The goal of the alchemists was to turn base metal into gold and discover the key to immortality. In both the Islamic world and Europe, alchemy became increasingly scientific, ultimately developing into chemistry.

Who Was Marie Curie?

Radioactivity—as a source of power, for medical imaging and diagnosis, and as a method of treating serious illness—is now a part of our everyday lives, but the phenomenon was discovered little more than a century ago. Marie Curie was one of the early pioneers, and she devoted her life to scientific research, working her way to the top and winning acclaim in a field that was almost exclusively a male preserve.

*

The dangers of radioactivity are now much better understood, and this symbol is used worldwide to denote a radiation hazard.

Maria Skłodowska was born in Warsaw in 1867, at a time when that part of Poland was under the control of the Russian Empire. Women were excluded from university education, but after high school she continued her studies in secret while working to earn the money to study in Paris. In 1891 she traveled to France and enrolled at the Sorbonne university, changing her name to Marie. Despite her informal education, she earned master's degrees in physics and math in just three years while working as a tutor to pay her way, and won a scholarship to carry out research into the magnetic properties of steel.

In the course of her research she met Pierre Curie, who shared her interest, and they became good friends. She returned to Poland, but the University of Krakow in her native Poland refused her entry (because she was a woman), and she returned to France. She and Pierre were married in 1895.

The Radiation Trail

The following year, Henri Becquerel discovered that uranium emitted radiation similar to X-rays, and Marie Curie decided to research this phenomenon with a view to gaining a doctorate. Using equipment developed by Pierre Curie's brother, she was able to show that the amount of radiation from a sample of a uranium compound was proportional only to the amount of uranium present and was independent of what the particular compound was or what form it was in. This was hugely significant. All other properties of elements were known to be due to their interactions with other chemicals, but radioactivity was clearly a property of the atoms themselves.

In the course of her research into a uranium ore called pitchblende, she found that the element thorium was also radioactive, and she also discovered the presence of another element far more radioactive than uranium. This was so intriguing that Pierre abandoned his own research and joined

FACT: *During World War I, Marie Curie persuaded wealthy people to donate their cars so that mobile X-ray machines could be used to locate shrapnel and bullets in wounded soldiers. She also pioneered the use of radioactive material, in the form of small tubes of radon gas, to destroy diseased tissue.*

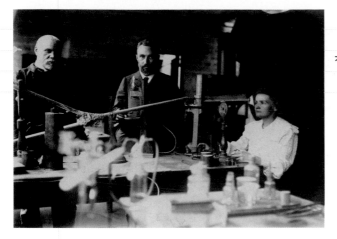

Marie Curie, her husband, Pierre (left), and their assistant, Petit, in their laboratory in a shed on the Rue Lhomond, Paris, where radium was first discovered.

Marie in hers. It was to prove extremely difficult, as the element formed only a tiny fraction of the ore, but in 1898 the two scientists published joint papers announcing the discovery of two new radioactive elements—polonium, named after Marie's homeland, and radium. The Curies were also the first people to use the word "radioactivity."

Well-Deserved Recognition

In 1903, under the supervision of Henri Becquerel, Marie Curie gained her doctorate, and in the same year Marie, Pierre, and Becquerel were jointly awarded the Nobel Prize in Physics, the first time a woman had received the honor. The Curies were suddenly hot property, and the Sorbonne provided them with a laboratory, giving Pierre a professorship and making Marie director of the laboratory, where they were able to work on isolating radium from pitchblende. In 1904 Marie gave birth to their second daughter, but in the spring of 1906 tragedy struck. Pierre fell while crossing a road in Paris and was killed by a horse and carriage.

The Sorbonne took the extraordinary step of giving Pierre's academic post to Marie, making her the first female professor at the university, and she immersed herself in her work. By 1910 she had found a way to separate pure radium from the ore, and in 1911 she became the first person to receive a second Nobel Prize, this time for Chemistry. This accolade enabled her to persuade the French government to build the Radium Institute, now the Institut Curie.

FACT: *In the latter part of her life, Marie Curie had various medical problems, probably as a result of her work with radioactive material. In 1934 she died of aplastic anemia, a disease of the blood linked to radiation exposure, and she was buried next to her husband. In honor of the couple's dedication to science, their remains were transferred to the Panthéon, in Paris, in 1995.*

SUMMARY

Marie Curie (1865–1934) was born Maria Skłodowska in what is now Poland. She overcame considerable financial difficulties and male prejudice to become one of Europe's leading scientists, and is most famous for her discovery of the intensely radioactive element radium.

Where Do Diamonds Come From?

These scintillating gems have fascinated us since time immemorial. They are the subject of endless myth and folklore, the gifts of kings and queens, a treasure for which people have died throughout the ages. But are they really so valuable? Do their beauty and rarity explain their fantastic worth? Are they really that rare, or is that just another myth? And are they really forever?

What do diamonds and the "lead" (actually graphite) in your pencil have in common? The answer is that they are both made of pure carbon, and yet an ounce of graphite is worth a few cents, whereas an ounce of diamonds will cost you hundreds of thousands of dollars. The physical differences lie in their molecular structure. The carbon atoms in graphite are arranged in layers of carbon lattices that can slide over each other. Graphite is soft, it is a good electrical conductor, and it can be used as a lubricant. Diamond, on the other hand, has a regular and rigid crystal structure that gives it immense strength. Indeed, diamond is the hardest naturally occurring mineral, which is why low-quality diamond is used in a host of industrial applications for cutting and grinding. And, unlike graphite, diamond is an electrical insulator.

Earthly Origins

Diamonds are formed under conditions of extremely high pressure and temperatures of about 2,000°F (1,000°C). These conditions are found about 100 miles (up to 200 km) down in the thicker parts of Earth's crust. Some diamonds are created from natural carbon deposits in the rock, and others are composed of organic material that has been carried down into the crust by the subduction of one tectonic plate beneath another. The diamonds are brought to the surface by volcanic activity, and most diamonds are thought to be between one and three billion years old.

The regular molecular structure, made up of carbon atoms with strong bonds between them, gives the diamond its hardness, high melting point, and insolubility.

Diamonds can also be formed as the result of meteorite impact, although such stones tend to be microscopic.

Sources of Diamonds

Diamonds were first discovered almost 3,000 years ago in river gravel in India's Golconda region, and this remained the primary source until the eighteenth century, when diamonds were discovered in Brazil. In the nineteenth century, rich deposits were found in South Africa, and southern Africa remains one of the main diamond-mining areas. In the 1960s, Siberia began to produce large quantities of small diamonds, and in the late 1970s vast deposits were discovered in Western Australia.

FACT: *The word "diamond" comes from the Greek **adamas**, which means "unconquerable." (The word "adamant," meaning resolute and immovable, has the same root.) One of the many beliefs surrounding this gemstone is that it confers invincibility. Medieval knights wore diamonds to protect them, and the hilt of Napoleon Bonaparte's sword bore a large diamond.*

Diamond Quality

Our fascination with diamonds stems mainly from their optical properties, as they split white light into the colors of the spectrum. The value of an individual stone depends on four principal qualities, known as the four Cs:

The unit used to express the weight of a diamond is the carat, once based on the weight of a carob seed but now fixed at ¹⁄₁₄₂ ounce (0.2 g). The price per carat depends on the size of the diamond, so a one-carat gem costs far more than two half-carat stones.

We tend to think that diamonds are colorless, but most stones have a tinge of yellow through to brown. Some, known as fancy diamonds, have shades of amber, red, green, or blue. Colorless diamonds are the most valuable.

Very few diamonds are totally clear, and most have "inclusions" of carbon that has not crystallized, reducing the value.

The way in which a diamond is cut has a major effect on the way that light is refracted and reflected, and it takes a skilled cutter to bring out the full beauty of the gem.

Cut Diamonds

- Star facet
- Table
- Upper girdle facet
- Bezel facet
- Lower girdle facet
- Girdle
- Pavilion facet

QUOTE:

"Diamonds are a girl's best friend."

Marilyn Monroe in the film

Gentlemen Prefer Blondes *(1953).*

FACT: *From the 1930s until the end of the twentieth century, the marketing of diamonds was managed by the De Beers group, which controlled the supply of the gems and manipulated demand through a worldwide advertising campaign to depict diamonds as a token of romance and eternal love. The company's slogan "A diamond is forever" helped dissuade private owners from selling their diamonds, which could have disrupted the artificially high market value.*

SUMMARY Diamonds are made of pure carbon. They are formed deep in Earth's crust under heat and pressure. The diamonds that are being mined now—chiefly in South Africa and Australia—were created between one and three billion years ago.

When Does a Solid Become a Liquid?

Most elements and chemical compounds can exist in both solid and liquid forms. The change from one state to the other occurs when the solid reaches a certain temperature, but what actually happens, and what is the difference between a solid and a liquid?

Most substances can actually exist in three states: solid, liquid, and gas. At a given temperature, when a substance is solid, its volume and shape are fixed; as a liquid, the substance has a fixed volume, but its shape depends on the shape of the vessel that contains it; in gaseous form, the substance expands until it uniformly fills the confining container. These three states, or phases, differ at the molecular level. In a solid the attractions between the molecules keep them in fixed positions relative to each other; in a liquid the molecules are still attracted to each other but are not held tightly; in a gas the molecules move independently of each other.

Heat and Latent Heat

So what causes these differences? The answer is "energy," which is why the state of a substance changes with temperature. The molecules in a solid vibrate, but they don't have enough energy to overcome the attractions between them. As the solid is heated, a point is reached at which the molecules do have enough energy, and the substance becomes liquid. Further heating gives the molecules enough energy to break away from each other completely and enter the gaseous phase.

The transition from solid to liquid and from liquid to gas requires the input of extra energy. The transition from solid to liquid requires the input of the substance's "latent heat of fusion" (*fusion* means "melting"), and the transition from liquid to gas requires the input of its "latent heat of vaporization" (turning to gas). *Latent* means "hidden," and the term is used because this extra energy does not change the temperature. Water and water vapor can both exist at 212°F (100°C), but water vapor has far more energy, and this energy is given out when it condenses and becomes liquid. This is why a steam burn is far more serious than a burn from boiling water. In the case of a cooling liquid, the latent heat of fusion is given out when the liquid becomes a solid.

FACT: *The melting point is, theoretically, the same as the freezing point, the temperature at which a liquid becomes a solid. However, if they are kept very still, many substances can be "supercooled" well below the freezing point without becoming a solid. For this reason, the melting point is a more accurate indication of a substance's characteristics.*

FACT: *It's fortunate for life on Earth that ice is less dense than liquid water. The surface of a lake freezes in winter because of the cold air above it, and the ice layer effectively insulates the water below. If water were to contract when it becomes solid, as most substances do, the forming ice would continuously sink to the bottom, cooling the depths and causing a lake to freeze from the bottom up, potentially killing all the life in it.*

A solid becomes a liquid when it reaches its melting point. At that temperature, with the input of the substance's latent heat of fusion, the movement of the molecules becomes sufficient to overcome some of the attraction between the molecules, the rigid structure of the solid breaks down, and the substance becomes liquid.

Melting and Vaporizing

When the melting point of a substance is given, you will usually see the words "at one atmosphere of pressure," or "at normal atmospheric pressure." This is because pressure affects the melting point. As most substances expand when they melt, an increase in pressure causes them to remain solid at a higher temperature. Water is exceptional in that it contracts when it melts, so an increase in pressure causes water to melt at a lower temperature.

The boiling point of a liquid is affected even more by pressure, as the change in volume from a liquid to a gas is much greater. An increase in pressure raises the boiling point of a liquid. This is how a pressure cooker works: food cooks more quickly because it is in water that is boiling at a temperature significantly above 212°F (100°C). Conversely, a climber at the top of Mount Everest would have to boil an egg longer, as the atmospheric pressure is much lower and the water, therefore, boils at a lower temperature.

In a solid, the molecules are bonded to each other and are in fixed positions relative to each other.

In a liquid, the bonds between molecules are weaker and the molecules can move to some degree.

In a gas, the molecules are no longer bonded to each other and can move freely and independently.

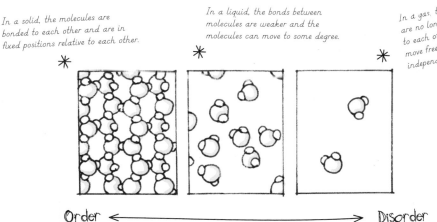

Order ⟵——————————————⟶ Disorder

Why Is Water a Solvent?

So many chemical compounds readily dissolve in water that it has been called the "universal solvent," but its importance goes way beyond its uses in the home or in industry. In the natural world, water performs a vital function in every living cell, and without it life on this planet could not exist in the form it does. So how does water do this?

The answer lies in the molecular structure of water. Each water molecule is composed of two hydrogen atoms and one oxygen atom, hence H_2O. The hydrogen atoms are held to the oxygen atom by a covalent bond, which means that each hydrogen atom shares an electron with the oxygen atom, but they don't share equally. The two shared electrons stay closer to the oxygen atom, and as electrons have a negative charge, this means that the oxygen atom is slightly negatively charged and the hydrogen atoms have a slight positive charge. A molecule that has positive and negative regions (these are called "dipoles") is called a polar molecule, and polar molecules have special properties.

Breaking Bonds

One of those properties is the ability to act as a solvent in which other compounds will dissolve, especially other polar molecules and ionic compounds— compounds whose molecules are composed of atoms attracted to each other by having opposite electrostatic charges. Common table salt (sodium chloride) is a good example of this. Each molecule is composed of a positively charged sodium atom (Na^+) and a negatively charged chlorine atom (Cl^-), the positive and the negative attracting each other in an ionic bond. The polar water molecules, which are much smaller, make their way into the crystal structure of the salt, surround the atoms, and break the ionic bonds between them, separating the sodium and the chlorine atoms and dissolving the salt. As a result of their relative charges, the water molecules line themselves up differently around the sodium and the chlorine.

FACT: *Water is virtually unique in that it exists in all three states of matter (solid, liquid, and gas) within the temperature ranges found on this planet.*

Oil and Water

As we know, oil and water don't mix, so oil is certainly not soluble in water. This is because oil and grease are nonpolar molecules and water cannot bond with them. And yet we remove oil from clothes by washing them in water. The solution, as it were, lies in the soap or detergent. These substances are known as *surfactants* (short for "surface-acting agents"), and they have long molecules with one polar end and one nonpolar end. The nonpolar ends attach to a molecule or globule of nonpolar grease and surround it, while the polar ends of the molecules are attracted to water. In this way the grease is removed.

FACT: *If you thought that the blue color of lakes and ocean's was caused by reflection of the sky, think again. Not only is the color really there but it has a unique source. Whereas color is normally caused by interactions between photons and the electrons in a material, recent research shows that the blue color of water is caused by the absorption of red light by particles in the nuclei of the water molecules, changing the speed of their vibration. Water is the only known case of this phenomenon.*

Surface Tension

The positive and negative dipoles of the water molecules don't only attract charged atoms of other compounds—they also attract each other. In the solid form, ice, there is a strong bond between the water molecules. The bond is weaker in liquid water, but the force of the attraction still exists, and can be seen at the surface. Whereas the molecules in the body of the liquid are being pulled equally in all directions, those at the surface are being pulled only sideways and down; this creates "surface tension," which can appear to act almost like a skin. This is what causes water to form beads on a shiny surface, to form spherical drops when in free fall, to rise up the sides of a glass, and to have a convex surface when a glass is overfilled. Surface tension also allows water boatmen (sometimes called water skeeters) to walk on water without sinking.

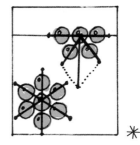

Below the surface, water molecules pull each other equally in all directions. At the surface they pull each other downward and sideways, creating surface tension.

Surface tension pulls a water droplet into a sphere, which has the smallest surface area for a given volume.

Life as We Know It

All life on this planet is water-based; if water didn't have its peculiar properties, life as we know it could not exist. Its solvent properties are key, because biochemical processes rely on aqueous (water-based) solutions to transport nutrients and waste material and carry out chemical reactions. But without its other remarkable qualities, water could not fulfill these tasks. If it were generally a solid or a gas, for example, its solvency would be useless. Fortunately, it stays in the liquid phase through a wider range of temperatures—32°F (0°C) to 212°F (100°C)—than almost any other substance. It is runny enough to flow, but has sufficient surface tension to rise through the tiny tubes in a plant's stem. And, being made from two of the most abundant elements in the universe, there's plenty of it!

SUMMARY

Water is a solvent—and a very good one—because its molecules are polar. This means that they have positive and negative regions, enabling them to bond with other polar chemicals and with compounds whose molecules have ionic bonds (bonds between positively and negatively charged atoms). Water molecules also bond with each other.

When Did the Olympics Begin?

The answer to this question depends on what you mean by "the Olympics." The Games have had two incarnations, ancient and modern. Both versions have common features that demonstrate how little human nature has changed over time: novelty, cheating, and politics. Sport has never been without these features, and the Olympics is no exception.

The five rings represent the Americas, Europe, Asia, Africa and Oceania

FACT: The modern Olympics retained a direct link to the ancient Olympics through the manner of its opening. The flame that burns throughout the Games is first lit at Olympia, traditional home of the ancient Olympics. The flame is then carried by torch to the site of the modern Games.

The exact starting date for the ancient Olympics is unknown, but many scholars place it some time around 776 B.C.E., in ancient Greece. At this time, Greece was not a single nation but a loose network of city-states, sometimes warring with each other, sometimes allied against an external foe. It is easy to understand the two impulses that may have encouraged the foundation of the Games in those turbulent times. First, life was pretty unpredictable, so appeasing the gods was an attractive idea. Second, young men needed a reason to stay fit and skilled for warfare. What could be better than an athletic event that served both purposes? An additional benefit, possibly unintended, was that the Games presented themselves as a nonviolent form of competition between the Greek city-states, allowing them to demonstrate prowess without resorting to arms.

Modern Revival

Dating the modern Olympics is less difficult. They began in 1896 as the brainchild of the French historian Pierre de Coubertin. The late nineteenth century is sometimes defined as the "age of empires." The states of Europe scrambled for land in a nationalistic bid to outdo each others' imperial ambitions, and this rivalry threatened to spill over into direct conflict. Plans were already afoot for renewed conflict between France and Germany, and a naval arms race between Great Britain, Germany, and the United States was well underway. To Coubertin, a revival of the Olympics seemed to offer a way to diffuse the situation. He asserted that, for the competitors, representing their country should be more important than determining which of them was the supreme athlete in their event, stating that: "L'important n'est pas de gagner, mais de participer." (The important thing is not to win, but to take part.) Others perceived the matter rather differently, considering the Games as an opportunity to demonstrate national superiority through the martial qualities of manhood.

Athletes at the ancient Olympics usually competed naked as a celebration of the abilities of the human body.

FACT: *The founder of the modern Olympics, Pierre de Coubertin, was French. As a result, the official language of the Games is French, so wherever in the world the opening and closing ceremonies occur, the speeches given by the Chairman of the International Olympic Committee are in French. Less well known is that Coubertin had been inspired by the work of Dr. William Penny Brooks, who had attempted an earlier revival of the Olympic Games in Britain.*

SUMMARY

The Olympics can be said to have two starting dates: 776 B.C.E. and 1896 C.E. The events, size, cost, and expectations of the Games have greatly changed over time, but their human qualities, both villainous and heroic, have not.

Sporting Values, Ancient and Modern

The ancient Olympics were abolished in the fourth century C.E. because they were believed to be a pagan practice in what was by then a Christian Roman world. However, the Games had not progressed to that point without being the subject of criticism that seems very familiar to the modern Games. From the outset, running was the main sport of the Games, but very quickly events were added, broadening the appeal and introducing more disciplines that had a military application. Purists were critical of some new events, believing that they detracted from the purity of the Games (critics of events such as synchronized swimming as a sport worthy of the Olympics have ancient allies). Cheating was as much of a problem for the ancients as it is in our time. Fines were levied against those athletes caught cheating, but these, and even the threat of flogging, failed to solve the problem. The adoption of a nationality of convenience is also not a modern phenomenon. Banned from the Games for a breach of treaty, one Spartan athlete, Lichas, entered the Games as a Boeotian. When the truth was discovered, he was banned and flogged for his trouble. The most prominent medical criticism of the Games came from the first-century physician, Galen. He argued that the athletes were overtraining, overeating, and generally having an adverse effect on their well-being.

The Games were then, and are now, big business. Training manuals, spectator revenues, merchandise, and sponsorship were as familiar to the ancient Greeks and Romans as they are to followers of the modern Olympics, although the modern Games have sought to exploit every opportunity to generate revenue and market the Games to a truly global audience.

FACT: *The first Olympic Winter Games were held in 1924, when the International Olympic Committee sanctioned an "International Winter Sports Week" at Chamonix in France. The Winter Games were held in the same years as the Summer Olympics until 1994, when the schedule was changed so that they alternate every two years.*

<u>Who</u> Broke the Four-Minute Mile Barrier?

Ever since accurate records have been kept—and that's more than 150 years for many sports—athletes have been running faster, jumping higher and farther, and generally getting better at every form of competition. One of the most important milestones ever reached was the breaking of the four-minute mile, but who was the first man to break this most famous of sporting barriers?

Back in 1886, a professional British runner named Walter George set a time of 4 minutes 12.75 seconds for the mile (1.6-km) run, and this record stood for almost thirty years, finally beaten by a fraction of a second by an American amateur, Norman Taber, in 1915. This was steadily eclipsed over the next thirty years until, thanks to Swedish runner Gunder Hägg in 1945, it stood at just 1.3 seconds above the four-minute mark.

The Miracle Mile

At that time, a British schoolboy named Roger Bannister was already attracting attention with his performances on the running track. He worked hard at school, too, and won himself a scholarship to Oxford University, where he studied medicine. Determined to break the four-minute barrier, he used his medical knowledge to develop his own training methods, and by 1954 both he and the Australian runner John Landy were getting very close. On May 6, aided by his two friends Chris Brasher and Chris Chataway, who acted as pacemakers, Bannister went for it. At the three-quarter distance, Chataway was still setting the pace, and then, in the final 200 yards, Bannister sprinted ahead for a finishing time of 3 minutes 59.4 seconds, going into the record books as the first person ever to run the mile in less than four minutes.

Roger Bannister breasts the tape in Oxford, England, to become the first person ever to run a mile in under four minutes. ✳

***FACT**: In August 1954, the two sub-four-minute men met in competition at the Commonwealth Games in Vancouver. Landy held the lead for most of the race, but on the last bend he looked back over his left shoulder to check Bannister's position and the Briton passed him on the right to win with a time of 3 minutes 58.8 seconds, 0.8 seconds ahead of Landy.*

FACT: *Women can't run as fast as men, but they're getting closer. In 1921, the women's record was two minutes, or 50 percent, slower than the men's. In the year that Bannister broke the four-minute mile, Diane Leather broke the five-minute mile, 25 percent slower. And the current women's record of 4 minutes 12.56 seconds, set by Svetlana Masterkova of Russia in 1996, is just 13 percent slower than the current men's record. Watch out, guys!*

Ever Faster

It had taken ten years for a runner to shave 1.5 seconds off the world record, but Bannister was to remain the fastest man on Earth for just six weeks! That's how long it took John Landy to shave off the next 1.5 seconds. The record now stands at just 3 minutes 43.13 seconds, set by Moroccan Hicham El Guerrouj in 1999, but no doubt that, too, will be beaten sooner or later. So what is going on?

There are several factors that explain the continued improvement of top athletes, but the most important is probably training. At the start of the nineteenth century, athletes believed that too much practice was a bad thing and almost amounted to cheating. Indeed, men whose work was manual labor were banned from certain sports because they were felt to have an unfair advantage. Roger Bannister proved that a training schedule could produce results, and all successful sportsmen and women now pay careful attention to their preparation.

The growth of professional sports has meant athletes can devote more of their time to improving fitness and technique without having to squeeze training in around other work. Athletes tend to have longer careers, staying in the sport longer and continuing to improve. Finally, technological advances in equipment, such as low-friction swimwear, can make the vital difference. All in all, we can look forward to more records being broken until we reach the true limit of human performance.

FACT: *In 1968, at the Mexico Olympics, Bob Beamon astonished the spectators with a jump of 29 feet 2 1/2 inches (8.90 m), adding 21 3/4 inches (55 cm) to the previous world long jump record. His achievement remained unbeaten for the next twenty-three years.*

SUMMARY

The first person to run the mile in under four minutes was Roger Bannister of Great Britain. His time of 3:59.4, set on May 6, 1953, was beaten just forty-six days later by John Landy of Australia, and runners have been getting faster ever since. The record for the mile is now 3:43.13, set by Hicham El Guerrouj of Morocco on July 7, 1999.

QUOTE:

"You have destroyed this event."

Defending Olympic long-jump champion Lynn Davies, speaking to Bob Beamon in 1968.

Why Are Soccer Balls Round?

The idea of a competitive game involving kicking, throwing, carrying, or hitting an object goes way back beyond recorded history. A stuffed spherical linen ball was found in an ancient Egyptian tomb, the ancient Greeks and Romans played a range of round-ball games, and the Mayans of Central America used a round elastic ball to play a game that could end in death. So what is the appeal of the sphere, and why are some balls oval?

We don't know much about the rules of ancient Egyptian "football," but the Greeks certainly allowed throwing and kicking in a game they called *episkyros*. In addition to solid balls made of cloth and hair, they used a much lighter ball called a *follis* that consisted of an inflated pig's bladder wrapped in animal skin. The Romans adapted the Greek game and called it *harpastum*. This was played by two teams on a rectangular field that had a center line, and the idea was to keep the ball in your own half, and to steal it back from the opposition if they took it. There was less kicking, but plenty of tackling and, because you could only tackle the one who had the ball, plenty of passing, too.

A Brief History of Football

When the Romans invaded Britain, they tried to introduce harpastum and even played against the British, but it didn't catch on. By the ninth century, various local forms of ball games were being played throughout the British Isles and in northern France, but some of these were more like a battle than a sport. In "mob football," which was played in the Middle Ages to celebrate festivals such as Shrove Tuesday and may have had its origins in pagan ritual, entire villages or town neighborhoods fought to get the ball into the opposing territory. There were virtually no rules, and there are records of players being killed in the fray. Several British monarchs from the fourteenth century onward tried to have football banned because of its riotous nature.

FACT: *Three thousand years ago, the Olmec people of Mesoamerica were playing a ball game that was passed on to the Aztecs and the Mayan people, and which still exists today in a form called "ulama." Originally played in a stone-built enclosure (several still exist throughout Mexico), the game involves keeping a heavy solid rubber ball in play using just your hips, and players gird themselves with a wide leather belt to reduce bruising. In the Aztec version, players tried to pass the ball through a stone circle on the wall, and it is thought that members of the losing team were sacrificed to the gods.*

FACT: *The use of an inflated pig's bladder as a football continued until 1870, when Richard Lindon, ball maker to Rugby Boys' School, introduced the rubber bladder. Until this time, the shape and size of each leather-clad ball had depended on the particular bladder, and balls were generally plum-shaped. The introduction of the rubber bladder allowed "rugger" balls to be made to a standard form, and the shape was deliberately elongated.*

Soccer
22 cm across

By the nineteenth century a slightly more civilized game, involving both kicking and handling the ball, was being played in British schools, most notably at Rugby School, which drew up rules that were generally accepted. However, there was also a movement toward a kicking-only game, and in 1863 the London Football Association separated the sport of Association Football (later known as soccer) from that of rugby football and created a set of rules that banned handling the ball. In the United States, a form of rugby football was taken up by universities such as Princeton and developed into collegiate and professional American football.

American football
28 cm long, 17.8 cm wide

The Shape of the Ball

When you think about it, a ball needs several qualities. It must be light enough to be kicked or thrown a distance. It has to be strong enough to survive the rigors of the game. It should bounce. And it needs to be made of available materials. But should it be round?

Rugby union
30 cm long, 20 cm wide

A round ball is predictable: it rolls in a straight line; kick it in the middle and it flies straight; bounce it on a flat surface and it comes off at the opposing angle. When throwing, passing, and catching are important, an elongated ball is actually easier to handle. There's even an added excitement in not knowing which direction the ball will bounce when it lands. But when it comes to a game that's all about kicking and footwork, you need a round ball if you want a game of skill rather than chance.

Rugby league
27 cm long, 19 cm wide

Australian football
28 cm long, 17.5 cm wide

SUMMARY

At the end of a long history, the balls used for soccer and almost every other ball sport are round because the regular shape produces regular performance— smooth rolling, straight flying, and predictable bounce. The ancient Egyptians knew this, and so did the Greeks and Romans. Modern technology makes it possible to have roundness at the same time as the right weight, size, and bounce to suit any sport. And now that we have complete predictability, every pitcher, kicker, batter, and bowler is working hard to induce spin and curve to fool the opposition!

Where Was Wrestling Invented?

As a form of primitive dispute resolution, wrestling has no doubt been around for as long as people have been pushing and shoving, but even as a competitive sport it has a long and glorious history. Images of grappling wrestlers are found in ancient art, and there are accounts of hand-to-hand battles in some of the earliest epic writing.

Wrestling as a sport dates back more than 4,000 years. Paintings on the walls of ancient Egyptian tombs depict wrestlers using holds and throws that are all found in modern-day "freestyle" wrestling, and in China at that time there was a rather painful form of martial art called *shuai jiao*, in which the grappling combatants wore horned helmets and tried to wound each other by head-butting. By 1000 B.C.E., the ancient Greeks had developed a slightly less violent form, and this was included in the Olympic Games of 708 B.C.E. Points were scored for throwing your opponent on his back, making him concede defeat (presumably by inflicting pain), or forcing him out of the ring. The rules banned hitting and kicking, gouging out the eyes, and grasping the genitals, but all other means were allowed. Score three points and you were the winner. Wrestling was also an integral part of Greek education and military training.

The Romans adopted and adapted the Greek style of wrestling, but whereas the Greeks fought naked, the Romans insisted on the wearing of a loincloth, which provided additional (legitimate) parts for grabbing.

FACT: Many regions of the world have their own indigenous forms of hand-to-hand combat, known collectively as "folk wrestling." The Icelandic national style is called **glima**, and it is thought to be more than a thousand years old. Each combatant wears belts around his waist and thighs, connected by straps. The aim is to hold your opponent by these straps and throw him to the ground.

✳
This marble relief, found in Athens, is thought to depict athletes wrestling in Olympics that took place around 500–400 B.C.E.

FACT: *Mongolia boasts a long history of wrestling, which is one of the "three manly sports" featured (together with horse-riding and archery) at the midsummer **Naadam** festivals. Competitors wear a midriff-revealing long-sleeved sweater, briefs, and cowboy boots.*

SUMMARY

Wrestling as a form of unarmed combat seems to have arisen in all cultures and in all ages, but the various modern forms of amateur wrestling can trace their ancestry back through European styles to the Greeks and Romans. American collegiate wrestling and its younger brother, scholastic wrestling, have strong ties with "catch-as-catch-can," which became popular in the northwest of England in the eighteenth century.

Europe and America

Over the next thousand years, wrestling took on many forms as it spread across Europe, each region developing its own rules and styles, and the sport became very popular. Indeed, when the kings of England and France held a lavish diplomatic meeting in 1520 on the "Field of the Cloth of Gold," Henry VIII challenged Francis I to a bout of wrestling—which he lost.

By the nineteenth century, several distinct styles of amateur wrestling were recognized, and two of these became modern Olympic sports. In Greco-Roman wrestling, which bears little resemblance to the rough and tumble of ancient times, no contact below the waist is allowed, and the sport is all about using holds and throws to control and force your opponent into contact with the mat. Extra points are earned for dramatic "high-amplitude" throws.

Freestyle wrestling, in which attacks to the legs are allowed, has a shorter but more direct connection to an earlier form. "Catch-as-catch-can" wrestling developed in Lancashire in northwest England, and became popular at fairs from the eighteenth century on, not only in Britain and Europe but also in the United States, where it was brought by early settlers. In Europe it evolved into freestyle wrestling, which is now an Olympic sport, whereas in the United States it became what we now know as collegiate wrestling, sometimes called "folkstyle" because of its origins. New York City hosted the first U.S. national wrestling tournament in 1888, and several U.S. presidents, from George Washington to Theodore Roosevelt, practiced versions of this sport. In both freestyle and collegiate wrestling the emphasis is on pinning your opponent to the mat for an instant win, and this results in intense bursts of action.

Professional Wrestling

Professional wrestling is a noncompetitive form of theatrical entertainment that uses a mixture of wrestling and boxing moves. Its origins lie in the nineteenth-century carnival sideshows of North America, but it boomed in the television age, becoming a multibillion-dollar industry after the 1960s. Particularly popular in the United States, United Kingdom, Japan, and South Africa, it has a range of styles from comic farce to super-violent, but it always features dramatic moves and plenty of in-the-air action.

What Is the Fastest Swim Stroke?

We may not have evolved with the sole focus of traveling through water, but we are nonetheless able to do quite a good job of it. Cave paintings from the Stone Age, and written references from the time of the Egyptian pharaohs, show we've been swimming for a long time, and of course, like most other human activities, it was eventually made competitive—but not for speed alone.

In many track and field sports, such as running or the high jump, you can do it any way you like. The aim is to run as fast or jump as high as possible, and no one tells you how you are allowed to move your arms or legs—but swimming isn't like that. In swimming, speed isn't everything—there are many different styles, or "strokes," and each one has its own history, rules, and records.

In the first swimming competitions, in Europe more than 200 years ago, swimmers used the breaststroke, and this remained the case for decades. The breaststroke involves pushing the hands out in front and then sweeping them out to the sides and back while the legs make a froglike movement. It is one of the slowest means of propulsion, but its undemonstrative style suited the Victorians. When the Swimming Society invited two Native Americans to an international competition in London, England, in 1843, everyone was shocked at the splashy and most ungentlemanly performance of the foreigners. Not only did they use an overarm swimming stroke and a kicking motion of the feet, but they were also considerably faster than the sedate Europeans who, of course, stuck to their guns and continued with the breaststroke for another thirty years.

Captain Matthew Webb, followed by his safety boat, approaches the French coast after swimming the English Channel in 1875.

FACT: *Four strokes are recognized in Olympic swimming. In descending order of speed, these are: freestyle (or crawl), butterfly, backstroke, and breaststroke. The sidestroke was an Olympic event from 1968 until 1984; all the sidestroke records were set by Australian Stephen MacKenzie at the FINA World Swimming Championships held at Guayaquil, Ecuador, in 1982.*

FACT: *Several swimming styles are used specifically for lifesaving. To search for someone in trouble, rescuers can keep their eyes above the water with a "heads-up" version of the crawl or breaststroke. To tow a person to safety, lifeguards swim on their backs, using just the leg movement of breaststroke, or use sidestroke, in which one arm does all the work, allowing the swimmer to hold the person with the other.*

SUMMARY

Although controversial when introduced into competition, the front crawl, or freestyle stroke, is both the most natural and the fastest swim stroke. The butterfly stroke is the next fastest, followed by the backstroke and breaststroke.

The Americans' swimming style was not new; it was the way that coastal native people around the world moved through the water because it was efficient and quick. The overarm stroke was finally taken seriously in Western competitive swimming after John Arthur Trudgen, having learned it in South America, won the English 100-yard race in 1875 with this arm movement, although he used a scissor kick of the legs rather than the more showy up-and-down flutter kick. This "Trudgen" style became very popular for a time, but in 1902 the full version of what we now call the front crawl, or freestyle stroke, entered the competitive arena, performed by Richard Cavill. This was, and still is, the fastest of all swimming strokes.

Breaststroke Variations

The original competitive stroke still kept its place, especially for longer distances, as it was felt that the crawl was too exhausting. Indeed, Captain Webb was using breaststroke when he became the first man to swim across the English Channel, in the same year that Trudgen introduced his stroke.

The downside of the breaststroke, and one of the reasons why it is slow, is that the arms have to be extended forward under water (the part of the stroke called the "recovery") before they can be used to propel the body. In the 1930s this was overcome by bringing the arms out of the water and throwing them forward, a stroke that became known as the butterfly. It proved to be faster than the breaststroke, and was improved further by a new leg movement that was called the "dolphin fishtail kick," involving a beating motion with the legs together, with two kicks to each arm stroke. The butterfly was regarded as a variant of the breaststroke, and the dolphin kick was therefore ruled illegal, until 1952, when it was recognized as a stroke in its own right.

Although the peak speed of a butterfly swimmer's stroke, as the arms pull through the water, is higher than that of a freestyle swimmer, the overall speed is slower. This is despite the fact that the butterfly stroke requires more energy.

Knowledge: *the ability to recall information*

1) When was the U.S. Constitution first drawn up?
- **a.** 1777
- **b.** 1787
- **c.** 1797
- **d.** 1807

2) When was the "Glorious Revolution?"
- **a.** 1650
- **b.** 1600
- **c.** 1695
- **d.** 1688

3) When was George Washington inaugurated as president?
- **a.** 1789
- **b.** 1787
- **c.** 1750
- **d.** 1800

4) Which amendment to the Constitution limited a president to serving a maximum of two terms in office?
- **a.** 7th
- **b.** 20th
- **c.** 22nd
- **d.** 5th

5) Why did George Washington eventually decide to salary the position of president?
- **a.** Because he had begun to run out of money
- **b.** So that the office did not become the preserve of the wealthy
- **c.** So that the president could live like a monarch
- **d.** To attract more people

6) For how long has Damascus been continually inhabited?
- **a.** 500 years
- **b.** 1,000 years
- **c.** 1,500 years
- **d.** 1,700 years

7) In which year did Syria gain independence?
- **a.** 1945
- **b.** 1946
- **c.** 1949
- **d.** 1960

8) On which ship did Roosevelt and Churchill meet in August 1941?
- **a.** HMS *Pinafore*
- **b.** HMS *Belfast*
- **c.** HMS *Prince of Wales*
- **d.** HMS *Dreadnought*

9) When does the United Nations celebrate its birthday?
- **a.** October 24th
- **b.** August 20th
- **c.** January 1st
- **d.** November 14th

10) What was the name of Marx's friend and coauthor of *The Communist Manifesto*?
- **a.** Antonio Gramsci
- **b.** Josef Stalin
- **c.** Vladimir Lenin
- **d.** Friedrich Engels

11) Approximately how many citizens were killed in the Paris Commune?
- **a.** 10,000
- **b.** 20,000
- **c.** 30,000
- **d.** 100,000

12) When was *The Communist Manifesto* written?
- **a.** 1847
- **b.** 1850
- **c.** 1864
- **d.** 1971

Understanding: *the ability to interpret information and make links between different aspects of it*

1) Why is it misleading to describe the British constitution as "unwritten"?

2) What is the purpose of a constitution?

3) Why was George Washington not a member of a political party?

4) What precipitated Damascus's decline in the early Middle Ages?

5) How was industrialization linked to the formation of new pan-national diplomatic bodies?

6) Why did later communists actively seek to precipitate revolution?

Knowledge: *the ability to recall information*

1) What adjective is used to describe fish that migrate up rivers from the ocean to spawn?
 a. Pelagic
 b. Demersal
 c. Catadromous
 d. Anadromous

2) Which butterfly migrates the length of the United States?
 a. Painted Lady
 b. Monarch
 c. Red Admiral
 d. Swallowtail

3) What delayed exploration of the White Nile?
 a. Impassable mountains
 b. Dangerous wild animals
 c. Impenetrable wetlands
 d. Lightning storms

4) Who was the first European to discover Lake Victoria?
 a. John Hanning Speke
 b. Dr. Livingstone
 c. Richard Francis Burton
 d. Henry Morton Stanley

5) In what year was the most distant source of the White Nile discovered?
 a. 1858
 b. 1862
 c. 1967
 d. 2006

6) The Great Barrier Reef is located off the coast of:
 a. Africa
 b. South America
 c. Australia
 d. Antarctica

7) Some corals have a "symbiotic" relationship with algae, which means that:
 a. One benefits at the expense of the other
 b. Both benefit
 c. Neither benefit
 d. They harm each other

8) Which of these is a kind of coral?
 a. Brain
 b. Staghorn
 c. Star
 d. All of these

9) What makes the McMurdo Dry Valleys an unusual kind of desert?
 a. They are below sea level.
 b. They are in the middle of a lake.
 c. They are in Antarctica.
 d. They are on top of a mountain.

10) Winds that blow downward are described as:
 a. Katabatic
 b. Anabatic
 c. Catatonic
 d. Apocalyptic

11) Most of the Grand Canyon is located in:
 a. Nevada
 b. Utah
 c. Arizona
 d. California

12) Rock that has been deposited in layers under water is described as:
 a. Volcanic
 b. Sedimentary
 c. Igneous
 d. Metamorphic

Understanding: *the ability to interpret information and make links between different aspects of it*

1) Why does some sea life migrate vertically through the ocean?

2) What are the principal reasons for animal migration?

3) Name some of the achievements of the Ancient Egyptians, and discuss what made these achievements possible.

4) Describe what a coral polyp looks like, and explain how it feeds.

5) There are four main factors that create desert. Explain three of them.

6) Why are the walls of the Grand Canyon striped, and what gives the rock its various colors?

Knowledge: *the ability to recall information*

1) Most of Isaac Newton's writing was about:
   a. Gravity
   b. Astronomy
   c. Light
   d. Alchemy

2) Which of these scientists combined alchemy with medicine?
   a. Roger Bacon
   b. Paracelsus
   c. Jabir ibn Hayyan
   d. Robert Boyle

3) Marie and Pierre Curie published their discovery of radium in:
   a. 1798
   b. 1848
   c. 1898
   d. 1948

4) The Curies worked with another eminent scientist in the field of radioactivity. His name was:
   a. Henri Becquerel
   b. Malcolm X
   c. Albert Einstein
   d. Enrico Fermi

5) The element polonium was named in honor of:
   a. The islands of Polynesia
   b. An American sausage
   c. Poland
   d. The North Pole

6) What is diamond made of?
   a. Carbon, hydrogen, and oxygen
   b. Feldspar
   c. Quartz
   d. Carbon

7) The word "diamond" comes from a Greek word meaning:
   a. Unconquerable
   b. Colorless
   c. Rare
   d. Valuable

8) What effect does color have on the value of a diamond?
   a. Diamonds never have any color.
   b. Red and green diamonds are the most valuable.
   c. Shades of yellow or brown increase the value.
   d. Any color reduces the value.

9) An increase in pressure:
   a. Lowers the boiling point of a liquid
   b. Increases the volume of a solid
   c. Raises the boiling point of a liquid
   d. Has no effect on the boiling point

10) Why is a water molecule polar?
   a. It has a net positive charge.
   b. It has a net negative charge.
   c. It has a net zero charge.
   d. The ends of the molecule have slight positive and negative charges.

11) Which of these statements is true?
   a. Water is a solvent and table salt is a solute.
   b. Table salt is a solvent and water is a solute.
   c. Water and salt are both solvents.
   d. Water and salt are both solutes.

12) Water is essential for life as we know it because:
   a. It is a good solvent
   b. It is a liquid throughout a wide temperature range
   c. It is abundant
   d. All of these

Understanding: *the ability to interpret information and make links between different aspects of it*

1) What were the alchemists of Medieval Europe trying to achieve?

2) What was the most significant finding that Marie Curie made about radioactivity?

3) What unit is used to express the weight of a diamond, and what is its origin? What is the equivalent of this unit in ounces or grams?

4) What are "the latent heat of fusion" and "the latent heat of vaporization?"

5) Although they are theoretically the same, why can the melting point and freezing point of a substance differ?

6) What property of detergent molecules enables us to remove grease from clothes by washing?

146

Knowledge: *the ability to recall information*

1) The first Olympic Games took place about:
- **a.** 1,000 years ago
- **b.** 100 years ago
- **c.** 2,000 years ago
- **d.** 200 years ago

2) The first Winter Olympic Games were held in:
- **a.** Greece
- **b.** Rome
- **c.** Sweden
- **d.** France

3) The first person to run a mile in less than four minutes was:
- **a.** Chris Brasher
- **b.** Roger Bannister
- **c.** John Landy
- **d.** Chris Chataway

4) Who first brought football to Britain?
- **a.** The Americans
- **b.** The Chinese
- **c.** The Romans
- **d.** The Argentineans

5) What did the Greeks wear during wrestling matches?
- **a.** A toga
- **b.** A knee-length skirt
- **c.** Short shorts
- **d.** Nothing at all

6) Who won when the kings of England and France wrestled on the "Field of the Cloth of Gold?"
- **a.** Francis I
- **b.** Louis XVI
- **c.** Henry VIII
- **d.** William the Conqueror

7) American collegiate wrestling developed directly from:
- **a.** Greco-Roman wrestling
- **b.** Professional wrestling
- **c.** Fairground wrestling
- **d.** Chinese Shuai Jiao

8) Which of these is not one of the Mongolian "three manly sports?"
- **a.** Wrestling
- **b.** Horse-riding
- **c.** Archery
- **d.** Running

9) Which is the fastest swimming stroke?
- **a.** Crawl/freestyle
- **b.** Breaststroke
- **c.** Butterfly
- **d.** Backstroke

10) Who was the first person to swim across the English Channel?
- **a.** John Arthur Trudgen
- **b.** Stephen MacKenzie
- **c.** Captain Matthew Webb
- **d.** Mark Spitz

Understanding: *the ability to interpret information and make links between different aspects of it*

1) What are the reasons behind the fact that athletes' performances are steadily improving?

2) What are the relative advantages of a round ball and an oval ball?

3) What is distinctive about the Icelandic "glima" style of wrestling?

4) What aspect of the breaststroke makes it inefficient?

5) What styles of swimming are used for life saving, and why?

Thursday

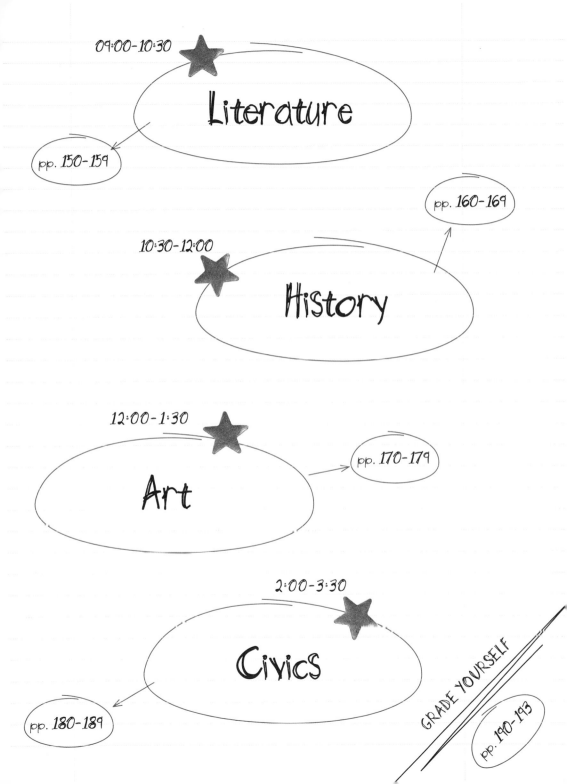

09:00-10:30

Literature

pp. 150-159

pp. 160-169

10:30-12:00

History

12:00-1:30

Art

pp. 170-179

2:00-3:30

Civics

pp. 180-189

GRADE YOURSELF

pp. 190-193

When Did Tolstoy Write War and Peace?

War and Peace is renowned as a difficult book: many readers set out with good intentions, but few manage to reach the end, and unfinished copies decorate many a bookshelf. In the case of War and Peace, the problem is its sheer size, epic scale, and seemingly infinite cast of characters; but all these factors, which undoubtedly can seem offputting, are a product of the period in which Tolstoy lived.

By the 1860s, Tolstoy was already an acclaimed author with three novels to his name. As the titles suggest, *Childhood* (1852), *Boyhood* (1852), and *Youth* (1857) drew heavily on his life, which had been marked by tragedy. Tolstoy's mother died when he was only two, and his father was murdered when he was nine. The family was a wealthy one, owning large estates, but such appalling experiences must have scarred Tolstoy and left their mark on his work.

The War

Tolstoy had served in the Russian army during the Crimean War (1854–1856). The war was part of a long-running contest between the Great Powers for control of the countries on Russia's borders. France and Britain were unwilling to see Russia gain complete control of the Black Sea and the access to the Mediterranean that it would bring. All three nations wanted to exert control over the declining Ottoman Empire, but they were also rivals in the Middle and Far East. These themes of rivalry and the impact of war run through *War and Peace*.

FACT: *In Tolstoy's time, the Ottoman Empire was widely known as "the sick man of Europe." Centered on modern-day Turkey, the empire was regarded as crucial because it controlled the Bosporus Straits at Constantinople. Without a warm-water port in the Black Sea and access to the Straits, the Russian navy was effectively trapped.*

The Peace

Domestically, the 1860s were a period of change for Tolstoy. In 1862 he had married Sofya Andreevna Behrs. He was thirty-four and she was nineteen. They settled on the family estate and had four children in the first seven years of their marriage. *War and Peace* deals with the massive impact of the Napoleonic wars through the lives of five aristocratic families. Tolstoy uses the intimate descriptions of individual lives as a tool for exploring huge issues such as social reform, death, and individual destiny.

SUMMARY

Lev (Leo) Nikolaevich Tolstoy wrote *War and Peace* in the middle of the nineteenth century. This was a time of great change for Tolstoy, and also for Russia, the country where he was born and lived. The novel reflects many of Tolstoy's personal experiences and the changes that were sweeping their way through Russia in the mid-nineteenth century.

The domestic context of Russia was a mirror for the issues that Tolstoy wrote about in *War and Peace*. Russia had achieved only limited industrial development by the 1860s. Russian agriculture still relied on the labor of serfs—virtual slaves who worked on vast estates. The tsar was the absolute ruler of the country, and the aristocracy held all positions of authority. Russia had grand ambitions but appeared to be slipping behind the other great powers. Intellectuals were divided about how Russia should respond to the changing world of the nineteenth century. Those who were known as "Slavophiles" believed in a uniquely Russian approach to development, reflecting Russia's particular history. The other school of thought was that of "Westernizers." They believed in the reform of Russian society and the introduction of a more liberal form of government. In *War and Peace*, Tolstoy was critical of authoritarian government and seemed to support reform. One of the central characters, Pierre Bezukhov, frees all of his serfs and introduces new methods of production to his estate (although he ends up bankrupt).

QUOTE:

"War is not a polite recreation but the vilest thing in life, and we ought to understand that and not play at war. We ought to accept it sternly and solemnly as a fearful necessity."

Leo Tolstoy, War and Peace, **book ten**

Leo Tolstoy
(1828–1910)

✳

Nations and Individuals

War and Peace was published in five parts between 1856 and 1869. The novel was greeted with popular success and critical acclaim. The extraordinary conflict between Napoleonic France and Russia provided a perfect backdrop for Tolstoy to explore issues that were significant to him and to Russian society in the 1860s, although he appeared to acknowledge the immensity of the task when he wrote in the epilogue: "History is the life of nations and of humanity. To seize and put into words, to describe directly the life of humanity or even of a single nation, appears impossible."

<u>**Who**</u> was Eric Arthur Blair?

The name might sound familiar, but you would be
forgiven for not knowing who Eric Arthur Blair is; he is
better known by his pen name: George Orwell. Born in
1903, his life was cut short by tuberculosis in 1950. The
life history of Eric Arthur Blair is bound up with some of
the key events of the twentieth century and tells the
story of the decline of a particular type of Englishness.

Eric Arthur Blair did not adopt the pen name George
Orwell until 1933. By that time his experiences had
shaped many of the views that were to influence his
major works. Born in India, he arrived in England
with his mother and older sister at the age of one. His father, Richard Blair,
worked for the civil service in India, and returned to his family only twice
between 1904 and 1912. A bright boy, the young Eric went to two private
schools, St. Cyprian's and then Eton. After finishing at Eton, he too found
work abroad in the British Empire, serving in Burma (now Myanmar) as
part of the Indian Imperial Police. During World War II, he worked at the
British Broadcasting Corporation (the BBC), working on programs aimed at an
Indian and Far Eastern audience. However, while he appeared to be part of the
establishment on the surface, this hid a much more complicated explanation of
who Eric Arthur Blair was.

George Orwell
(1903–1950)

The Hidden Story

On returning from India, the Blair family were comfortably off, but not
wealthy. The two private schools that the young Eric attended were the
consequence of scholarships—he was a bright student, not a rich one. His fees
were partly paid by his uncle, the only member of the family who seems to
have encouraged the young man to develop his intellect. At Eton he made
social contacts that were far beyond his family's social circle, but he was
unable to afford to go on to a university.

FACT: *The decline of English society is a regular theme in
Orwell's novels. Two of the most famous are* **A Clergyman's
Daughter** *(1935) and* **Keep the Aspidistra Flying** *(1936).
An aspidistra is a type of potted plant, regarded in the novel as an
indication of social respectability.*

Aspidistra

FACT: *Nineteen Eighty-Four* included many powerful images and introduced many new words to the English language, including "room 101," "doublethink," "thought police," and, most famously, "Big Brother."

Although Orwell spent five years in the service of the British Empire, he grew to despise everything that it represented. His first works were largely autobiographical, cutting straight to the futility, hypocrisy, and brutality of imperial rule. The most famous work from that period is *Burmese Days*, which depicts the claustrophobia and racism of the ruling class. Leaving the Imperial Police cost Orwell dearly. His life in England during the late 1920s and early 1930s was marked by poverty and ill health. Indeed, it is possible that the tuberculosis that finally killed him was contracted during this period. Although Orwell served the empire again through his work in the BBC, it proved too much for his conscience and he resigned in 1943.

Later Years

Orwell's experiences led him to form a firmly left-wing perspective. He was prepared to carry his beliefs into practice, even at the risk of his own life. When the Spanish Civil War broke out, Orwell, who was already a member of the Independent Labour Party, joined the Workers Party of Marxist Unification in Spain to fight against Franco's Nationalists. In 1937 he was shot in the neck, and he returned to England later that year. His account of the Civil War, *Homage to Catalonia*, was published in the following year.

In the short period of life left to Orwell after World War II, he produced his two most famous novels. *Animal Farm* (1945) retells the Russian Revolution through the story of farm animals overthrowing their human masters. Gradually, the principles that bind them together are distorted until a new order emerges, this time with the pigs acting as the humans had. *Nineteen Eighty-Four* was written (in 1948) as a warning against totalitarian dictatorships of any kind. It is a brutal account in which Winston Smith, the main character, is uncovered, betrayed, and then systematically destroyed.

FACT: The Spanish Civil War is regarded by many as a precursor to a larger conflict between left and right, democracy and dictatorship. It was fought from 1936 to 1939, causing lasting scars in Spanish society.

SUMMARY

Middle-class, privately educated, and firmly part of the British establishment; a fair portrait, perhaps, of Eric Arthur Blair. Subversive, antiestablishment, and true to his principles might be a better description of George Orwell.

<u>**What**</u> *Is Moby-Dick?*

Everyone thinks that they know the answer: *Moby-Dick* is a novel about a huge whale and the hunt to kill it; Captain Ahab and the eponymous leviathan are linked forever in the public imagination. Sure, that is one answer; but, like the whale, we can go much deeper.

Moby-Dick is not just any whale. Moby-Dick is *Physter macrocephalus*, the sperm whale. On average, an adult male like Moby-Dick will be between forty and fifty feet (12–15 meters) long, weighing anything up to forty-five tons. All that bulk needs a ton of food a day, made up of squid, octopus, and fish. A whale like Moby-Dick doesn't reach maturity until he has lived in the oceans for ten years or more. The family groups are almost always made up of females and calves. The males join family groups only for a brief time and a sole purpose: to breed.

An Adventurous Life

Moby-Dick (1851) is the title of the sixth book by Herman Melville. Melville's youth was every bit as adventurous as his novels. He was born in New York City in 1819 and sailed for the first time as a cabin boy on a merchant ship at the age of nineteen. The year-long voyage left a lasting impression, and when money became scarce just over a year later he returned to the sea, this time on a whaling ship. During the voyage, Melville was marooned on a Polynesian island, where he lived with the local cannibals. Later, he served in the U.S. Navy. All of these experiences were used by Melville in a series of novels including *Typee: A Peep at Polynesian Life* (1846) and *White-Jacket, or The World in a Man of War* (1850).

*Herman Melville
(1819–1891)*

✳

FACT: *Moby-Dick was not very popular when it was first published, something that may have contributed to Melville giving up writing as a profession.*

SUMMARY

Moby-Dick is part myth, part novel, and part symbol. As a creation of Melville's imagination, it was appreciated by few at the time of publication, but has been dissected ever since and has become the great white whale known to all.

A Lost World

The novel *Moby-Dick* is 135 chapters long. Although it has grown in fame and popularity since the death of its author in 1891, many readers find it difficult and tedious in places. The novel is set against a highly detailed account of life on a whaling ship, the *Pequod*. The narrator, Ishmael, signs up for the voyage with a chance companion, a South Sea harpooner named Queequeg. At the end of the novel, the *Pequod* is smashed and sunk, with the loss of all aboard except Ishmael.

Moby-Dick provides an insight into a form of whaling that had already passed its peak when it was written. The great sailing ships of the whaling fleets were relics of a pre-industrial age; the products derived from the whales were increasingly being replaced by artificial chemicals. By 1880, whaling as described in *Moby-Dick* was dead.

In the novel, Moby-Dick is a sperm whale, sought after by Captain Ahab, who seeks revenge for being maimed by this huge white whale. Ahab uses terror and bribery to drive the crew beyond the limits of endurance in the hunt. He offers a gold doubloon, which he literally nails to the mast, for the first man to sight the whale. Ahab has a special harpoon created to kill Moby-Dick, which is "baptized" in the blood of the ship's harpooners.

Critics of the novel have sometimes reinterpreted it as an allegory of the twentieth century: the *Pequod* represents society and Ahab the despot who is prepared to inflict any cost to achieve an extreme end. It could be argued that *Moby-Dick* warns of the fate that awaits societies that surrender their democratic values. In the early twenty-first century, this idea has been recast in an ecological light, and *Moby-Dick* has been portrayed as an allegory for the consequences of environmental destruction. Today's sperm-whale population is approximately 360,000, which is perhaps less than a third of the levels before commercial whaling.

Why Are Books Sometimes Banned?

What do the following have in common: the tale of a lady's affair with her gamekeeper; a nineteenth-century story of a dog lured to the arctic landscape of North America; and a twentieth-century novel set on a desert island populated only by a group of schoolboys? That's right: *Lady Chatterley's Lover*, *The Call of the Wild*, and *Lord of the Flies* have all, at some point, been banned. Is there a reason why? Yes, there was at the time, but history makes a lot of the reasons look weak in hindsight.

To ban a book means, in effect, to withdraw it from circulation. To wipe a book from existence is virtually impossible. Only in the pages of a novel such as Geroge Orwell's *Nineteen Eighty-Four* is a government sufficiently omnipotent to ban a book so completely (coincidently, *Nineteen Eighty-Four* was banned until 1990 in the USSR). In almost all cases, banning means removing the book from libraries, bookshops, catalogs, and schools. This gives a clear indication of who most frequently bans books: a government.

Oppressive Regimes

Some of the most prolific lists of banned books have come from regimes seeking to assert and maintain totalitarian control. On May 10, 1933, thousands of Germans participated in the burning of books declared to be "un-German" by the Nazi government. This effort was led by the National Socialist German Students' Association and resulted in the destruction of books regarded as "degenerate" by authors such as Ernest Hemingway and Erich Maria Remarque. Jack London enjoyed the honor of being banned by Hitler in Germany, Mussolini in Italy, and Stalin in Russia. In his case, the favorite target was his 1908 novel, *The Iron Heel*.

Political, Religious, and Ethical Objections

The formal banning of books by authority has a very long history. Books have often been banned because they were regarded as treasonous or heretical, and this remains common in some parts of the world. A current example is *The Satanic Verses* by Salman Rushdie, which (as of 2009) is banned in Singapore, India, Bangladesh, and Iran because the religious authorities feel it to be a direct challenge to their faith, or at least insulting to it.

QUOTE:

"Where they burn books, they will ultimately also burn people."

Heinrich Heine (1797–1856), Almansor

FACT: *Ray Bradbury's famous dystopian novel **Fahrenheit 451** takes its name from the temperature at which paper spontaneously combusts. It is set in a future society in which all books are banned, and if found are burned.*

In modern Saudi Arabia, customs officials are unlikely to look favorably on the Bible, unless it is carried by a Western family and appears to be solely for personal use. Books dealing with Tibetan culture or the Falun Gong sect will be seized by Chinese border officials, and in countries such as Austria, Germany, and France, Holocaust denial can be grounds for prosecution and the banning of a book.

In a modern context, a more common reason for banning a book is that it is regarded as socially or morally unacceptable. The First Amendment offers some protection in the United States; but, contrary to popular belief, it is not an open invitation to write with impunity. In the States, it is also the case that books are sometimes challenged at the community level, often with the intention of removing a certain book from the local education system. Among the books to have fallen foul of numerous challenges are Philip Pullman's *His Dark Materials* trilogy (because of political and religious controversy), J. D. Salinger's *The Catcher in the Rye* (sexual content and offensive language), and the *Harry Potter* series by J. K. Rowling (accusations of occultism).

Jack London (1876–1916)

✳

Voluntary Withdrawal

Beside the formal restriction or destruction of books, some are voluntarily withdrawn. Novels written in the eighteenth and nineteenth centuries can include language that seems unacceptable in some modern societies. Should, some people ask, books such as *Gone with the Wind*, *Uncle Tom's Cabin*, or *Huckleberry Finn* be allowed in schools and public libraries when the terminology employed in them is widely thought of as racist and offensive? Plays such as *The Merchant of Venice* and novels such as *Oliver Twist* have encountered similar opposition on the grounds that their portrayal of Jews is anti-Semitic.

SUMMARY Books have been banned, for a host of different reasons, ever since they were first produced, and the habit doesn't seem likely to disappear in the near future. But does it work? It is human nature to seek out those things that are forbidden, and the banning of a book gives it a sort of credibility that can work against the very reason for trying to suppress it in the first place.

Where Is the World's Most Comprehensive Library?

The world's most comprehensive library is located in Washington, D.C. It is the Library of Congress. The technical details of the Library of Congress are impressive, but a rival is on the horizon and very soon the world's most comprehensive library may be somewhere else entirely.

The Library of Congress was established by an act of Congress in 1800. The clear and limited intention was to provide "such books as may be necessary for the use of Congress." If the members of Congress didn't need to know it, it didn't need to be in the library. That might help to explain why the collection had only just reached 3,000 books by 1814. In that year the British Army destroyed most of the Capitol and the entire library.

FACT: The War of 1812 was caused by tensions between Britain and the United States over British rule in Canada and the interception of American ships breaking the Royal Navy's blockade of Europe.

At this point the retired president, Thomas Jefferson, offered his library as the starting point for a new Library of Congress. His private collection consisted of over 6,000 books. However, the collection changed the concept of "what was necessary for the use of Congress." Jefferson's library contained works of literature, scientific studies, foreign-language editions, and volumes about philosophy. By adopting his collection as the beginning of a new library, Congress began a process that led ultimately to the creation of the world's most comprehensive library.

*

The Thomas Jefferson Building, which is oldest of the three Library of Congress buildings, was built between 1890 and 1897.

FACT: *The Library of Congress currently handles 22,000 items every working day. Of these items approximately 10,000 are added to the collection. That is just over twenty items for every minute of the working day!*

Modern Expansion

Since 1815 the Library of Congress has expanded to become one of the dominant features of the Capitol. Its core building was opened to the public in 1897 and is called the Thomas Jefferson Building. In 1980 a fourth building, the James Madison Building, was opened. The Library of Congress in Washington, D.C., contains 650 miles (1,050 km) of bookshelves holding more than 138 million items. This includes 61 million manuscripts, 12.5 million photographs, more than five million maps, and 32 million books. By comparison, the British Library holds 14 million books, 920,000 journal and newspaper titles, 58 million patents, and 3 million sound recordings; the National Library of Australia holds 5 million items.

Washington, D.C., is not the only location of the Library of Congress. Motion-picture preservation and storage facilities are situated in Dayton, Ohio. The Library of Congress has faced criticism for being too focused on the English language and sources derived from the English-speaking world. In 1962 the library began to maintain international offices as well. Today these can be found in Brazil, Kenya, Pakistan, Indonesia, Egypt, and India.

SUMMARY

The U.S. Library of Congress is the largest in the world, holding more than 138 million items. It may soon, however, be overtaken by digital libraries, such as UNESCO's World Digital Library, which went live in April 2009.

FACT: *It is a myth that the Library of Congress holds one copy of every book published in the United States. The Library has an entitlement to receive copies of every work registered for copyright but does not exercise that right and does not keep all copies indefinitely.*

So the Library of Congress is currently the most comprehensive library in the world, but it is working in partnership with the United Nations Educational, Scientific, and Cultural Organization (UNESCO) and other national libraries to create something even bigger. The World Digital Library (WDL) will become the world's most comprehensive library during the twenty-first century. Although the WDL's aim can never be fully achieved, it is to be a free library containing a catalog of all human wisdom. The prototype has been operating since 2007 and the WDL went live in April 2009. Most of the WDL's resources are in Arabic, Chinese, English, French, Portuguese, Russian, and Spanish.

Where Was the Bubonic Plague From?

There are two ways to think about this question. One is to consider where, in a geographical sense, the bubonic plague broke out before racing through the human population. The other is to consider where, biologically, a disease so deadly to humans evolved.

Society depends on agriculture and trade. From the nomadic groups to the first settled communities, humans and animals lived in very close proximity. Most diseases that affect us have come from the animals that we rely on or from the pests that infect them. In the case of the bubonic plague, it has been suggested that the disease came from pigs. These animals suffer from a disease similar to the plague that is transmitted by fleabites. It is not difficult to imagine that fleas infecting pigs could have also been drawn to cats, dogs, and rats, eventually transferring the disease to humans. There has long been an awareness that the bubonic plague might have come from animals. In the Old Testament, the book of Samuel suggests that mice carried the disease.

The Black Death

When we think of the bubonic plague, we usually mean the "Black Death" of the mid–fourteenth century. In fact, there is evidence to indicate that the plague had broken out in different societies over a much longer period. An Egyptian medical text refers to a plague-like disease as long ago as 1500 B.C.E., and archeological evidence suggests that outbreaks had occurred 2,000 years before even that. The Byzantine Empire was rocked by a plague in the sixth century C.E. that, at its height, may have killed as many as 10,000 people a day in Constantinople.

The difficulty is that we cannot be sure that these plagues were the same "bubonic" plague that broke out in the Middle Ages. Some scientists argue that what we call the bubonic plague today may not have been the disease that swept across Europe in the fourteenth century. They note that the bubonic plague is a bacterial infection and is slow to be transmitted. It has been proposed that the plague of the Middle Ages was a viral infection, more like Ebola—and every bit as deadly. This is a minority view at present.

* **Flea**
  (not to scale!)

FACT: *The bacteria that cause bubonic plague are carried in the gut of the flea. As the bacteria thrive, they begin to block the gut, causing the flea to become hungrier and so bite more often. Every bite transfers bacteria to the victim.*

FACT: *The bubonic plague is estimated to have killed 25 million people in Europe during the fourteenth century. This was approximately a quarter of the population.*

The rate of mortality fluctuated in different epidemic waves, but one in four is probably a good average.

From East to West

Geographically, the most likely place that the bubonic plague came from was Central Asia. There were three factors that allowed it to spread into the wider world, the most important of which was trade. The overland route from Asia to Europe, the Silk Road, had been established for centuries and was supplemented by sailing routes across the Indian Ocean and the Mediterranean. Trading caravans and merchant vessels almost certainly carried the infection from its starting point.

The migration of the disease was made easier by two other factors. In the Islamic Middle East and Christian Europe, pilgrimages were seen as a religious duty. The pilgrims made excellent hosts for the bubonic plague as they returned to their homes. The mid–fourteenth century was also a period marked by conflicts that enhanced the potential for a new disease to spread. In the trading port of Kaffa on the coast of the Black Sea, the Tartars besieged traders from Genoa and Venice. When the attackers were afflicted by bubonic plague, they catapulted the dead bodies into the city. The disease broke out there and was carried in the trading ships as people fled in 1347. The survivors later introduced the Black Death to mainland Europe, with catastrophic consequences.

FACT: *The first recorded Ebola virus outbreak in humans occurred in 1976. The mortality rate for the virus is between 50 and 90 percent. The speed with which victims succumb often means that small communities are virtually wiped out, preventing a more extensive spread of the disease.*

SUMMARY

It seems most likely that the medieval outbreak of the bubonic plague came from somewhere in Central Asia and spread outward. We know that it was the result of close interaction of humans and domestic animals, and we know that it has been more virulent at some times than others. We also know that it is still with us, and that the World Health Organization (WHO) records about 3,000 cases a year—so one day it could be coming to a place near you.

<u>Why</u> Was the Magna Carta Important?

You probably know the name, Magna Carta. It may even have been mentioned in your history lessons, though perhaps only in passing, and yet the Magna Carta is one of the most important documents in human history, not because of what it said but because of the process it started.

Many historians argue that England's King John has been unfairly represented. King Richard the Lionheart was not a hands-on monarch, and his English realm did not prosper, leaving his brother John some very awkward problems. Chief among these was the growing strength of the English barons. As the burden of paying for the Crusades and the wars with France grew, the barons, led by Robert FitzWalter, demanded a greater share in government. They were prepared to challenge the king and the manner in which he exercised power—with force, if necessary. They were neither popular nor successful; but John was even less so. When London opened its gates to the rebels, the balance of power tipped against the monarch, and he entered into negotiations.

FACT: *King Richard I ruled from 1189 to 1199. In that time he spent only six months in England itself.*

The Balance of Power

In June 1215, at Runnymede (to the west of London), King John signed the Magna Carta presented to him by his rebellious barons. Most of the document deals with Church issues, finances, and the feudal system. But one section asserts the rights of free men under Common Law. King John didn't value the Magna Carta or consider it to represent a defeat because he had no intention of honoring it. Neither did the barons, and within months the rebellion was underway again. John's fortunes waxed and waned for the following two years until his death from dysentery in 1217.

It is at this point that the Magna Carta's impact becomes clear: the barons offered the throne of England to John's son, the future King Henry III, but only after he had reissued the Magna Carta. It was confirmed in law by King

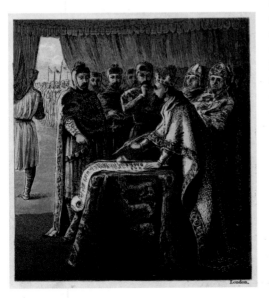

King John signing the Magna Carta at Runnymeade, outside London, in 1215, with the barons looking on.

FACT: *Magna Carta is Latin for "Great Charter." A charter is a form of contract, in this case between the state, represented by the monarch, and its citizens.*

SUMMARY

The Magna Carta was signed by King John in 1215. It established the principle that the powers of the state are limited and that individual citizens have rights that should be protected in law. The concept of human rights has grown to be widely accepted and is enshrined in the Universal Declaration of Human Rights.

Edward I in 1297. This was important because it asserted that the powers of the monarch were both limited and conditional. Both the state and its citizens had rights and responsibilities. The principle that the state has limits to its power, combined with the concept of individual rights in law, forms the basis of much that we recognize in the modern world.

A Blueprint for Revolution

In 1776, rebellious colonists in North America rallied to the Declaration of Independence, which announced that the freedoms it proposed were "self-evident." Chief among the causes was a belief that King George III's government was failing to respect the freedoms granted by the Magna Carta. From that declaration sprang the Constitution and the Bill of Rights. The seed sown by the Magna Carta had grown into a structure for a new nation.

In 1789, the revolutionary National Assembly of France issued the Declaration of the Rights of Man, asserting the rights or freedoms that were, henceforth, to be protected in law and offered to the citizens of any country "liberated" by France. Among these was the assertion that there should be no taxation without representation, a direct reference to the causes of the earlier American Revolutionary War. But the French document went further by presenting these rights not as God-given or bestowed by a monarch, but as natural. The modern understanding of human rights had begun.

More recently, in 1948, the United Nations General Assembly approved the Universal Declaration of Human Rights. Its thirty articles assert the rights of every human. Although many governments still fail to respect the UDHR, it is a yardstick of dignity and freedom, an ideal that has its roots in Runnymede.

FACT: *There are several contemporary copies of the Magna Carta. In 2007, one of these sold at auction in New York for $21.3 million.*

QUOTE:

"The flames kindled on the Fourth of July, 1776, have spread over too much of the globe to be extinguished by the feeble engines of despotism; on the contrary, they will consume those engines and all who work them." **Thomas Jefferson (1743–1826), third president of the United States**

<u>When</u> Was the Printing Press Invented?

By "printing press," we usually mean a moveable-type press. A German goldsmith named Johannes Gutenberg is generally credited with inventing this new form of printing in the early 1440s. It was to have an impact far beyond his expectations.

For much of human history, the reproduction of documents has been done by hand. This was a slow and expensive process, requiring resources that only institutions like the state and the church could provide. As a result, these institutions controlled information and ideas to a great extent. This control and the expense of producing documents made literacy of limited use. Most ordinary people were illiterate, and even those with power and influence were often only barely literate. The invention of the printing press would alter that situation entirely.

Forerunners

Presses of different sorts have existed for much of human history. They have been used in the making of wine, cheese, olive oil, and paper. Combining press technology with the reproduction of text was not new to Gutenberg's era. Woodblock printing had been used in the West from the thirteenth century, having arrived from China, where it had been used for the reproduction of pictures and small quantities of text since before 200 c.e. One of the main uses for woodblock printing in China had been the production of paper currency. The carving of the mirror-image wood blocks required skilled craftsmen, and the blocks had a limited lifespan as the wood began to split. The blocks could be used by hand and didn't necessarily require a press.

Gutenberg's Breakthrough

Johannes Gutenberg (1398–1468) made his breakthrough in the city of Strasburg and applied it commercially when he returned to his home city of Mainz. With its access to the Rhine and Main Rivers, the city had long been important. It was a center for trade and culture, as well as an administrative hub for the Catholic Church. Gutenberg had experience as a stonecutter and goldsmith, providing skills that helped him to develop a practical form of moveable-type printing. He invented an alloy for the type blocks that was reliable and hard-wearing, and adapted a woodblock printing press to suit the production of printed sheets using racks of his moveable-type characters.

Gutenberg's creation took time to perfect, so he had to look for financial backers and projects to generate profit as quickly as possible. He tried printing Papal indulgences, then

Gutenberg's Press *

FACT: *Although Gutenberg did independently invent the printing press, he was not the first. Four hundred years earlier, in 1041, a Chinese inventor named Bi Sheng created a form of moveable-type press that used characters produced in porcelain. He is probably less well known because the complexity and number of characters in the Chinese language made his breakthrough less influential than Gutenberg's.*

the *Poem of the Last Judgment*, and a calendar for 1448. Sadly, Gutenberg was a clever inventor but a poor businessman—these projects helped him to perfect the printing press, but they did not make much money.

The breakthrough project was the production of the Bible. Mainz was the seat of an important diocese, with a powerful archbishop at its head. It was a massive potential market. Gutenberg printed two hundred copies of the Bible using his groundbreaking moveable-type press. The two-volume editions were first sold at the 1455 Frankfurt Book Fair. The Bible seemed like an ideal moneymaking opportunity for Gutenberg, but its production left him heavily in debt, and he was forced to sell out to his most important backer, Johann Faust. Faust went on to develop color printing and turn the project into a profitable affair. Gutenberg had tried to keep the precise details of his breakthrough secret, but within thirty years of his death (in 1468), cities right across Europe had established printing industries.

*

The printing press was an information revolution that changed the world, just as the Internet is doing today.

SUMMARY

Gutenberg's printing press changed the world with incredible speed. Education, law, government, and commerce were all revolutionized by the invention of the printing press. Books became less expensive and more widely available, new ideas could be circulated far and wide, and literacy became a useful skill for a much broader section of society. Established institutions began to feel threatened and weakened by the changes. Gutenberg had started an information revolution.

What Did Columbus Do in 1492?

As everyone knows, Columbus set sail from Spain in 1492 with a fleet of three ships—the *Niña*, *Pinta*, and *Santa Maria*—in search of a new route from Europe to the Far East. If this could be achieved, the boost to trade would make Columbus and his royal sponsors incredibly wealthy. Instead of finding a nautical alternative to the overland route to China, however, Columbus discovered America. That's the standard tale, anyway. And it's wrong. Columbus did not discover America. So what did he really do in 1492?

FACT: Columbus Day is a public holiday in the United States. It used to be held on October 12 (the day of first landfall), until 1971, when it became the second Monday in October.

Columbus set sail in August 1492 and, after spending nearly a month in the Canary Islands to replenish his supplies, found signs of land in late September and early October. Seven or eight weeks of sailing was about the time that Columbus had proposed as sufficient to reach China from Spain by the new westerly route, and most authorities agreed with the estimate.

So one of the things that Columbus did in 1492 was to demonstrate that the world was much bigger than Europeans had previously believed. He did not, however, prove that it was round. We are usually told that people in the Middle Ages thought the world was flat. This is wrong. Most educated people—and any sailor worthy of the name—knew that the world was round. In fact, it had been clearly demonstrated since the time of the ancient Greeks.

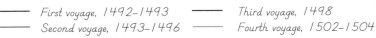

—— First voyage, 1492–1493   —— Third voyage, 1498
—— Second voyage, 1493–1496   —— Fourth voyage, 1502–1504

FACT: *Columbus never set foot in North America. He actually made landfall in the Caribbean, although he thought that he had arrived somewhere near the East Indies (known today as Southeast Asia). His next stop was in Cuba, which he thought likely to be part of China.*

Not the First

Nor did Columbus discover the Americas. For a start, Viking ships had already landed there in around 1000 C.E. More important, he couldn't "discover" the Americas because both were home to complex and thriving civilizations, and had been for thousands of years. One thing Columbus did do in 1492 was—inadvertently—to bring disaster to these native peoples.

Long cut off from the other continents, North and South America had developed a range of unique cultures. Their isolation had also left them without sufficient immunity to diseases that were commonplace in Europe and Asia. European visitors such as Columbus introduced the New World to the killer diseases of the Old World. We cannot be sure how many natives perished (often without even being directly aware of European contact), but the estimates run to many millions.

New-World Wealth

The end of the fifteenth century was scarred by continuing conflict between Christians and Muslims. In Spain and Portugal, a bloody reconquest had taken place; Christians had won back the Iberian Peninsula from the Moors. However, the balance of power around the Mediterranean as a whole remained quite delicate. Islam largely controlled access to the resources of the East, and so Columbus had no hesitation in presenting his epic voyage as an attempt to break free from that hold.

This made financial sense, as the Spanish monarchy (who funded the expedition) would have been attracted to such an idea, but it was also a firmly held conviction of Columbus that he was striking a blow against those whom he believed to be infidels.

On his return from his first voyage, Columbus brought with him enough wealth to demonstrate the vast economic potential of his discovery. Fueled by rivalry, the powers of Europe, led by Portugal and Spain, struck out westward in the wake of Columbus. In doing so they began to tip the geopolitical balance in favor of the Christian West.

SUMMARY

In 1492, Columbus did much more than sail the ocean blue. He did not "discover" America, which was already populated. What he did do was to change our understanding of the globe, bring deadly diseases to the native populations, and alter the balance of power in Europe. Not bad for three ships, a couple of months' sailing, and a mistaken landfall.

<u>Who</u> Was Thomas Paine?

**Thomas Paine can rightly be given the title of "the father of revolutions."
His influence on the world of politics and reform was central to two key revolutions
that shaped our world. He was also a writer, a political philosopher, a radical, and
largely self-taught.**

At the age of forty-seven, Thomas Paine left England for the American
colonies. Up to that point, his life had been unremarkable. He had come from
a humble background and received only a basic education. However, Paine
clearly had a thirst for knowledge. He read and wrote with an energy that
remained with him for most of his adult life. His second marriage had come to
an end on the eve of his departure from England, and he had no children.
The New World seemed to offer Paine a new life.

Shaping the New World

In the 1770s, the British colonies in America were in a rebellious mood.
They were secure and wealthy, they were making an ever-increasing
contribution to the wealth of Britain, and the untapped potential of the vast
American hinterland was becoming clear. In the home country, most people in
the ruling classes regarded the colonies as a resource, not a partner. This
attitude caused growing resentment. Thomas Paine captured the essence of
the fermenting revolution in an essay called *Common Sense*, which he had
published in 1776. It had three clear themes, and was written in the simple and
accessible style that was to be Paine's trademark. *Common Sense* argued that
the primary function of government was to
serve the common good. In order to do that,
the government needed to be free from
corruption. This was only possible if the
government was democratically elected, and
that in turn meant that hereditary government
by monarchs had to be abolished. It was
music to the ears of the American rebels, and
100,000 copies of the pamphlet were sold.

*Thomas Paine
is often depicted
as a Romantic
visionary, but
the truth is less
glamorous.* ✳

QUOTE:

*"Every person of learning is
finally his own teacher."*

Thomas Paine (1737-1809)

FACT: *Thomas Paine may have been a political genius, but he was a financial failure. He owned a shop in the small town of Lewes, in southeast England, that went bust; he needed handouts from the newly independent American government; and he lost money trying to design new iron bridges and smokeless candles.*

SUMMARY

Thomas Paine was a highly principled and intelligent man. He was able to dissect and critically assess common assumptions about government, religion, and human rights. In doing so, he helped to forment two revolutions, one that reshaped the Old World and another that shaped the New World. His writings are still engaging, controversial, and relevant today.

Reshaping Europe

By 1787, Thomas Paine had returned to England. He had become a famous and divisive figure. Radical ideas were swirling through British society. In France, revolution erupted in 1789, quickly bringing the downfall of King Louis XVI. Many in Britain welcomed the change, but the government favored a fierce and repressive reaction. In the face of such a challenge, Paine produced his most influential work, *The Rights of Man* (published in two parts, in 1791 and 1792). Paine had been a student of French politics and society since the 1780s. Just as *Common Sense* had caught the essence of the rebellious colonies, *The Rights of Man* captured the fundamental ideals of the French Revolution. He presented a carefully constructed case for the natural rights of the individual, including government intervention to end social and economic inequality, protected by a formal constitution.

Such was its success that Thomas Paine became a French citizen in 1792, and was elected to the National Assembly—an amazing achievement given that he couldn't speak the language! His time in France was not, however, happy. Surprisingly for a declared republican, he opposed the execution of Louis XVI and was critical of the ultra-revolutionary Jacobins. They turned on him and he was imprisoned. When in prison, Paine wrote the two-part book *Age of Reason* (1794 and 1795), which attacked organized religion in general and Christianity in particular. For many people in late eighteenth-century society, this was too revolutionary by far. Many radical groups in Britain, already under pressure in a repressive atmosphere, distanced themselves from Paine. Friendless and isolated, he became a political outcast. He returned to America in 1802, but few people were interested. He died in New York in 1809, sick, miserable, and drunk.

FACT: *Paine was buried in unconsecrated ground. Ten years later, the English campaigner, William Cobbett, who was an admirer of Paine's work, had the bones returned to England to be placed in a special memorial. Sadly, the memorial was never built and Paine's bones were lost in the mists of time.*

<u>**Who**</u> *Took the First Photograph?*

The first person to take a photograph in the modern sense was Joseph Nicéphore Niépce. It shows the view from an upper-story window at his home Le Gras, the family estate in France. A grainy image of a building, a tree, and a barn may not sound all that spectacular, but it was groundbreaking in 1826.

Niépce was born in 1765. He lived a comfortable middle-class life, and, like many gentlemen of his era, he took an active interest in science. With his brother, he worked on several developments, but two in particular came to dominate his time and money. The first was an early form of internal-combustion engine that could be used to power boats. Working examples were used on the River Saône, near the family estate, and on the Seine. Joseph and his brother patented the idea in 1807, and they spent a further two decades attempting to improve the invention. The second project was to create a permanent photographic record.

FACT: Although they cannot be considered photographs in the modern sense, the Dutch artist Johannes Vermeer made use of the camera obscura to capture an intensely lifelike perspective and quality of light. **Officer and Laughing Girl** *is a particularly good example.*

Historical Developments

The first photograph was the culmination of many early developments. Leonardo da Vinci is sometimes credited with the principles of the camera obscura, which was used largely for entertainment in the seventeenth and eighteenth centuries. The camera obscura allowed the viewer to see an inverted scene projected onto a flat surface but not preserved. In 1802, Thomas Wedgwood, like Niépce a gentleman of independent means, and Humphrey Davy presented a paper describing their attempts to produce an image using a camera obscura and chemicals that reacted when exposed to light. In the catchily titled "An Account of a Method of Copying Paintings upon Glass and of Making Profiles by the Agency of Light upon Nitrate of Silver," the two inventors explained that they had been able to create a reverse image, but were unable to "fix" it. When exposed to light, the image degraded to the point of total obscurity.

The first cameras may have looked simple, but the chemistry was very complex.

FACT: The images taken by Thomas Wedgwood in 1802 lost their clarity so quickly, it was said that he had to view them in a dark room by candlelight.

A Permanent Record

Niépce was certainly aware of these developments. He experimented with light-sensitive chemicals in an attempt to copy engravings. In doing so, he discovered that a polished pewter plate coated in a type of bitumen captured an image and fixed it. Combining this with the camera obscura, he invented a form of pinhole camera that took the world's first photograph in the summer of 1826. It took eight hours of exposure for the image (above) to be formed. Proud of his discovery, Niépce had the opportunity to present it to the Royal Society in London during the following year. Aware of the potential commercial applications of his invention, he decided not to disclose the full details of his breakthrough, and in response the Royal Society refused to validate it.

Back in France, Niépce formed a partnership with Louis-Jacques Daguerre. They tried to improve the process of *heliography* until Niépce died in 1833. Six years later, Daguerre revealed the daguerreotype. Using a thin copper plate with a silver coating that had been made light-sensitive, it required only a few minutes' exposure and was much more robust than the earlier heliographs. Daguerre became famous, and his invention laid the foundation for photography as we know it today.

The name Joseph Nicéphore Niépce is largely unknown today, but his place in the creation of the modern world deserves to be better appreciated. From his breakthrough we can trace the developments in image capture and storage that are taken for granted today. Left in obscurity until 1952, the first photograph was rediscovered by a historian of photography, Helmut Gernsheim. It is now on display at the University of Texas.

<u>Why</u> Did Van Gogh Cut Off His Ear?

Let's not get carried away. If you're imagining a gaping hole where his ear had been, you're way off the mark. On Christmas Eve, 1888, Vincent van Gogh cut off part of his left earlobe—far from cutting his ear off, but by no means a normal (or sensible) thing to do. The exact reasons for his extraordinary action are unknown, but there are lots of interesting theories.

Throughout the mid-1880s, Van Gogh had been busily working in Paris. The art capital of the world had been rocked by the Impressionist revolution (see pp. 76–77) and Van Gogh was leading a new "Post-Impressionist" wave of painting. But life was becoming a burden to the artist. The pressures of long hours at work, a close and critical artistic community, and the squalor of the city were beginning to tell.

Hoping to make a fresh start, he moved to Arles, in southeastern France, in the spring of 1888. In late autumn he was joined by fellow artist Paul Gauguin. At first their collaboration worked well, but bitter differences gradually emerged that were to culminate in a fierce argument. Van Gogh snatched up a razor and chased after Gauguin. When he failed to catch his intended victim Van Gogh turned the blade on himself. Gauguin wisely got out as soon as possible and never saw Van Gogh again—and who could blame him?

FACT: *Van Gogh wrapped the bloody earlobe in newspaper and took it to a local brothel. There he placed it in the care of a prostitute called Rachel, telling her to "guard this object carefully."*

SOLD for $49m. (£27 m.)

Sunflowers were the subject of many of Van Gogh's paintings and also provided the background for others.

FACT: *One of the treatments for epilepsy in Van Gogh's time was digitalis. This drug is derived from the common foxglove. It can cause yellow-tinted vision or yellow spots. This may account for the swirling features in* **The Starry Night** *(1889) and the yellow tones in some of Van Gogh's other paintings.*

Driven by Ill-Health

Van Gogh was known to suffer from epilepsy, and the attacks caused him to become violently depressed. His lifestyle is another possible factor. Often very poor, he probably suffered from malnutrition. He was not much of a ladies' man, but does seem to have known his way around a brothel or two. Some experts have gone as far as to suggest that Van Gogh's mental instability could be linked to the symptoms of syphilis. He was also fond of absinthe, a strong (up to 74 percent alcohol by volume) and very popular form of alcohol among the bohemians of Paris. Absinthe contains a substance called thujone, which has been shown to act in a distinctive manner in those who have epilepsy, causing hallucinations and insomnia. Depressed, argumentative, sleep-deprived, and intoxicated; could this be the mix that led Van Gogh to turn a razor on himself?

However, there are as many as thirty possible explanations for Van Gogh's self-harm, ranging from a form of bipolar disorder (formely known as "manic depression") to periodic porphyria, a disease that famously afflicted King George III, to a form of lead poisoning from his lead-based paints. (One symptom of lead poisoning is a swelling in the retina that can create a halo effect in the sufferer's vision. This could explain both the act of self-mutilation and the characteristic art Van Gogh produced.)

The Aftermath

Van Gogh was hospitalized after the incident and later returned to the north of the country following the closure of his home in Arles by the police. His outbursts and erratic behavior had prompted a petition from thirty local people, in which they called Van Gogh a "redheaded madman." In the hospital, Van Gogh endured long periods of isolation that forced him to paint from memory, reinterpreting earlier work or painting scenes entirely from memory rather than observation.

SUMMARY

Increasingly depressed and largely unsuccessful as an artist, Vincent van Gogh shot himself on July 27, 1890, dying two days later. His art was to become recognized and cherished around the world. As for the incident with the ear and the razor, many theories have been put forward, but two weeks after the event Van Gogh described it in a letter to his brother Theo as "simply an artist's fit"; perhaps that should be explanation enough.

What Is Pop Art?

The expression "pop art" comes from the shortening of the word "popular." This implies that it is accessible to ordinary people. It refers to art that is linked with popular culture. Despite its name, however, pop art is far from universally popular.

The term "pop art" was first used in 1958, but the trend had been developing since the early 1950s. Emerging quickly from World War II as a global superpower and leader of the free world, the United States exuded a brash optimism that had an impact in Europe and beyond. A prosperous and growing middle class enjoyed the benefits of mass production. Early pop art drew its inspiration from these consumerist and materialist factors, using mass-produced objects such as beer and soup cans and taking well-known images such as the Stars and Stripes and forcing the viewer to consider their meaning and significance. Pop art was eye-catching, bold, bright, and full of color. It seemed to be a break from the drab war years.

*

Andy Warhol had a distinctive sense of personal style that influenced the development of pop art.

QUOTE:

"In the future everyone will be world-famous for fifteen minutes."
Andy Warhol (1928–1987), American painter

From Optimism to Irony

In the mid-1950s pop art's emphasis was upbeat. The British artist Richard Hamilton and the "Independent Group" of artists organized exhibitions such as "Man, Machine, and Motion" and "This is Tomorrow." In the second exhibition, Hamilton showed what some people consider to be the first true piece of pop art: *Just What Is It That Makes Today's Home so Different, so Appealing?* Images from magazines, television, and advertising were used as the inspiration for a new wave of art. Gradually, however, optimism gave way to irony. At first, pop artists intended to take the elitism out of art, but they soon used their art to criticize popular culture and perhaps establish a new artistic elite.

FACT: The expression "pop art" is often attributed to the English art critic Lawrence Alloway and his 1958 essay, **The Arts and the Mass Media**. In fact, the term he used was "popular mass culture," and the first recorded use of "pop art" in print dates from an earlier (1955) article produced by a London-based arts collective called the Independent Group.

For and Against

Andy Warhol's screen prints of Marilyn Monroe and Roy Lichtenstein's comic-strip paintings are two of the most famous examples of pop art. Lichtenstein deliberately mimicked the format and themes of popular comic books, leading some to ask if this was just garish sensationalism with no real intention to express a deeper meaning. Warhol's prints of Monroe have been interpreted as an assertion that fame in the modern era is also a mass-produced item, packaged and prepared for the consumer. Was pop art imitating life or mocking it? Critics demanded to know.

The most common criticism of pop art is that it had double standards. It drew from popular culture and yet seemed to be critical of it. At first it was a reaction against the perceived elitism and intellectualism of abstract art, but it quickly developed its own philosophy, which critics argued was just as elitist and intellectual. The price of pop artwork certainly quickly exceeded anything that an ordinary person could afford.

Supporters of pop art argue that the artists can hardly be blamed if popularity made their art expensive. Critics and collectors snapped up these ironic statements about mass production, putting them in art galleries where they seemed to be the very opposite of the fine art that viewers had previously expected to find.

A Lasting Legacy

Supporters also point to the enduring popularity of images such as Warhol's *200 Campbell's Soup Cans*. But the success of pop art was part of its undoing. In breaking down boundaries and undermining concepts about what art was, pop art became the inspiration for the very forms of media that it first drew inspiration from. It became reabsorbed into commercialism and lost its ability to shock the artistic world. By the late 1960s it was disappearing as a distinct artistic approach, but its influence lives on.

> ## *QUOTE:*
>
> *"Style is something you can use, and you can be like a magpie, just taking what you want."*
>
> *David Hockney (b. 1937), English painter*

Warhol used the semi mechanized silkscreen process to create striking works of art in which one image was repeated with variations.

✳

SUMMARY

Pop art is art fused with popular culture, the images and ideas that surround us in a modern society. It breaks down the divide between commercial art and fine art, and challenges concepts about what art is and what art is for. As a movement, pop art drew inspiration from advertising, television, popular music, cinema, and magazines, but it influenced them in turn. The techniques used in pop art have gone on to change the way in which images are presented in the modern world.

<u>Where</u> Is the World's Largest Gallery?

If you were thinking the Louvre, think again. Standing on the bank of the River Neva, in the heart of the Russian city of St. Petersburg, is the world's largest museum of art and culture. The State Hermitage museum is two-and-a-half centuries old and can rightly claim to hold the largest collection of paintings in the world.

The Hermitage is made up of six main buildings, but the centerpiece of the complex is the Winter Palace. This spectacular building was designed by the architect Francesco Bartolomeo Rastrelli and built between 1754 and 1762. The Winter Palace was the official residence of the Russian royal family, but it has now become the home of an amazing collection of artifacts. The gallery began as a private museum for Catherine the Great (Empress of Russia from 1762 to 1796). Founded in 1764, it acted as a royal haven, a place that connected the Russian capital with the art and culture of Europe. The Hermitage was opened to the public by Tsar Nicholas I (who commissioned the New Hermitage building to house part of the expanding collection) in 1852.

FACT: The name for the gallery is believed to have originated from a reference by Catherine the Great to her little retreat. She was a reclusive monarch who relished the fact that "Only the mice and I can admire all this."

St. Petersburg

❋

The striking northern façade of the Hermitage dominates the embankment of the River Neva in St. Petersburg.

FACT: *Walking the gallery complex would involve visiting 365 rooms and 322 galleries, a journey of 15 miles (24 km). It is said that the Hermitage contains three million items, and that it would take a year of nonstop viewing to see the entire collection.*

SUMMARY

The Hermitage is a truly impressive collection of massive proportions. It can justly hold claim to being the world's largest gallery and it is unlikely ever to be surpassed. The Hermitage is a must-see location for any art lover, telling as it does the history of art and the changing nature of its home country.

Collecting Collections

The Hermitage has acquired other collections from its earliest days. Indeed, Catherine the Great purchased 200 paintings from the Gotzkowsky collection in 1763 to found the gallery. In the nineteenth century, particular attention was paid to acquiring items from the ancient world, and the New Hermitage was principally constructed to house the collections from antiquity. After the Russian Revolution in 1917, the Hermitage, like other royal palaces, became the property of the state. The collections of wealthy individuals and the other works acquired by the Russian royal family were seized and brought to the Hermitage. This greatly increased the size of the collection, as well as its diversity.

The Hermitage collection has not expanded continuously throughout its history. The communist government of the USSR cared little for the "decadent art of capitalism." In the late 1920s and through to the 1930s, over two thousand works of art were lost to the collection as the dictator Stalin sold them abroad in return for much-needed hard currency. The Soviet state also redistributed some parts of the collection to other galleries across Russia.

FACT: *The Hermitage contains one of the premier collections of gold from the ancient world, including treasures from the ancient city of Troy that were discovered by the German archeologist Heinrich Schliemann.*

Controversial Exhibits

One of the most controversial parts of the current collection dates from the conclusion of World War II, when the victorious Red Army seized all kinds of resources from defeated Nazi Germany. The argument was that these seizures compensated in some small way for the terrible blood price paid by the USSR. Among the "reparations" were works of art taken from German industrialists. These were thought to have disappeared, perhaps destroyed in the confusion surrounding the end of the conflict. In fact, they were held in the Hermitage and finally revealed to the public in 1995. To prevent them from being taken from Russia, the Duma (parliament) passed a law banning the return of the art on the grounds that the original owners financed the Nazi dictatorship.

When Will La Sagrada Familia Be Finished?

You might not recognize the name, but you will certainly recognize the appearance of La Sagrada Familia. It is one of the most famous churches in the world even though it hasn't even been finished yet, which is somewhat surprising when you consider that construction started in 1882!

Estimates for the completion of La Sagrada Familia vary by quite a margin. It could be as soon as 2025, or it might be as late as 2041. Perhaps a little sooner, maybe a bit later, it's difficult to tell exactly; but there is an explanation for the extraordinary length of the project.

One Man's Vision

One year after the building began, a revolutionary young architect was appointed to lead the project. His name was Antoni Gaudí, and the church was to become his life's work—the focus of his endeavors for forty-three years until his death in 1926. Progress since that point has been a bit inconsistent.

La Sagrada Familia is an iconic building that has become firmly associated with its home city of Barcelona, Spain. The church has been described in all kinds of ways. Some call it an organic construction because it has developed and been amended during its long period of construction. Others refer to it as modernist, or neo-gothic, or baroque. All of these reflect Gaudí's influences. He was particularly drawn to the ideas of the English philosopher and writer John Ruskin, who argued that there was a close relationship between architecture and ornament. Whatever it is defined as, La Sagrada Familia is certainly an incredible sight.

FACT: Antoni Gaudí was born in 1852. He was a keen student of nature, loved music, and showed an early talent for geometry. He was also very pious. Most of Gaudí's architectural work was built in Barcelona. He died there in 1926 after being knocked over by a tram, and is buried in the crypt of La Sagrada Familia.

Antoni Gaudí was a visionary architect, and his Modernist style has shaped the city of Barcelona.

QUOTE:

"It is a work that is in the hands of God and the will of the people."

Antoni Gaudí (1852–1926), Spanish architect

One Day at a Time

The church is being built on a huge scale, and on completion it will be capable of holding 13,000 worshipers. What makes the project even more amazing is that it is being financed entirely from donations, which provides at least one reason for the slow rate of construction. Fortunately, it doesn't matter. Gaudí designed the entire edifice to be constructed in distinct stages, and thought that each generation would be able to contribute something distinct to La Sagrada Familia.

*

The unfinished Sagrada Familia viewed from above.

It is difficult to assess quite what he intended, though, because not many of his original plans remain. His workshop was covered in photographs, models, and drawings, but a lot of what he left was destroyed during the Spanish Civil War. The war provides the second reason why the pace of construction hasn't been very consistent. Construction came to a halt in 1936 when the workshop and crypt were damaged by fire, and building did not recommence for sixteen years.

Different architects have continued the work begun by Gaudí, trying to remain true to the principles that he established—although some critics have argued that the church is emerging in a form that Gaudí could not have anticipated and may not have approved of. Toward the end of the twentieth century and into the twenty-first, estimates for the completion of the church have been steadily reduced as computer-aided design, new building techniques, and modern materials speed up the process of construction.

FACT: On completion, La Sagrada Familia will have eighteen towers and ten domes. It will be 312 feet (95 m) long and 197 feet (60 m) high. The final tower to be completed will be the Tower of Jesus.

SUMMARY

The current estimate is that the church will be completed in 2036. You don't have to wait that long to visit it, though. The church is already a UNESCO World Heritage Site and is open to visitors. Visitors can admire over a century of construction, and there is a museum, tours of the site, and an opportunity to witness building taking place. They would probably welcome a donation, too.

<u>**Why**</u> Do We Vote?

Whether you think it's a chore or a privilege, voting is a way in which you, as an individual, become linked to the interests of wider society. The motivations for voting vary: some people vote because they seek personal gain through the outcome; others because they believe it is a social responsibility; and, in some countries, people vote because they are obliged to by law.

Whether governments are elected (democratic), inherited (a monarchy), or imposed (dictatorship), they all crave legitimacy. A monarch may claim that a divine right, or the will of a god (or gods), provides sufficient legitimacy, but democracies and dictatorships prefer to find more earthly reasons to justify their existence. Both therefore employ some type of voting system to support their right to rule. This can come in the form of an election. It can also come in the form of a show of popular feeling, or from a vote on a particular issue (known as a "referendum").

Practical Motives

Practical reasons for voting can come in all shapes and forms. The most obvious is that it provides the voter with some share in the governance of society. In the democratic city-states of ancient Greece, this reason was direct and apparent to all. The citizen could vote and did so because the consequences had an immediate impact. For example, if a vote went in favor of war, the electorate would have to pick up their shields and swords before heading out to do the fighting. (In modern states, the connection between the individual vote and the actions of government is less direct.) Another practical reason for voting is personal gain. Aspiring Members of Parliament in Britain at the end of the eighteenth century, party bosses of American cities in the nineteenth century, and rural politicians on the Indian subcontinent in the twentieth century all appreciated the power of money in gaining votes.

> ### QUOTE:
> *"We do not say that a man who takes no interest in politics is a man who minds his own business: we say he has no business here at all."*
> *Pericles (c.495–429 B.C.E.), Athenian general and statesman*

QUOTE:

"Democracy is the worst form of government except for the others." Winston Churchill (1874–1965), British Prime Minister (1940–1945 and 1951–1955)

SUMMARY

In broad terms, there are three reasons why we vote. First, we vote for practical reasons (it gives us a share in power). Second, we vote for ethical reasons (it is the right thing to do). Third, we vote because we have to. Not all of these reasons apply in every country, but, in one combination or another, they do explain why we vote.

Civic Duty

Many people vote because they regard it as the right thing to do. This is sometimes referred to as a civic duty. Participation in the electoral process establishes a contract between the voter and the representative. Once elected, the representative has an implicit obligation to stand for the electorate, even when some of them voted for other candidates. The same applies in a referendum. Once the people have been asked to vote on the issue, the result acquires a moral force. This is partly why some states rarely hold them, because there is an argument that it undermines the supremacy of the legislature.

Registering to vote, paying even a modest degree of attention to the issues, and then voting requires the individual to make an effort. The chance that one vote will make a discernable difference to the outcome is negligible, and for many the natural inclination is to not bother participating, so where does this sense of civic duty come from? It may simply come from social expectation. Moreover, enormous sacrifices have been made to establish the right to vote. Wars have been fought at the cost of countless lives to defend the principles of democracy, and women and different racial groups have struggled to achieve the right to vote. This history creates a value in voting, even for those people who might have only a hazy notion of the issues.

Compulsory Voting

The simple fact is that fewer and fewer people in many democracies vote. Many voters feel isolated from the electoral process. Others refuse to give legitimacy to a system that they do not believe serves their needs. In Indian-administered Kashmir, political parties in favor of independence encourage potential voters not to participate. In South Africa, a campaign among the landless poor was focused on the slogan "No land! No house! No vote!" with the intention of placing pressure on the government by not voting.

To combat this, some democracies require potential voters to participate in elections. The most famous example is Australia; and Mexico, Brazil, and Belgium also make voting a legal requirement. Those who support this stance believe that ensuring widespread participation is vital to a vibrant democracy, whereas opponents argue that a compulsory vote is anti-democratic in itself.

Where Do Laws Come From?

This is one of those topics that seem straightforward. Laws come from the government, right? Well, yes and no. In truth, there is no simple answer. Laws are instruments of government, and they govern our conduct as a society, but that doesn't mean that all laws come from a society's government.

The type of law that most people think of is that which comes from the legislating body of a nation-state. This legislature is an assembly intended to create and validate legislation. There are many different forms of legislature, with wide variations in their powers. In one-party states, the legislature is little more than a validating assembly. It rubber-stamps whatever proposed legislation is put before it by the head of state, sometimes with a show of debate and at other times in unanimous approval. Other countries have extremely powerful legislatures, which counterbalance the power of the executive arm of government (the head of state or head of government, depending on the system). A legislature can sometimes be split into two houses, and this is called a "bicameral legislature." The intention is to foster debate and improve representation while preventing one political party from becoming dominant. These, too, can have wide variations. In France and the United States, for example, both houses are elected; whereas in the United Kingdom, Parliament's lower chamber (the House of Commons) is elected but the upper chamber (the House of Lords) is unelected. Whatever the arrangement, the primary purpose of the legislature is the creation of statutory law.

FACT: *There are also international laws, such as maritime law, which are adopted by a legislature even though they originate from outside the state.*

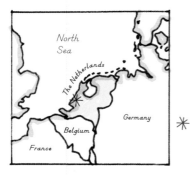

North Sea

The Netherlands

Germany

Belgium

France

The Hague in Holland has been the site of international trials concerning events such as the Lockerbie bombing and the wars in former Yugoslavia.

FACT: *In the modern era, the highest court might not be in any given country, but outside it. International law courts now rule on many issues, especially those relating to human rights. A legal issue about employment rights in Germany or Portugal, for example, might eventually be settled in the European Court of Justice.*

Written Constitutions

Statutory law is not, however, all-powerful, and it is not the only place that legislation comes from. Many countries have a written constitution that limits the power of statutory laws. This creates a potential conflict, and in most cases some form of constitutional court exists to deal with such problems. A famous example is the Supreme Court, which rules on the constitutionality of laws brought before it. The difficulty of this arrangement is that it reflects the majority view of the judges who make up the court, which can be engineered through the appointment of judges with a particular philosophy or can simply occur through the passage of time. The end result is the same: an assessment of a law as unconstitutional in one generation can be overturned in the next. So, constitutional law may be superior, but it is not consistent.

Scales are often used to represent the concept of justice, and the balance between the competing sides.

Case Law

At another level, courts also create a legal framework through the decisions that they make. This is called case law. All courts arrive at a decision or ruling. These decisions create a sort of legal sediment, building up one layer on top of another. This is called "precedent." A decision is made in a court, which goes to appeal. At the appeal court, that decision might be reversed or upheld. Either way, the judgment could go up and up until it reaches the highest court in the land. At each stage, it is the final appeal decision that outweighs all of the other earlier decisions.

Secondary Legislation

Just as some laws can come from judgments about laws, others can come from the application of the law. This is sometimes called "secondary legislation" or "administrative regulation." Where a situation is dynamic or complex, statutory law can include options for those enacting the law to create, over time, additional regulations that have the force of law. This secondary legislation is considered to be essential to the running of government by some, and by others as an invitation for the power of government to creep ever deeper into our lives. Secondary legislation is usually very specific and comes from the broader principles of statutory legislation, rather than establishing any wider point.

SUMMARY Laws come from several places. They all serve the purpose of governing society, but their origins can be quite different. In a constitutional document they can be set as the overarching principles for the rights and responsibilities of a state and its citizens. Parliamentary laws deal with the ever-changing demands of society, and can empower governmental agencies to create specific secondary regulations. All laws, whatever their origin, have to be judged in a court of law, where precedent establishes a fourth place from which laws come.

What Is the Separation of Powers?

The separation of powers is the division of government that prevents one branch from becoming more powerful than the others. At least, that's the theory. In practice, the separation of powers can be a little more difficult to define, but here goes....

Modern government tends to divide into three branches. Even the most tyrannical dictators—Stalin, Hitler, and Mao—maintained the three institutions of government, albeit as farcical imitations of the real thing.

The *executive branch* is the decision-making body, usually led by a prime minister or president and composed of some kind of cabinet, with a civil service dedicated to administering its decisions. Next is the *legislative branch*, the law-making body. The legislature is the supreme branch of government when it is composed of elected representatives, and what it decides can be described as the "will of the people." The legislature is usually made up of one or two chambers, introducing a further balancing separation. (A parliamentary system is one in which the executive branch is drawn from the legislative branch.) Last we have the *judicial branch*, which administers justice according to its interpretation of the laws passed by the legislature. It may also refer to a constitutional document as a benchmark.

FACT: *The Greek philosopher Aristotle considered the separation of powers to be the balance between a monarch, the aristocracy, and the ordinary people. Our modern definition of the separation of powers has its origin in the writings of the French political theorist Charles de Montesquieu.*

Creating a Safeguard

So far, so good: we have three branches, each with distinct roles. The separation of powers creates a system of checks and balances that prevents tyranny. The executive branch needs the legislative branch to create the laws; without its support, a budget cannot be formulated and implemented. The legislative branch needs the leadership that the executive offices provide; without this the legislature is a debating chamber with no clear sense of direction. Both the executive and the legislative branches require the judiciary to arbitrate in the inevitable disputes that arise when a law is enforced. The separation of powers means that each branch needs the others; but, at the same time, each has reasons to be antagonistic.

QUOTE

"The accumulation of all powers, legislative, executive and judiciary, in the same hands, whether of one, a few, or many, and whether hereditary, self-appointed, or elective, may justly be pronounced the very definition of tyranny."

James Madison (1751–1836), fourth president of the United States

The White House

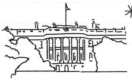

* As the home of the President, the White House is the seat of executive power.

Putting Theory into Practice

That is all very well in theory, but in practice the separation of powers becomes blurred. In the United States, Japan, France, and other democracies with codified constitutions, the theory holds up well. In more dubious democracies, such as Iran, Egypt, and Russia, the power of the president or the influence of religious authorities warps the checks and balances, favoring one branch of government over the others. In such cases the executive branch usually comes out on top, although the extraordinary transfer of President Putin to become Prime Minister Putin in Russia demonstrates the capacity for a charismatic leader to alter the balance of power to suit his or her own ends. In dictatorships such as North Korea and the People's Republic of China, the separation of powers is a complete fiction, as the most powerful state institution is the party. If the judicial, executive, and legislative branches are all drawn from the same political party, all checks and balances disappear.

The U.S. Capitol

* The U.S. Capitol is the location of the legislative bodies: the House of Representatives and the Senate.

The Supreme Court

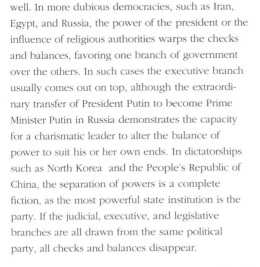

* The Supreme Court is the judicial branch of government in the United States.

Monarch and Parliament

Although many systems of government have arisen as a reaction against the hereditary rule of monarchs—for example, the French Revolution overthrew Louis XVI—some countries retain a vestige of monarchical rule in the form of a *constitutional monarchy*. Such a consitutional monarch as found in Belgium, the United Kingdom, and Thailand, among other nations, holds powers that tend to be greater in theory than they are in practice; for example, in the U.K. the monarch must give a bill "royal assent" before it can pass into law, but no king or queen since the beginning of the eighteenth century has refused his or her assent.

SUMMARY

The separation of powers divides the three branches of government. The best practice is for the separation to be absolute so that each branch of government acts as a check against the others. In this way, power remains balanced. In practice, however, the separation of powers can be less clear-cut, or even a complete fiction. When this happens, it is ordinary people who ultimately pay the price.

<u>**Who**</u> Is Nelson Mandela?

Nelson Mandela is one of the most courageous and visionary statesmen of the modern era. He was a leading figure in the transformation of South Africa, and his conduct has made him a world statesman whose opinions still carry weight even though he has been retired from public life since 2004.

The humble origins of Nelson Mandela gave few clues about the impact that he was to have on the world stage. He was born in 1918 in a small village on the Eastern Cape. His father died before Mandela reached the age of ten. Life was not easy, but education was seen as the way out of poverty. Through education came awareness of the injustices that the black majority suffered in South Africa, and that in turn led to political activism. In 1943, Mandela joined the African National Congress (ANC).

QUOTE:

"I am not a messiah, but an ordinary man who had become a leader because of extraordinary circumstances."

Nelson Mandela (b. 1918), first black president of South Africa

Political Activist

In common with the Congress Party in India, the ANC was attempting to promote human rights. It took inspiration from the example of Gandhi, presenting a legal and peaceful challenge to the ruling elite. By the time that Nelson Mandela qualified as a lawyer and set up a joint practice with his colleague Oliver Tambo, he had risen to be president of the ANC's youth wing. There was much to campaign against.

Through the 1950s and 1960s, tensions were steadily increasing as the ruling National Party implemented a legal framework for apartheid. The "pass laws" restricted the movements and rights of non-whites. Opportunities for blacks were few and far between, and the level of oppression was severe. In 1960, the Sharpville massacre of sixty-nine black people—shot dead by the South African police force—grabbed the attention of the world. That year also marked the end of a four-year trial in which Nelson Mandela had been rounded up, along with other leading figures in the anti-apartheid movement, and accused of treason by the government. The government also banned the ANC, ending all hopes of peaceful reform. At this point the ANC switched

The Y-shape evident on the flag of the Republic of South Africa represents the unification of its diverse society.

✳

FACT: *Apartheid was a legal structure that defined all South African citizens on the basis of race, which determined their human rights and levels of economic opportunity.*

tactics and attempted to undermine the economy of the state. The reaction was swift and brutal. Some ANC leaders, such as Oliver Tambo, escaped into exile, whereas Nelson Mandela was among those arrested.

Prison Years

In 1964, Nelson Mandela was sentenced to life imprisonment. He was to spend the next thirty-six years in jail. At the trial, Mandela accepted full responsibility for his resistance to apartheid. In doing so he risked the death sentence, but he also secured moral leadership of the movement. In prison, Mandela set an example of leadership and dignity. To the wider world, he became a symbol of the injustice and oppression of apartheid. South Africa became increasingly isolated and impoverished because of its adherence to racial segregation.

A Fresh Beginning

Eventually, in 1990, President F. W. de Klerk released Nelson Mandela from custody and restored the legal status of the ANC. This was a prelude to talks that were to lead to the creation of a multiracial democracy. The two men shared the Nobel Peace Prize in 1993, and in the following year Mandela was elected as the first black president of the Republic of South Africa. He served in that capacity until 1999.

Mandela's life has been marked with personal tragedy. He experienced two difficult divorces, most notably in 1992 from Winnie Mandela after she had been found guilty of charges that included kidnapping. His mother and eldest son died while he was in prison, and he was not permitted to attend the funerals. More recently, he has battled prostate cancer. In 2005, an HIV/AIDS-related illness resulted in the death of his second son. He has become increasingly frail and attends few public functions. Despite this, Nelson Mandela has never lost the qualities that sustained him through the apartheid years.

SUMMARY In short, Nelson Mandela is an inspirational leader. He led South Africa through its transition to a multiracial democracy, eventually becoming its first black president. He remains a global symbol of triumph against oppression.

When Was the Age of Revolution?

We all learned about the American Revolution in class, and you've probably heard of the French Revolution, too, but do you know the extent to which they were connected? They both fit into the "Age of Revolution," which ran from the early decades of the eighteenth century to the middle of the nineteenth century. During this time of political, economic, and technological upheaval, the foundations of the modern world were laid down.

When this period is taught in school, much attention is paid to the Industrial Revolution. There is much to catch the imagination: new factories, the first steps toward mass production, canals, steam locomotives, and more. Often neglected, however, is the Agricultural Revolution: the enclosure of fields that had been occurring since the time of the Tudor monarchs. This concentrated land in the hands of the aristocracy, including King George III, who, having grown wealthy from "triangular trade" (see right), were inclined to invest in the development of scientific farming in search of greater profit. This included experimenting with crop rotation, improving the condition of the soil, and the selective breeding of domestic livestock. Agricultural production increased and the population exploded, creating a new labor force and a new market. From the Agricultural Revolution came the Industrial Revolution.

FACT: *The terrible and tragic "triangular trade" involved goods being used to purchase slaves on the west coast of Africa, who were then shipped to the Americas. Their labor, particularly in the fields of sugar, tobacco, and cotton, produced the raw materials that were sent to Europe, generating enormous profits for European industrialists and landowners.*

✳

John Trumbull's depiction of Major General Charles Cornwallis surrendering to French and American forces after the Siege of Yorktown.

FACT: *The opening conflict between the American revolutionaries and British forces at Lexington is sometimes described as "the shot heard round the world."*

SUMMARY

Lasting from the mid-eighteenth to the mid-nineteenth centuries, the Age of Revolution was not a period of steady transformation. It was a series of explosive changes, sometimes secured and sometimes lost, that cumulatively created the global commerce and industry that we accept as inevitable. It also established the modern concepts of human rights and democracy that are cherished to this day.

The First Shots

During the same period, three world-changing political revolutions took place. The first of those was the American Revolution, or War of Independence, from 1775 until the signing of the Treaty of Paris in 1783. In asserting the Declaration of Independence and cementing it with the U.S. Constitution, the Founding Fathers took revolutionary concepts and showed that they could be successfully applied in practice. The relationship between the state and the individual, the concept of human rights, and the power of democracy all found form in the new country; a revolution in the new world, it was to change the old one as well.

Liberty and Fraternity

The French Revolution began in 1789. King Louis XVI was bankrupt and France was mired in debt. Anxious to find a way out of the crisis, Louis called the Estates-General (a general assembly) and promptly lost control over it. A National Assembly was formed and power slipped away from the monarchy, beginning a revolution that was to alter not only France but all of Europe.

Monarchies across Europe were threatened by the ideals of the revolution and the military power of the Garde Nationale. First the National Convention and later Napoleon swept aside the old order. However, at the end of the Napoleonic Wars, the old order reasserted itself, conservatism and autocracy were reinforced, and the ideals of political revolution appeared to be largely snuffed out . . . but there was more to come.

The New Order

As the nineteenth century reached its middle years, the flames of revolution were fanned once more; in 1848 another revolution broke out in France and there were uprisings across Europe. New nation-states emerged, most notably an increasingly unified Germany, and revolution in Italy brought the reunification of the peninsula. The old order had been unable to suppress change. An emerging middle class and an angry working class proved too powerful to resist. Wealth acquired through industry and trade stripped the old aristocracy of power based on land ownership. Cities were melting-pots for radical ideas, and, ultimately, in many states religious authority and monarchism gave way to liberalism, socialism, nationalism, and new constitutions.

Knowledge: *the ability to recall information*

1) The early life of author Leo Tolstoy was:
   a. Mundane
   b. Joyful
   c. Unhappy

2) Tolstoy served in the army of:
   a. Russia
   b. Persia
   c. France

3) The novel *War and Peace* is set in:
   a. The Napoleonic War
   b. The Crimean War
   c. The Russian Revolution

4) George Orwell was the pen name of:
   a. Arthur Fredrick Blair
   b. Arthur Eric Blair
   c. Eric Arthur Blair

5) George Orwell was born in:
   a. China
   b. India
   c. Britain

6) George Orwell was wounded in the:
   a. Russian Revolution
   b. Spanish Civil War
   c. Second World War

7) Herman Melville served as a sailor in the navy of:
   a. The United States
   b. Canada
   c. Great Britain

8) The captain of the *Pequod* in *Moby Dick* was:
   a. Allan
   b. Ahab
   c. Aaron

9) Nazi Germany and Soviet Russia both banned the novel:
   a. *Nineteen Eighty-Four*
   b. *Uncle Tom's Cabin*
   c. *Iron Heel*

10) It is wrongly assumed that complete freedom of expression is protected by which amendment of the U.S. Constitution?
   a. The fifth
   b. The first
   c. The second

11) Every working day the Library of Congress handles:
   a. 22,000 items
   b. 4,000 items
   c. 40,000 items

12) The initial core of the Library of Congress was the personal collection of:
   a. President Thomas Jefferson
   b. President George Washington
   c. President Theodore Roosevelt

Understanding: *the ability to interpret information and make links between different aspects of it*

1) What tensions and issues did Tolstoy explore in *War and Peace*?

2) Why is *Nineteen Eighty-Four* portrayed as a visionary novel?

3) What are the allegorical messages that readers have seen in *Moby Dick*?

4) What is the difference between informal censorship and formal censorship?

5) Why did the Library of Congress have a false start in 1800?

6) Which digital project is the Library of Congress currently engaged in?

Knowledge: *the ability to recall information*

1) Which animal is the bubonic plague thought to have come from?
- **a.** Pigs
- **b.** Sheep
- **c.** Cows
- **d.** Horses

2) Which animal is thought to have carried the bubonic plague, particularly during the Black Death?
- **a.** Cats
- **b.** Rats
- **c.** Mice
- **d.** Fleas

3) How many people are estimated to have been killed in Europe during the fourteenth century?
- **a.** 20 million
- **b.** 25 million
- **c.** 30 million
- **d.** 35 million

4) *Magna Carta* is Latin for?
- **a.** Big book
- **b.** Great Document
- **c.** Great Charter
- **d.** Big promise

5) Where and when did King John sign the Magna Carta?
- **a.** Bristol in 1213
- **b.** London in 1215
- **c.** York in 1217
- **d.** Runnymeade in 1215

6) Where did Gutenberg make his breakthrough with the moveable-type printing press?
- **a.** Berlin
- **b.** Strasburg
- **c.** Hamburg
- **d.** Freiburg

7) What was Gutenberg's breakthrough project?
- **a.** The production of the Bible
- **b.** The printing of papal indulgences
- **c.** The *Poem of the Last Judgment*
- **d.** The printing of paper money

8) Where did Columbus land in 1492?
- **a.** North America
- **b.** Canada
- **c.** The Caribbean
- **d.** South America

9) Who financed Columbus' expedition?
- **a.** The Portuguese government
- **b.** The Spanish Monarchy
- **c.** The English Monarchy
- **d.** The Vatican

10) Which of these was not one of Columbus' ships?
- **a.** The *Santa Maria*
- **b.** The *Nina*
- **c.** The *Golden Hind*
- **d.** The *Pinta*

11) How many copies of Thomas Paine's pamphlet *Common Sense* were sold?
- **a.** 10,000
- **b.** 50,000
- **c.** 100,000
- **d.** 200,000

12) When did Paine become a French citizen?
- **a.** 1776
- **b.** 1789
- **c.** 1792
- **d.** 1799

Understanding: *the ability to interpret information and make links between different aspects of it*

1) What factors aided the spread of disease during the fourteenth century?

2) Why was the Magna Carta not seen as significant at the time of its signing?

3) How was the Magna Carta linked to the rebellion of the British Colonies in America over five centuries later?

4) Why was the invention of the printing press so revolutionary?

5) Why didn't Columbus discover America?

6) Why did Thomas Paine die alone and friendless?

Knowledge: *the ability to recall information*

1) When was the first photograph taken?
- **a.** Summer 1826
- **b.** Winter 1825
- **c.** Autumn 1820
- **d.** Spring 1830

2) How much exposure was needed for the photograph to form?
- **a.** 2 hours
- **b.** 4 hours
- **c.** 8 hours
- **d.** 12 hours

3) When did Van Gogh cut off part of his ear?
- **a.** Christmas Day 1885
- **b.** Christmas Eve 1888
- **c.** New Year's Day 1891
- **d.** New Year's Eve 1880

4) Who was the artist with whom Van Gogh fell out before cutting off part of his ear?
- **a.** Seurat Monet
- **b.** Cézanne
- **c.** Pissarro
- **d.** Gauguin

5) Which disease was Van Gogh known to suffer from?
- **a.** Diabetes
- **b.** Epilepsy
- **c.** Tuberculosis
- **d.** Cancer

6) What is "pop art" short for?
- **a.** Popping art
- **b.** Proper art
- **c.** Popular art
- **d.** People art

7) Which of these figures was not a pop artist?
- **a.** Andy Warhol
- **b.** Roy Lichtenstein
- **c.** Salvador Dali
- **d.** David Hockney

8) Who opened the State Hermitage to the public?
- **a.** Catherine the Great
- **b.** Francesco Bartolomeo Rastrelli
- **c.** Josef Stalin
- **d.** Tsar Nicholas I

9) How many rooms are there in the State Hermitage Gallery?
- **a.** 255
- **b.** 315
- **c.** 365
- **d.** 400

10) Which famous architect was appointed to lead the construction of La Sagrada Familia?
- **a.** Antoni Gaudí
- **b.** Christopher Wren
- **c.** Antonio Palacios
- **d.** Adolfo Moran

11) How did Antoni Gaudí die?
- **a.** He fell off scaffolding.
- **b.** He drowned at sea.
- **c.** He was hit by a tram.
- **d.** He died of tuberculosis.

12) What is the earliest predicted completion date for La Sagrada Familia?
- **a.** 2018
- **b.** 2025
- **c.** 2032
- **d.** 2041

Understanding: *the ability to interpret information and make links between different aspects of it*

1) Why isn't Niépce better known?

2) How has Van Gogh's health been connected to his style of art?

3) Why did pop art fade away as a distinct artistic approach?

4) Where is the name State Hermitage thought to have originated?

5) Why is one of the collections in the State Hermitage politically controversial?

6) Why is the construction of La Sagrada Familia taking such a long time?

Knowledge: *the ability to recall information*

1) In which of these countries is voting not a legal requirement?
- **a.** Belgium
- **b.** France
- **c.** Australia
- **d.** Mexico

2) Who said that "Democracy is the worst form of government except for the others"?
- **a.** Winston Churchill
- **b.** Plato
- **c.** Pericles
- **d.** George Washington

3) Which of these bodies is unelected?
- **a.** The U.S. Senate
- **b.** The U.K House of Commons
- **c.** The U.S. House of Representatives
- **d.** The U.K. House of Lords

4) Where is the European Court of Justice?
- **a.** England
- **b.** France
- **c.** Germany
- **d.** The Netherlands

5) Which of these is not one of the traditional branches of state power?
- **a.** The executive branch
- **b.** The legislative branch
- **c.** The directive branch
- **d.** The judicial branch

6) The modern view of the separation of powers comes from:
- **a.** Aristotle
- **b.** Adolf Hitler
- **c.** Charles de Montesquieu
- **d.** President Putin

7) Which of these countries does not have a codified constitution?
- **a.** The United States
- **b.** France
- **c.** Britain
- **d.** Japan

8) In what year was Nelson Mandela born?
- **a.** 1900
- **b.** 1915
- **c.** 1910
- **d.** 1925

9) What does Nelson Mandela's African name "Rolihlahla" mean?
- **a.** President
- **b.** Peace
- **c.** Troublemaker
- **d.** Holy one

10) In what year did Nelson Mandela win the Nobel Peace Prize?
- **a.** 1990
- **b.** 1993
- **c.** 1999
- **d.** 2004

11) In what year did revolution break out and uprisings begin across Europe?
- **a.** 1776
- **b.** 1815
- **c.** 1848
- **d.** 1889

12) When was the Treaty of Paris signed, which ended the American War of Independence?
- **a.** 1775
- **b.** 1776
- **c.** 1783
- **d.** 1789

Understanding: *the ability to interpret information and make links between different aspects of it*

1) What are some of the reasons people don't vote?

2) What is case law?

3) In what sense is the British monarchy a "constitutional monarchy"?

4) What is the ANC?

5) What is apartheid?

6) What was "triangular trade"?

Friday

09:00-10:30

Religion

pp. 196-205

pp. 206-215

10:30-12:00

Science

12:00-1:30

Earth Sciences

pp. 216-225

2:00-3:30

History

pp. 226-235

GRADE YOURSELF

pp. 236-239

<u>Why</u> Is Zeus also Jupiter?

Have you ever heard the phrase, "by the beard of Zeus"? Well, the same guy was also called Jupiter. It might seem unusual for a god to have two names, but it was all because of the Romans. As a nation, the Romans were acquisitive. They conquered land and took wealth, and they valued the learning of other cultures as well. They were even happy to borrow their gods.

There was a time when Rome was not unrivaled in its power and Roman might did not strike awe in the hearts of all. Rome was once part of a fractured Italian peninsula in which different kingdoms were sometimes rivals and other times allies. The Romans, like other ancient peoples, had a belief system that involved a large pantheon of gods. However, these deities lacked personalities as such; they were an expression of natural forces, and sometimes of the places most closely associated with those forces (for example, Vulcan was the god of fire and was believed to dwell beneath the volcano Mount Etna). Because of this, the early Romans did not develop a strong narrative around their gods. There was no real mythology, and Rome's pantheon of divinities was meager and formless.

Competing Mythologies

The dominant Italian power in Rome's early days was the Etruscan civilization, and several of Rome's kings were, in fact, Etruscan. The Etruscans had built up a stronger mythology and forged a closer association between the forces of nature and the personalities of their gods. From further afield came the influence of Greece: the Greeks developed a commercial network on the Italian Peninsula, spreading their systems of learning and beliefs. The Greeks had also developed a strong sense of the human nature of their gods. Olympus, the home of the gods, resembled the setting of a daytime soap opera, with lovers, vengeful spouses, murder, and intrigue. At the head of this pantheon was Zeus, the supreme god of Greek mythology. Under the influence of these rival cultures, the Romans began to borrow a mythology for their own gods from around the sixth century B.C.E.

FACT: The most influential shrine in the city of Rome was the temple of Jupiter. It was dedicated to Iuppiter Optimus Maximus, the "best and greatest" of the gods.

The great Greek god ✱ Zeus has inspired art and sculpture around the world, even as far away as Hawaii, where this fountain can be found.

FACT: *The symbols of Zeus and Jupiter included thunderbolts, the oak tree, bulls, and eagles. Jupiter was regarded as the king of the gods, and all acts of government in Rome were dedicated to the god Jupiter.*

In the ancient world, dramatic natural phenomena were often attributed to the gods. Zeus/Jupiter was supposedly able to hurl lightning bolts.

The Triumph of Jupiter

For the Romans, Jupiter was a sky god. He was associated with lightning and rain. Both of these elements are strongly linked to the fortunes of early societies. Fire and water are essential for agriculture. A failed crop meant starvation and ruin. As a result, many cultures developed a deity who controlled these elements. Lightning strikes on hilltops sometimes resulted in Jupiter being worshipped at prominent points. Zeus and Jupiter were both shown with lightning bolts and were believed to control the weather and fertility. It was not difficult for the characteristics to merge.

The tipping point was to come later in Roman history. Greece was overwhelmed by the expanding power of the Roman Republic. Greek culture and learning remained significant across the ancient world, and the Romans maintained a generous attitude toward the beliefs of the peoples that they conquered. The assimilation of new peoples into the empire could be very effective: trade with Rome could bring great prosperity; the road network meant rapid communication. Jupiter became Zeus, and Zeus became Jupiter.

Jupiter had a significant place for the Romans. Indeed, Jupiter was too powerful for even the emperors to overthrow. As the Roman Empire expanded and the days of the republic passed, it became common for the deceased emperors to be deified. But Jupiter was untouchable and the emperors adopted him as protector of Rome in general and themselves in particular.

FACT: *Jupiter was also called Jove by the Romans, hence the phrase "by Jove." It is from Jove that we also derive the word **jovial**, meaning merry or good-spirited in a robust sort of way.*

Both the Greek and Roman civilizations had their roots in a period when science was much more primitive and the mysterious forces of nature were appeased and explained by invoking gods. The Greek god Zeus and the Roman god Jupiter were the supreme gods of their respective pantheons. The fact that they shared so many characteristics gives us a clue to the capacity of the Romans to conquer different cultures and then absorb their ideas.

Where Does Hinduism Come From?

Hinduism presents some unique difficulties for anyone trying to provide a definite location and date for its origin. It has no central charismatic figure (in the way that Christianity has Christ, Buddhism has Buddha, or Islam has Muhammad), and although it has many sacred texts, their origins and transference from oral history are uncertain. There are two core theories, and a heated contemporary debate, but no firm answers.

The usual date given for the origin of Hinduism is at some point between 1500 and 1000 B.C.E. This date is usually taken from an assessment of the four groups of texts called the Vedas, which are sacred to the Hindu religion. Astrological references in the oldest texts provide a good chronological reference point. The difficulty is that the Vedas probably had a long oral tradition before they were written down, and this makes specific dating uncertain. The most important text, the Ramayana, was not written until the first century C.E. but had probably existed in an oral form for 600–800 years before that. The problems of dating Hinduism make it all the more difficult to name a specific source, leading to competing theories about its origins.

QUOTE:

"Those who imbibe the knowledge of the Vedas and bring them into practice, they enjoy prosperity and happiness." Samaveda

Conquest and Fusion

The traditional theory is that Hinduism arose from the conquest of the Indus Valley in the northwest of the Indian subcontinent. The fertile plains of the Indus provided a starting point for a culture that was overwhelmed by a mass migration around 1500 B.C.E. The new arrivals were Aryan peoples from the vast steppes of central Asia. Restless and acquisitive, they conquered the Indus Valley and forged a new faith from a fusion of the two cultures. According to this theory, therefore, Hinduism can be said to have come from Aryan roots.

The fertile Indus Valley provided an excellent site for early settlements, but an inviting prize for invaders.

Pakistan

India

The Indus River

FACT: *The term "Hindu" may have come from a Persian word for the Indus.*

FACT: *The Vedas, the oldest sacred Hindu scripts, consist of hymns, descriptions of rituals, moral stories, and incantations. The four groups of texts are named the Rigveda, Samaveda, Yajurveda, and Atharvaveda.*

SUMMARY

We can say for sure that Hinduism is an ancient religion, and it almost certainly emerged from the complex and populous region of the Indus Valley in the northwest of the Indian subcontinent. The idea that its origins lie in a migration or invasion from central Asia is less widely held, but the exact cultural origins will probably continue to be the subject of dispute.

The traditional theory is supported, in part, by the sacred Vedas, which describe people of Aryan descent. There are also some linguistic traits in the Vedas that may point to origins beyond the Indus Valley. However, there is little archeological evidence of Aryan migration. The tribes of central Asia were dependent on the mobility provided by horses, giving these animals a central place in their culture, but there is no archeological evidence for the same in the Indus Valley. Horses and chariots do not appear to have made any social or military impact.

Decline and Recovery

An alternative theory argues that Hinduism originated from the indigenous cultures of the Indus Valley. It is accepted that some form of decline occurred between 1800 and 1500 B.C.E., but this is ascribed to natural disasters, not an invasion. The most likely explanation is a prolonged period of flooding, which would have disrupted agriculture, had an adverse impact on trade, and spread disease. During the recovery that followed, Hinduism could have emerged as a unifying force, weaving together different cultural influences.

This revisionist theory draws on the lack of archeological support for Aryan migration. There is, however, evidence for Vedic rituals throughout the period. It dismisses linguistic links with central Asia as being the wrong way around: culture and anthropology should be used to understand the language, not language used to interpret cultural development. The theory's weakness is that it relies on an intervening factor such as flooding, for which evidence is scant.

The symbol "aum" is shared by Hinduism and a number of other Indian religions. It represents many things, including, when chanted, the living sound of the universe.

Wider Implications

The traditional theory of an Aryan migration was formed during the nineteenth century. Its main proponents were Western archeologists, historians, linguists, and anthropologists. Their work was rooted in the preconceptions of racism and imperialism. The revisionist theory gives greater status to the indigenous Indus Valley culture. It now seems that this society was much larger and more sophisticated than previously believed. It may well have had trade links to the rest of the Indian subcontinent and Babylonia. For modern Indians, the concept of Hinduism arising without the intervention of an external invader is attractive. As such, the question of where Hinduism came from has developed political and national implications, making it all the more controversial.

When Did Buddha Live?

Buddhism is followed by up to 1.6 billion people across the globe. Its center lies in Asia, but there are adherents in most places and it is growing quickly in Western countries. The actual dating of Buddha's life is uncertain, though, reflecting the development of different forms of Buddhism. Different scholarly traditions tend to accept that Buddha lived for about eighty years before his Mahaparinibbana (death), but they differ radically in dating his birth.

FACT: *Buddha was born into a life of privilege as Prince Siddhartha Gautama; however, he left his palaces behind at the age of twenty-nine, and achieved enlightenment at thirty-five before preaching his teachings to the world.*

Let's start with the dating of Buddha's birth among the religion's most easterly adherents. It is given as 766 B.C.E. in the eastern Buddhist traditions of Korea, China, Vietnam, and Japan. There is an argument that this early date was established to make the life and teachings of Buddha fit with the Chinese philosopher and poet Lao-Tse, providing continuity with the core teachings of Chinese society.

An important source from Canton gives an alternative date for the birth of Buddha: 566 B.C.E. This is known as the "Dotted Chronicle" because it is supposed to show one dot for every year after the death of Buddha—975 dots up to the year 489 C.E. This date became more commonly accepted by Japanese scholars.

Indian Traditions

Moving westward, on the Indian subcontinent there are competing northern and southern traditions. The northern is based on the beliefs and scholarly efforts of Buddhists in Mongolia and Tibet, and offers a date around 961 B.C.E., which is considerably earlier than any other estimate, and for which there seems to be less credible evidence. The more widely accepted date comes from a southern Buddhist tradition, which suggests 623 B.C.E.—a date that has been adopted by the World Fellowship of Buddhists.

The "fat Buddha" is generally a depiction of the Chinese monk Budai (Hotei in Japanese), who in turn is regarded as an incarnation of Maitreya, the future Buddha.

QUOTE:

"All that we are is the result of what we have thought. If a man speaks or acts with an evil thought, pain follows him. If a man speaks or acts with a pure thought, happiness follows him, like a shadow that never leaves him." **Gautama Buddha**

Having achieved enlightenment, Buddha is often represented in a central position to indicate wisdom.

FACT: *Starting in 331 B.C.E., the conquests of Alexander the Great were monumental in scale, stretching from Egypt, across Persia, and into the Himalayas. Nineteenth-century European explorers were shocked to discover that his name was still recalled with loathing in Afghanistan.*

QUOTE:

"Believe nothing, no matter where you read it, or who said it, no matter if I have said it, unless it agrees with your own reason and your own common sense." **Gautama Buddha**

Western Perspectives

Shifting still further westward, the records of the ancient Greeks provide some evidence for another possible date. In his extraordinary conquests, Alexander the Great came into contact with Indian rulers. Greek records confirm a territorial agreement between Alexander's appointed ruler of Babylonia and an Indian emperor in 303 B.C.E. Using Indian records for the duration of previous imperial rulers, it is possible to establish a chronicle that dates the birth of Buddha as 563 B.C.E. This is the date most widely accepted by Western historians.

FACT: *Lao-Tse was born in 604 B.C.E. His writings teach about the nature of virtue and the role of man in the natural world. He is regarded as the first Taoist, one who seeks to accept the oneness of all things.*

SUMMARY

The fact that Buddhism has no single hierarchy and no single leading representative has resulted in the development of a wide range of regional variations, each adapted to the society in which it is based. This has, in turn, resulted in different scholarly traditions when it comes to dating the life of Buddha. We can be sure of his existence and teachings. What we cannot be sure about is exactly when he was born and when he died.

What Does Pantheism Mean?

The term "pantheism" was first used by John Toland in *Socinianism Truly Stated* (1705). It is formed from two Greek words: *pan*, meaning "all," and *theos*, meaning "god." Although he put a name to it, pantheism did not, of course, begin with Toland. Its history dates back to the ancient world, and it still influences our beliefs today.

What is god? It is a question that has been asked throughout human history. All cultures have formed belief systems that try to address that question, and in doing so they have raised other issues. If god can be defined, for example, what is the relationship between the divine and the physical worlds? Pantheism is an attempt to reconcile these two worlds, and it has existed in different forms for thousands of years.

The Material and the Spiritual

Pantheism argues that there is a unity between the material world (nature) and the spiritual world (god). There are many variations of this core belief. The two main forms of pantheism are theomonisticism and mysticism. The theomonistic view is that all beings—indeed, all life—are part of one divine being. The mystical perspective argues that divinity exists within all beings—the opposite side of the same coin perhaps, but that's theology for you!

Pantheism and Religion

Pantheistic beliefs date back to the ancient world. In Hinduism, Brahman is the original source of all existence. Elsewhere, Egyptian gods such as Osiris were associated with all living creatures. There seems to have been a progression from the worship of gods in the forces and forms of nature to a sense that divinity and nature are one and the same thing. In ancient Greece, the application of scientific understanding to the natural world created a tension between the divine and the physical. This found some reconciliation in forms of pantheism such as the Eleatic school of philosophy, which taught that the material world was an expression of spiritual unity.

✱ St. Augustine is one of the most important early Christian thinkers.

FACT: *Pantheistic ideas have influenced the works of many great artists, including Beethoven, Wordsworth, Mary Shelley, Walt Whitman, and D. H. Lawrence.*

John Toland coined the term *pantheism* three hundred years ago to define the question about the relationship between god and the physical world, but pantheistic beliefs have ancient origins and have developed many variations. It can be argued that pantheism has had a significant impact on human culture and that it continues to influence our concept of divinity and nature today.

Neoplatonism also developed from pantheistic schools of thought in ancient Greece. For Neoplatonists, a divine "Unknowable One" was the very source of the universe. This idea went on to influence early Christian theology, including that of Augustine. Some authorities in the early church argued that the Neoplatonists had begun to grasp the nature of God before the revelation of Christ. This meant that they were able to accept and incorporate ideas such as the science of Aristotle and the medical concepts of Galen. These, therefore, became standard texts in the Middle Ages, and their authority was not widely challenged until the Renaissance (see pp. 72–73).

A Modern Return

The Renaissance witnessed a reexamination of the ideas of the ancient world and a return to some pantheistic concepts. Two texts from the period laid the foundations for modern pantheism. These were the Dutch philosopher Spinoza's *Ethics* (1675) and Toland's *Pantheism: or The Form of Celebrating the Socratic-Society* (1720). The time was ripe for questions to be asked. Christianity in Western Europe was divided between Roman Catholic and Protestant teachings. The Americas had revealed huge civilizations, such as the Incas and Aztecs, who had totally alien belief systems. Trade with India and Asia had brought Europeans into direct contact with the ancient religions of the East. These new ideas fueled an inclination for some writers and theologians toward pantheism. It seemed to offer a belief system that reconciled many different views.

FACT: *The philosopher Plotinus (an Egyptian-born Roman of Greek descent) founded Neoplatonism in the third century B.C.E., basing it on the ideas of Plato.*

In some respects pantheism has changed contemporary spirituality even if it has not significantly changed traditional religions. Many people do not now attend regular services or profess to hold more than a loose connection to one religion. Instead, many believe that god is a part of all things, or that all things are a part of god—both of which are essentially statements of pantheism.

QUOTE:

"Every thing God, and no God, are identical positions."

Samuel Taylor Coleridge (1772–1834), English poet and philosopher

Who Were the Fathers of Western Philosophy?

The easiest way to look smart is to know a thing or two about philosophy, and the best place to start is with the three ancient Greeks who, between them, established the foundations of Western philosophy.

FACT: *Philosophy means "the love of wisdom."*

The three men in question are Socrates, Plato, and Aristotle. During their lifetimes, Greece was by far the most significant civilization in the ancient world. To be precise, though, there was no "Greece" as such—at least, not in the way that there is a single country called Greece today. Instead, there was a collection of city-states that were sometimes allied with each other (against external foes) and at other times in open conflict among themselves.

Greek Learning

Trading communities had been established around the ancient world, and Greek learning was gaining a positive reputation, but there were more cultured and sophisticated civilizations. The Egyptians, Phoenicians, and Babylonians all held great prowess in the fields of learning. It can be argued that the existence of these competitors drove Greek learning in a different direction, toward an investigation of the natural world without the deeply religious definitions and justifications of other cultures. Philosophy, as its founding fathers knew it, was more expansive than our definition today. To the ancient Greeks, philosophy—a term that they created—meant all forms of inquiry into the origins and processes of the natural world. This led to a search for fundamental laws that could explain and predict natural occurrences. To achieve this, philosophy emphasized inquiry, observation, experimentation, and analysis. These form the basis of the empirical approach that is fundamental to all modern science.

FACT: *Thales of Miletus is a good example of the very practical nature of Greek philosophy. For example, he attempted to work out how an observer on the shore could calculate the distance to a ship at sea.*

The Fathers of Western philosophy were Socrates, Plato, and Aristotle. Building on each other's concepts and practices, they established philosophy as being fundamental to human society. The principles of empirical inquiry have gone on to be the foundation of politics, science, mathematics, and much more.

Socrates (c. 469–399 B.C.E.)

Socrates was not the first philosopher. That honor is usually given to Thales of Miletus (c. 624–546 BCE). Socrates insisted that he had

Socrates

no wisdom but was forever in search of it. He became famous in his own lifetime for questioning all kinds of people about a wide range of topics. He was always probing at preconceptions and commonplace ideas. He worked to establish the nature of good in any field of human conduct and made many enemies by sticking to his principles, even at the cost of his life (see p. 26).

Plato (c. 428–c. 347 B.C.E.)

Plato was a devoted follower of Socrates' principles and practice. Thanks to Plato's accounts, we are able to read for ourselves the debates that Socrates held, but Plato went beyond his role model by founding the Academy of Athens. Here Plato developed the concept of "forms" from the philosophy of Socrates. Put simply, the idea was that Socrates had been searching for ideals—such as the ideal of goodness—but these do not exist in nature. Similarly, in other types of knowledge, humans seek the ideal, though in many cases we don't get very close. Plato described this as being like a man who lives in a cave and knows the outside world through the shadows on the cave wall. A philosopher steps outside the cave, seeking wisdom and purity of form, even at the cost of blindness. Whereas Socrates' inquiries had been at the individual level, Plato applied philosophy to political institutions and attracted the interest of powerful rulers.

Plato

Aristotle (384–322 B.C.E.)

Aristotle came to the Academy of Athens aged just seventeen but already noted for his precocious intellect. He remained a member for twenty years; but that didn't mean that he accepted all that was taught. Aristotle challenged the concept of forms and gave the philosophy of Socrates a complete overhaul, making it more systematic. In doing so, he created the discipline of logic. For Aristotle, everything had to be open to empirical inquiry. If something couldn't withstand rigorous investigation, it didn't have a place in his system; his philosophical understanding had no place for divine intervention.

Aristotle

The Role of Islam

The story does not end there. With the collapse of the Roman Empire in Western Europe, the teachings of Socrates, Plato, and Aristotle fragmented; but Islamic scholars of the Middle East kept the flame alive by collating, translating, and advancing their philosophy. Ideas such as Al-Khwarizmi's (780–850 C.E.) advances in algebra, and Avicenna's (979–1037 C.E.) development of medicine, as well as many others, spread to Europe during the Middle Ages, transforming European learning and kick-starting the Renaissance.

When _Did the Dinosaurs Die Out?_

Triceratops, a dinosaur that lived around 68 million years ago.

For more than 150 million years, the world was dominated by a wide range of dinosaurs that were able to occupy many different habitats around the globe, from tiny vegetarians to meat-eating monsters. Then, in a relatively short period of time, they disappeared from the face of Earth. So, when did this happen and why?

We know from the fossil record that dinosaurs first appeared some 220 million years ago (mya), at the end of the Triassic period (248–208 mya). These early dinosaurs were small, carnivorous creatures that walked on their hind legs and bore little resemblance to the giants that evolved later. During the Jurassic period (208–144 mya) many new dinosaurs evolved, including the brachiosaur, which weighed over 30 metric tons and was one of the largest creatures ever to have walked the Earth. Dinosaurs dominated life on land until the end of the Cretaceous period (144–65 mya), but during this period there were major changes; for example, flowering plants began to take over from the coniferous plants that had previously dominated. Dinosaurs don't appear to have evolved to take advantage of this change, whereas insects and mammals did.

About 65 million years ago, dinosaurs disappear quite suddenly from the fossil record, along with many other species. Altogether, around 85 percent of known species became extinct at that time, including all flying reptiles, most large marine reptiles, and many species of plants. So what happened?

A Wealth of Possibilities

Scientists have put forward many theories to explain the dinosaurs' extinction. Some suggest that their disappearance might have been due to an inability to adapt to changing conditions, or to some kind of biological inferiority when compared to other animals, in particular mammals. Were they simply too stupid or too cumbersome to survive against competition from the brainy, fleet-footed mammals? Today we even use the word "dinosaur" to suggest something outmoded and unable to change; but is that fair? At the time of their extinction, dinosaurs seem to have been flourishing; there are thought to have been thousands of different species, and some of the late-Cretaceous dinosaurs had the largest brains.

FACT: _Before dinosaurs became extinct, it is possible that one branch had evolved into a very different kind of creature. Many scientists believe that birds (of which there are almost 10,000 living species) evolved from a branch of the largely meat-eating theropod dinosaurs, with which they share many anatomical similarities. These include a three-toed foot, air-filled bones, and feathers in the case of some theropods._

FACT: *The term "dinosaur" was first used by the English anatomist Professor Richard Owen in 1841 at a meeting of the British Association for the Advancement of Science. It comes from the two Greek words **deinos**, meaning "terrible," and **sauros**, meaning "lizard."*

There are many other extinction theories, including dietary change, disease, and parasitic infestation, but these would be unlikely to affect so many different life forms simultaneously. Volcanic activity on a huge scale, or climate change as a result of Pangaea breaking up (see pp. 18–19) are possible explanations, but these would not cause the sudden extinction shown by the fossil record.

Luis Alvarez and his geologist son, Walter.

The K–T Boundary

One theory is favored by the majority of scientists: an "impact event." In 1980, the physicist Luis Alvarez and his geologist son, Walter, discovered a 65-million-year-old layer of rock in Earth's crust that contained an unusually high concentration of iridium, which is uncommon on Earth but is found in meteorites. They suggested that the layer was caused by the impact of a huge meteorite up to 8 miles (13 km) in diameter. This layer, which is at the geological boundary between the Cretaceous and Tertiary periods (known as the K–T boundary), has now been found in more than a hundred places around the globe, and other geological evidence supports the idea, especially the discovery of a gigantic crater 110 miles (180 km) across that is centered on the Yucatán Peninsula in Mexico. There are also other craters around the world that date from the same period and suggest a series of impacts.

Such a series of collisions would have blasted masses of debris into the atmosphere, covering the planet with dust, preventing the Sun's heat and light from reaching the surface. This would have caused the climate to change and damaged the plant and plankton life that is the basis of the food chain. It is thought that the dinosaurs were some of the many casualties.

FACT: *Don't be misled by popular Hollywood classics such as **One Million Years B.C.**, in which humans are pitted against ferocious dinosaurs in titanic battles. These amazing and diverse reptiles became extinct long before the appearance of any of the Homo species.*

SUMMARY

The dinosaurs died out about 65 million years ago, over a period of a few thousand years, which is a short time in biological terms. The most likely reason for their disappearance is that the impact of a very large meteorite affected the climate and the atmosphere, reducing the food supply. In the competition for the dwindling resources, the dinosaurs lost out to mammals, birds, and insects, and to other reptiles.

Who Was Carl Linnaeus?

Have you ever wondered how people around the world are able to refer to any plant, animal, fungus, or single-celled organism—regardless of what language they speak—and be absolutely certain that they are talking about the same thing? The answer lies in a foolproof system of classification that was invented in the eighteenth century by a truly great scientist named Carl Linnaeus.

Carl Linnaeus was born in southern Sweden in 1707. His father wanted him to become a clergyman, but Carl was more interested in botany, and the local doctor persuaded his father to send the young man to study at the University of Lund. After a year he moved to the University of Uppsala, where he published a paper on the classification of plants that earned him a position as a lecturer.

In 1732 he set out on a five-month expedition to Lapland, in the north of Sweden, funded by the Royal Society of Sciences in Uppsala, from where he returned with a wealth of research material, as well as great tales of adventure. He published a list of the plants of Lapland, organizing the plants according to his newly devised classification system, or "taxonomy."

In 1735 Linnaeus moved to the Netherlands and earned a degree in medicine before traveling to London, Oxford University, and Paris, meeting with many eminent botanists of the time and developing his classification of the living world in a work that he called *Systema Naturae.*

He returned to Sweden in 1738, opening a medical practice in Stockholm, then becoming a professor at the University of Uppsala, where his broad knowledge and infectious enthusiasm made him popular with students. He became well known for his research, and people sent plants and animals from around the world for him to examine and classify. In 1753 he published his naming system for plants, followed five years later by one for animals. Although there have been many changes since, the system that we use today is based on his work.

> **QUOTE:**
> "Linnaeus was in reality a poet who happened to become a naturalist."
> Swedish author August Strindberg

Carl Linnaeus, in a portrait by Hendrik Hollander, believed he had a God-given mission to classify the Creator's handiwork.
✳

Linnaeus's system was published in Latin in 1735, in a work entitled **Systema Naturae,** meaning "The System of Nature." ✳

SUMMARY

Carl Linnaeus (1707–1778) was a Swedish biologist whose studies of plants, animals, and humans led him to develop the first comprehensive system for classifying living things, based on shared physical characteristics. "Linnaean taxonomy" is the basis of the system that we use today, which gives every species a unique Latin name and places it in its evolutionary relationship with other species. Linnaeus is also one of the founders of ecology.

Modern Taxonomy

Linnaeus organized all things into groups according to similarities in structure, which he took to reflect the proximity of relationship. The most important aspect of his system was that every organism was given a two-part Latin name, or "binomial," consisting of a genus name that indicates the group of species to which it belongs and a species name that distinguishes it from all other organisms. If you've ever listened to a gardening program and heard plants referred to by their Latin names, such as *Bellis perennis*, you may have thought it sounds pretentious, especially when you realize that it's just the common daisy that's being discussed. However, the term "daisy" can be used to refer to several different species, and would mean nothing to someone who spoke French or German, whereas the binomial *Bellis perennis* refers to a specific plant and is understood by gardeners worldwide.

The theory of evolution by means of natural selection, proposed in the mid-1800s by Charles Darwin, had a profound effect on taxonomy, as scientists have since turned their attention to classifying all living things according to what are thought to be their evolutionary relationships rather than their structural similarities. However, Linnaeus's system was robust enough to be adapted and extended instead of being replaced.

The Way It Works

The system is constantly being amended as new species are found and new discoveries made, but the scientific community broadly divides the living world into five *kingdoms*: Animals, Plants, Fungi, Monerans (single-celled organisms without a nucleus, such as bacteria), and Protists (single-celled organisms with a nucleus, such as protozoa and algae).

Each kingdom is sub-divided; Animalia, for example, has more than thirty *phyla*, one of which is arthropoda (animals with an external skeleton, such as crustaceans and insects). Insecta (insects) is a *class* within arthropoda, and coleoptera (beetles) is an *order* within that. This is further divided into *families*, then *genera*, which are made up of various *species* and *subspecies*.

Why *Is Evolution Controversial?*

When, in 1859, Charles Darwin published his book *On the Origin of Species by Means of Natural Selection*, he fundamentally changed the way in which biologists understand the natural world. As well as explaining how all species of living things came into being and making sense of the fossil record, his ideas have provided a theoretical foundation for all the life sciences. Why then, more than 150 years later, is evolution still controversial?

✳

The English biologist Charles Darwin not only demonstrated that evolution had taken place but also put forward a theory of how this occurred.

At the time of Darwin's life-changing five-year journey to the coast of South America onboard HMS *Beagle*, the idea of evolution had already been posited. However, an enthusiastic observer and collector, and a keen student of both geology and biology, Darwin pieced together a wealth of information on his travels that gave fresh impetus for evolution by suggesting a mechanism that drove it. It was the writings of the British scholar Thomas Robert Malthus on the subject of human population growth and the "struggle for existence" that prompted Darwin to suggest that a process of "natural selection" led to the evolution of new species.

So What's Controversial?

At the heart of the theory of evolution is the idea that there is a certain level of genetic variation between generations within a species, and that some variations will positively affect the individual's ability to survive and reproduce. As a result, the number of individuals having this variation will tend to increase at the expense of those that do not. Over time, this leads to the development of a new species. Scientists are still investigating the details of the process of evolution, but the scientific community is virtually unanimous in agreeing that this is indeed the way in which life on this planet has come to be the way it is. However, there are several aspects of this argument that various groups have been unwilling to accept over the decades.

Darwin himself perceived that this means humans are simply a form of animal, and came into existence in just the same way as other animals, by evolving according to natural laws. He expanded upon these ideas in

FACT: *Science and religion are not always opposed on the issue of evolution. There are plenty of scientists with strong religious beliefs, and on the flipside of the coin there are those religious people who view creation stories as allegories and myths, and are able to accept the body of evidence that life on this planet has evolved.*

QUOTE:

"To use the Bible to support an irrational and an archaic concept of static and undeveloping creation is not only to misunderstand the meaning of the Book of Genesis, but to do God and religion a disservice by making both enemies of scientific advancement and academic freedom."

Little Rock Ministerial Association, 1968

✳ Gustave Doré's **Creation of Light**. Creationists who maintain that the Bible gives a literal account of how life on Earth came into existence can only do so by ignoring the wealth of geological, paleontological, and biological evidence to the contrary.

The Descent of Man, and Selection in Relation to Sex, in which he suggested we evolved from ancestors we share with the apes. Many find this uncomfortable, a thought that strikes against a sense of being special; but for many of those who believe we were created in the image of God, it is quite unacceptable.

Creationism

For Christians who maintain that the Bible contains the literal truth, there are other problems. The Book of Genesis says that Earth and the Heavens, and all things within them, were created in six days, and some "Creationists" insist that this should be taken literally, a view that is clearly opposed to evolution.

The processes of evolution are generally extremely slow, and the theory requires that life must have existed on Earth for hundreds of millions of years. Geological studies and the fossil record bear this out, but there are those who, basing their reasoning on the genealogies found in the Bible, claim that Earth cannot be more than 10,000 years old.

These views, based on a literal reading of the Bible, are clearly not scientific, but they don't claim to be. There is a school of thought, however, that asserts that some aspects of the universe — including the complexity and diversity of life—can only be explained by invoking "intelligent design." To support their case, and to justify their demands that Creationism be taught in schools, proponents put forward evidence that they claim is scientific, a claim that the scientific community utterly rejects.

SUMMARY

Evolution remains controversial for various religious groups that insist upon a literal interpretation of certain divine creation stories. Many are also unwilling to accept that, rather than being the pinnacle of created order, humankind is merely the temporary outcome of an undirected process.

What Is DNA?

DNA is found in almost every cell in every living thing. It carries the code or blueprint for life, and the discovery of its structure and the way it works has revolutionized our understanding of life processes. But what exactly is this remarkable chemical, and how does it carry and transmit all the information living things need to function?

The presence of a chemical in the nuclei of the cells of many different living things was discovered in the nineteenth century by a Swiss doctor named Johannes Friedrich Miescher (1844–1895), and it was given the name "nucleic acid." By the 1930s it was known that there were two forms of nucleic acid: shorter molecules containing a sugar called ribose, and longer ones containing the sugar deoxyribose. These molecules became known as ribonucleic acid (RNA) and deoxyribonucleic acid (DNA). Scientists knew that these substances were somehow responsible for carrying inherited characteristics, but the way in which they did this remained a mystery until the 1950s.

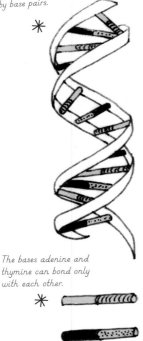

The structure of the DNA molecule is two spirals linked together by base pairs.

✳

The bases adenine and thymine can bond only with each other.

✳

✳ *Similarly, guanine and cytosine can bond only with each other.*

The Structure of DNA

In 1953 James Watson and Francis Crick proposed, correctly, that the DNA molecule is a double helix—two spirals wound around each other. They continued their research, making a major contribution to our understanding of what DNA does and how it works, and in 1962 they, along with Maurice Wilkins, were awarded the Nobel Prize.

Each strand of DNA is a long molecule that consists of repeating chemical units made of phosphates, sugars, and bases. These units are called nucleotides, and each includes one of four different bases—adenine, cytosine, guanine, and thymine. Each of these bases will bond only with one of the other three. Adenine bonds only with thymine, and guanine with cytosine, to form base pairs. The double-helix structure of DNA is formed in this way, with the two individual strands spiraling around each other, joined together like the two halves of a ladder with the base pairs acting as the rungs.

The wonderful thing about this structure is that it can replicate. If the two strands separate, each will attract a sequence of complementary nucleotides—the result is two complete and identical DNA molecules. This happens when cells divide, so each new cell has a complete set of DNA.

Working with data from other researchers, James Watson and Francis Crick solved the puzzle of the structure of DNA.

FACT: Crick and Watson owed much to the work of other scientists. Separate investigations by Rosalind Franklin and Maurice Wilkins using X-ray diffraction to analyze the structure of the DNA molecule provided vital clues in the puzzle. Maurice Wilkins shared the Nobel Prize with Crick and Watson in 1962, but Rosalind Franklin had died of cancer in 1959, and the rules did not allow the prize to be awarded posthumously.

SUMMARY

DNA, or deoxyribonucleic acid, is a complex molecule found in almost all living cells. Its structure is a double helix—two spirals bound together by four chemical compounds that link in pairs. The sequence of these compounds along the spiral acts as a code to carry information that enables the cell to assemble amino acids into proteins. In this way DNA directs the growth and function of cells.

Information in Code

We can think of the four bases as letters in a code. On the DNA strand these work in sequences of three, each of which is called a *codon*, and there are sixty-four possible codons or three-letter combinations. Some of these are used to instruct the cell to create specific amino acids, of which there are twenty, and these are then put together in different combinations to create thousands of different proteins. A section of DNA that codes for the building of a particular protein is called a *gene*.

Genes and Genomes

It is through processes controlled by the sequences of base pairs in the DNA that an organism grows and functions. Humans have about three billion base pairs in their DNA, and the DNA in a human cell exists as forty-six bundles called chromosomes.

An organism's complete set of genes is called its *genome*, and this determines not only what species it is but exactly how it looks and even some aspects of how it behaves. We inherit half of our genome from each of our parents, and this can be very obvious in our appearance.

FACT: In 1980, the U.S. Human Genome Project set out to map the complete set of genes that make up the human genome, identifying each gene and the base pairs that compose it, and to put all this information into a huge database. The project was expected to take fifteen years, but with research groups around the world contributing to the effort and great technological advances, the work was completed in 1993.

Where Does *Homo sapiens* **Come From?**

***Homo sapiens* is one of those Linnaean binomials (see pp. 208–209). It's the label for you and me: modern humans. The term has been applied to our species since the mid-1800s, and it sounds simple enough. But in those two words there's a wealth of information about how we evolved to become the dominant force on this planet.**

In the eighteenth century, Carl Linnaeus gave humans the binomial *Homo sapiens*, Latin for "men of wisdom," and grouped us with the great apes in the family Hominidae (hominids), but the exact relationship was unclear. Darwin's theory supported the possibility that we shared common ancestors, but no fossil evidence was found to support this—until the twentieth century.

Bones of Our Forebears

In 1925, Australian anthropologist Raymond Dart discovered the skull of a juvenile primate in rock from a limestone quarry at Taung in South Africa. On the basis of its teeth and evidence that it walked upright, he boldly

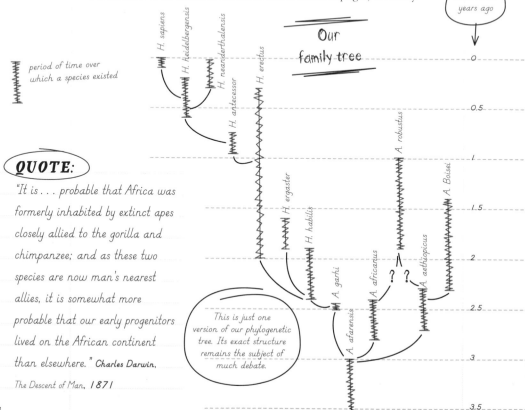

Our family tree

millions of years ago

period of time over which a species existed

QUOTE:

"It is . . . probable that Africa was formerly inhabited by extinct apes closely allied to the gorilla and chimpanzee; and as these two species are now man's nearest allies, it is somewhat more probable that our early progenitors lived on the African continent than elsewhere." Charles Darwin, The Descent of Man, 1871

This is just one version of our phylogenetic tree. Its exact structure remains the subject of much debate.

FACT: *A rival theory to the Recent African Origin suggests that* **Homo sapiens** *evolved in various forms (such as Asian and Caucasian) in several locations from geographically isolated populations of* **H. erectus***. However, DNA studies do seem to support a single origin some 200,000 years ago.*

hailed it as an evolutionary link between apes and humans, naming the new species *Australopithecus africanus*. Many contemporaries dismissed his claim, but several more Australopithecine finds eventually proved him right.

The Broader Picture

A wealth of fossil finds since that time has enabled scientists to piece together a fairly detailed picture, albeit one that is constantly refined in the light of new finds. The current view suggests that *A. africanus* lived two to three million years ago (mya), and that *A. afarensis*, which lived a million years earlier, was the ancestor of both *A. africanus* and the genus *Homo*, to which we belong. Some 2.5 mya, the first of the *Homo* genus diverged from the Australopithecines, with smaller molar teeth, a larger brain, and the ability to use tools, earning it the name *H. habilis* ("handy man"). It seems unlikely that *H. habilis* was our direct ancestor. Several other *Homo* species, with yet more refined teeth and a larger brain still, lived at the same time. *H. ergaster* (meaning "workman," as stone axes have been found with the fossils), existed from 1.9 to 1.4 mya and may well be our ancestor.

The fossils of all the species mentioned so far come from Africa, but those of *H. erectus* ("upright man"), dating from 1.8 to 1 mya, have also been found in Java, Vietnam, China, and Europe. Thought to be the first human to have left Africa, *H. erectus* is generally considered our direct ancestor. Evidence of several other human species co-existing with *H. erectus* includes Rhodesian man from Africa and Heidelberg man in Europe, which may have been the Neanderthals' ancestor.

The Arrival of Wisdom

The first modern humans (*H. sapiens*) appeared about 200,000 years ago in Africa, and the "Recent African Origin" theory proposes that this is where speciation from *H. erectus* took place, with groups of modern humans spreading out from Africa about 70,000 years ago. It is thought that, with their greater brain power, better use of tools, and higher degree of social organization, they displaced earlier species such as the Neanderthals and descendants of *H. erectus*. The earliest European example, Cro-Magnon man, dates from about 30,000 years ago, and by 14,000 years ago *H. sapiens* had reached America.

SUMMARY

Homo sapiens, meaning "man of wisdom," is the Latin name given to modern humans by Carl Linnaeus. The branches of the family tree that lead to us separated from the gorillas' branch some 8 million years ago, from the chimpanzees' branch 5 million years ago, from Australopithecines 2.5 million years ago, and from Neanderthals about 300,000 years ago.

<u>When</u> Did the Worst Earthquake Happen?

As we have seen, tectonic plates move relative to each other (see pp. 16–17 and 20–21); sometimes the motion is steady and gentle, but sometimes the edges of the plates get stuck. The plates keep moving, but at the boundary the rocks deform, and enormous energy builds up. Sooner or later, something has to give, and when it does the effect can be catastrophic.

The vast majority of earthquakes take place around the edges of the Pacific tectonic plate, in the so-called Ring of Fire, but earthquakes occur in many parts of the world where there is tectonic activity. The point at which the sudden movement takes place is called the *focus* or *hypocenter*, and this can be anything from 20 to 400 miles (30 to 700 km) beneath the surface. The point on the surface directly above the focus is known as the *epicenter*.

Energy from the earthquake travels through Earth's crust in the form of seismic shock waves that cause the ground to shake, buckle, and heave. The magnitude of an earthquake—the energy released by the initial event— can be calculated from the amplitude of these waves as measured by instruments called seismographs. Magnitude is measured on the Richter scale and, for larger earthquakes, the "moment magnitude" scale, which both run from 0 to 10. They are logarithmic scales, so the seismic waves in a magnitude 5 earthquake are ten times greater than those of a magnitude 4, and the energy released is about thirty-one times as great.

The 2004 tsunami hit a train in Sri Lanka, hurling it inland and killing more than 1,000 people. ✳

FACT: A tsunami can be more deadly than the earthquake itself. Moving rapidly across the ocean and gaining height as it moves into shallower water, a tsunami has huge destructive power when it hits the shore, and can travel far inland. The tsunami from the earthquake that occurred off the coast of Sumatra, Indonesia, on December 26, 2004, hit the coastlines of several Asian countries and killed more than 250,000 people.

The Most Powerful

The Great Chilean Earthquake—at 9.5 on the moment magnitude scale, the largest recorded in the world—occurred on May 22, 1960. The earthquake, which came on the heels of a much smaller one that took place the previous day, caused damage throughout more than 150,000 square miles (400,000 sq km) of Chile. The worst affected city was Valdivia, where soil subsidence caused buildings to collapse and a landslide blocked a river, causing a lake above the city to rise to dangerous levels. Tsunamis (waves produced by the earthquake) up to 80 feet (24 m) high struck the coast of Chile, and the main one hit the coastal community of Hilo in Hawaii, killing more than sixty people. It also reached Alaska in the north, Japan in the west, and New Zealand in the south. As many as 6,000 people died, mainly in Chile.

The epicenter in Valdivia, Chile.

Tsunamis from the Great Chilean Earthquake radiated out across the Pacific in all directions.

The Highest Death Toll

The magnitude of an earthquake is not always an indicator of the loss of life that it causes. When a magnitude 7.4 earthquake hit the industrial town of Izmit in northwestern Turkey in the early hours of the morning of August 17, 1999, more than 17,000 people lost their lives, mainly in collapsing multistory concrete buildings. When an earthquake of similar magnitude struck central Vancouver Island, Canada, in 1946, the death toll was just one. The area was far less populated than was the case in Turkey, but the big difference was that the majority of buildings in the region were wood-framed and only one or two stories tall.

The world's deadliest recorded earthquake occurred on January 23, 1556, in the central Chinese province of Shaanxi. In the city of Huaxian every single building was destroyed and tens of thousands died, but the death toll in the rural areas was also high. The area has silty soils, and many people were living in elaborate caves carved from the soft rock. The earthquake, thought to have had a magnitude of about 8, caused widespread landslides, and the fragile caves simply collapsed, bringing the total number of people killed to 830,000. In some areas, as much as 60 percent of the population died.

SUMMARY

The most powerful recorded earthquake took place in Chile in 1960. The magnitude 9.5 quake struck a relatively sparsely populated area, and the total death toll was about 6,000 people. The earthquake with the highest death toll struck central China in 1556. A large proportion of the 830,000 people killed by the Shaanxi or Jiajing earthquake were dwelling in caves that collapsed.

<u>Why</u> Is Tourism So Important?

The idea of traveling away from home for leisure, to relax and see the sights, began in Britain in the eighteenth century, at the time of the Industrial Revolution. Initially, only the wealthy could afford to take vacations, but the development of mass transport in the nineteenth and twentieth centuries has made tourism popular for working people throughout industrialized countries.

Looking just at international tourism, the figures are amazing—almost a billion tourists arrive at international destinations worldwide every year, and they spend almost a trillion U.S. dollars. Hardly a corner of the globe is unaffected, and there are certainly upsides to the international tourist industry. Few activities could be more educational or self-improving than experiencing other lands and other ways of life, helping us to understand and appreciate other cultures and our place in the world.

The Pros ...

Better
transportation?

Tourism doesn't benefit just the traveler; there are advantages for the people and the places that we visit. For example, tourism creates employment in restaurants and hotels, transportation, merchandising, and entertainment. In poorer countries, tourism often results in improvements to infrastructure, with increased investment in roads, water supply, electricity, and telecommunications. Improved infrastructure benefits residents and brings an increase in property values, so local people find their land and buildings are worth more. Foreign currency flows into tourist destinations, too, and wealth can be expected to trickle down through society. Cultural aspects of the society can also be expected to benefit, as societies treasure and preserve the culture that tourists come to see. This all seems very positive but, as with most stories, there are two sides to this one.

Merchandising
money

... and the Cons

Tourism undoubtedly creates many jobs, but often the highest-paid work goes to those who run the capital-intensive amenities such as hotels, who tend to be outsiders rather than local people. When local people are employed, the work is often poorly paid and may be seasonal, leaving many locals unemployed for much of the year.

Increased
carbon emissions

The majority of the money that people spend on accommodation and food never even enters the destination country, but is paid to vacation companies and tour operators based in industrialized countries. Improvements in the infrastructure may indeed result in increased wealth within a region, but the increases in property prices

Disturbed
wildlife

FACT: *Tapping into our fascination for the grim and the gruesome, "dark tourism" brings travelers to sites linked to death and tragedy, such as Nazi concentration camps, Ground Zero in New York City, battlefields, graveyards, and scenes of natural disaster, such as post-Katrina New Orleans. While growing in popularity, the sensationalizing of suffering raises a range of moral and ethical questions.*

SUMMARY

Tourism is important because it forms the backbone of many developing economies, and it provides a major source of revenue and employment in developed countries. By exposing travelers to other lands, peoples, and cultures, tourism at its best encourages a broader world view and promotes understanding. At its worst it can be destructive and exploitative.

often mean that the local people are no longer able to afford to live there. As for the argument that tourism preserves and enhances cultural diversity, sometimes it can have precisely the opposite effect, bringing outside influences into traditional societies, disrupting established economic and social relations, and turning vital elements of a culture into hollow theatrical performances.

The physical harm done to sensitive environments, wildlife habitats, and archeological treasures by thousands of visitors can also be huge.

There is also the question of carbon emissions. In an age of dramatic climate change (see pp. 224–225) and a worldwide move against the use of fossil fuels, burning vast amounts of fuel to reach the ultimate holiday destination is becoming increasingly unacceptable.

An Evolving Market

Aware that these issues could adversely affect the market, the tourism industry has been quick to address some of them, in word if not always in deed. The result has been the blossoming of niche tourism sectors.

Ecotourism advocates low-impact, small scale travel to sensitive areas, putting money into conservation and into local economies to have a positive impact on the host country. Unfortunately, the "eco" label is frequently misused. Voluntourism (volunteer vacations) combines volunteer help on projects, such as the building of schools or medical centers in developing countries, with an opportunity to experience the culture. Cultural-heritage tourism represents something of a return to the early days of international travel, focusing on the cultural treasures of other societies and hopefully reinforcing, rather than eroding, the identity of those societies.

FACT: *According to the World Religious Travel Association, religious tourism is worth some $18 billion annually. Much of it is focused on sacred sites in the Middle East, but every year shrines, tombs, churches, and temples around the world draw millions of visitors who combine pilgrimage and sightseeing.*

Who Was Gerardus Mercator?

Humankind has been drawing maps for at least 8,000 years, and the problem of making these representations true to reality has been tackled in a variety of ways. However, it was the contribution of Gerardus Mercator that was perhaps the most important.

Gerardus Mercator developed a method of mapping the spherical globe onto a flat surface.

In 1963, a large wall painting was discovered during the excavation of the ancient city of Catal Hyuk in Turkey. It shows a town plan of the area, and it is thought to date from about 6000 B.C.E. By at least 2500 B.C.E., the Babylonians (in what is now Iraq) were making small clay maps with inscribed place names, and by 600 B.C.E. they had attempted a world map. It didn't show much of the world we know, which appeared as a disk surrounded by ocean, but already the cardinal points (north, south, east, and west) were being shown.

In the second century B.C.E., detailed and fairly accurate maps were made by the Chinese, showing towns and cities, rivers, and the coast.

In the second century C.E., great advances were made by the Greek-born astronomer, mathematician, and cartographer Claudius Ptolemaeus, better known as Ptolemy. Using a wealth of personal observation and astronomical data, some of it from the Babylonians, he wrote an extensive work on astronomy, but he also collected a great deal of geographical information, which he presented in *Geographica*. He was convinced that the world was a sphere (although he also thought that the Sun revolved around Earth) and he used a grid system of longitude and latitude to define the locations of places.

He was the first person to tackle the problem of representing Earth's curved surface on a flat map. The 360-degree circle had been used since the Sumerians' time, but Ptolemy went further and divided the degree into minutes and then seconds, which we use today as divisions of both the degree and the hour.

FACT: *Mercator's projection has the drawback that, although relative distances are accurate at the equator, area becomes distorted as one moves north or south, reaching extremes at the poles, which are expanded to take up the whole width of the map. This renders maps fairly useless at latitudes greater than 70°.*

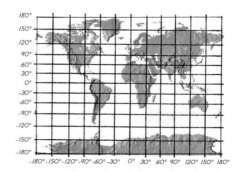

Mercator's projection means that the globe could be mapped onto a rectangle instead of two separate circles.

FACT: *For aviation purposes, an alternative projection called the Lambert conformal conic projection is generally used. This effectively projects Earth's surface onto the surface of a cone rather than a flat surface. A straight line plotted on the resultant map is approximately a section of a "great circle" (a circle with its center at the center of the planet), representing the shortest distance between two points.*

Through the Middle Ages

Geographical accuracy took something of a back seat to religious belief in the Christian West, and maps became highly stylized, but from the fourteenth century the boom in seafaring for trade and exploration led to a need for accurate maps. Commercial mapmakers, calling themselves "cosmographers," gathered information primarily from sailors and travelers, and the maps they made dealt largely with coastal trading routes and ports. These maps were to be used for navigation, so they needed to be carried onboard ship and show accurate distances. Globes, with horizontal lines of latitude and meridians connecting the poles, were used from the end of the fifteenth century, but an effective way of projecting Earth's surface onto flat maps was still needed.

Mercator's Projection

Gerardus Mercator produced his first map in 1538, mapping the spherical surface onto a flat plane by spreading out the lines of latitude as they approached the pole. By then straightening the meridians so that they intersect the lines of latitude at right angles, the stretching effect was equal in both directions. This kind of projection is called "conformal," which means that the scales are the same in both directions and the angles between objects on the map are true, making it well suited for navigation. However, it was not until the eighteenth century, with the development of accurate clocks (allowing mariners to calculate their longitude accurately) and the plotting of variations in magnetic north around the globe, that his maps truly came into their own. Mercator's projection is still in use today.

QUOTE:

"What's the good of Mercator's / North Poles and Equators, / Tropics, Zones, and Meridian Lines?' / So the Bellman would cry: and the crew would reply, / 'They are merely conventional signs!'"

Lewis Carroll, *The Hunting of the Snark,* 1874

Gerardus Mercator was a sixteenth-century mapmaker. His ground-breaking projection solved some of the problems of plotting our three-dimensional planet in two dimensions. Mercator's projection is well-suited for navigation; however, it does distort size, meaning that the view of the world we hold in our heads is not an entirely accurate one.

Where Is the World's Largest City?

Cities are synonymous with civilization, and humankind has certainly built some big ones. Which is the biggest? Like so many questions, this one hangs on an "it depends on what you mean by . . ."

To begin with, there is no single legal, cultural, or geographical definition of a city. We can all agree that a city is a large built-up area of residential and commercial buildings, with all the attendant infrastructure—roads, power, water, sewerage, public transit, and so on—but where do you draw the boundary? Many of the world's cities have grown to engulf their suburbs, smaller towns around them, and even other cities; so is the city the administrative municipality, the central part of the built-up area, or the full extent of the urban sprawl? And does "largest" mean the greatest area, or the highest population? Here we'll look at some alternative answers, but we'll focus on administratively defined districts with the largest populations.

The Most Populous

Given that many cities don't carry out a census every year and that in some parts of the world the population is growing rapidly, the figures are ever-changing, but the ranking of the top ten cities and their approximate populations looks like this:

1	Mumbai (Bombay), India	14 million		6	São Paulo, Brazil	11 million
2	Shanghai, China	13.5 million		7	Moscow, Russia	10.45 million
3	Karachi, Pakistan	13 million		8	Seoul, South Korea	10.42 million
4	Delhi, India	12.26 million		9	Beijing, China	10.12 million
5	Istanbul, Turkey	11.4 million		10	Mexico City, Mexico	8.84 million

FACT: Using a range of carefully chosen criteria, Mercer's Quality of Living survey ranks the world's top cities by how pleasant they are to live in. Interestingly, none of the current top five (Vienna, Austria; Zurich, Switzerland; Geneva, Switzerland; Vancouver, Canada; and Auckland, New Zealand) is in the top 150 by population size, suggesting that growth comes at a price.

SUMMARY

Taking "city" to mean a municipal administrative unit, the world's most populous city is Mumbai in India, with about 14 million. It also has one of the highest population densities in the world. If one takes "city" to mean the metropolitan area as a whole, Tokyo has the greatest population (33 million).

The Biggest in the United States

By any criteria, the U.S. city with the largest population is, unsurprisingly, New York City. With its five boroughs, New York City ranks thirteenth in the world, with a population of 8.3 million, an area of 300 square miles (790 sq km), and a population density of 27,700 people per square mile (10,450 per sq km).

Largest Through History

The largest city at any historical period reflects various shifts in power. The list of one-time largest cities contains many places that have surfaced in other lessons in this book, from Catal Hyuk in Turkey, which had a population of several thousand more than 8,000 years ago, through Babylon in what is now Iraq, to Memphis, Thebes, and Alexandria in Egypt. Alexandria was probably the first city with a population of over one million, achieved in about 100 B.C.E. Cities in China topped the list several times during the first millennium B.C.E.

In the Mediterranean, power moved to Rome—the world's largest city for the first centuries of the first millennium—with Constantinople (now Istanbul) in Turkey then growing to take first place until the Chinese city of Chang'an outstripped it in the seventh century C.E.

Pole position rotated between Baghdad in Iraq and the Chinese cities of Hangzhou, Jinling, and Beijing until the nineteenth century, when the Industrial Revolution in Britain fueled rapid urbanization, and London grew from a population of just over a million in 1820 to 6.5 million in 1900. New York took the lead in the 1920s, before losing it to Tokyo in the 1960s.

FACT: The region of Hulun Buir in northeastern Inner Mongolia, in the People's Republic of China, has the administrative status of a city. Covering an area of more than 100,000 square miles (260,000 sq km) and with a population of some three million souls, it is the world's largest city by area, and has one of the lowest population densities (30 people per square mile; 12 per sq km).

What Is Climate Change?

Even recently, politicians anxious to avoid unpopular decisions denied that climate change was taking place. That position is no longer tenable—the evidence that climate change is happening and that it's our fault is overwhelming. So what is happening, what is causing it, and what, if anything, can we do to rescue the situation?

The term "global warming" has largely given way to "climate change," because the processes that are occurring are much more complex than a uniform warming of the globe. Nonetheless, the key issue is that the average temperature of Earth's surface, the oceans, and the lower atmosphere is increasing. This is thought to be largely the result of a rise in the levels of "greenhouse gases," such as carbon dioxide (CO_2), in the atmosphere.

It is now more than twenty years since the Intergovernmental Panel on Climate Change (IPCC) began looking into the scientific evidence and reporting back to the world on its findings, and in its report *Climate Change 2007* the IPCC stated: "For the global average, warming in the last century has occurred in two phases, from the 1910s to the 1940s (0.63°F/0.35°C), and more strongly from the 1970s to the present (0.99°F/0.55°C). An increasing rate of warming has taken place over the last 25 years, and 11 of the 12 warmest years on record have occurred in the past 12 years [1995 to 2006]. . . . Confirmation of global warming comes from warming of the oceans, rising sea levels, glaciers melting, sea ice retreating in the Arctic, and diminished snow cover in the Northern Hemisphere."

Global Effects

An increase of less than 1°F (0.56°C) in the average global temperature doesn't sound like much, but it is enough to have dramatic effects on weather systems and the environment. At the International Scientific Congress on Climate Change in 2009, the world's top climate scientists presented evidence that the dynamics of the oceans and the polar ice sheets are changing, that oceans are becoming more acid (as a result of absorbing CO_2), and that there is an increase in extreme climatic events such as droughts, hurricanes, and heavy rainfall. The great concern is that these trends will accelerate, and that "tipping points," at which abrupt or irreversible shifts may occur, could be reached.

FACT: *The Intergovernmental Panel on Climate Change (IPCC) was set up in 1988 by the World Meteorological Organization (WMO) and the United Nations Environment Program (UNEP) to provide independent scientific advice on the issue of climate change.*

FACT: *Global warming may cause "positive feedback loops." For example, in Siberia a giant permafrost peat bog covering hundreds of thousands of square miles is already starting to melt. It contains billions of metric tons of methane, another greenhouse gas, which could accelerate global warming if released.*

The Human Cost

The effects of climate change vary around the globe. Some parts of the world may even see lower temperatures as ocean currents change, or increased snowfall as a result of greater evaporation from warmer seas. The impact on different societies will also vary, and some of the poorest developing countries could be the hardest hit. For example, if sea levels rise, the first to suffer will be people inhabiting low-lying areas such as Bangladesh and Pacific island nations. A major change in rainfall patterns could dramatically reduce crop production in many of the poorest parts of Africa.

Around the world, changes in temperature patterns are already leading to shifts in the distribution of plants and animals, pests, parasites, and diseases, having a major impact on food production and health, and creating problems that all societies will have to solve.

Causes and Solutions

Earth's climate has fluctuated, sometimes widely, throughout geological time, producing ice ages and much warmer periods than we are experiencing now. The factors that caused this in the past, such as changes in solar radiation and the movements of tectonic plates, are no doubt still at work, but the rapidity of the current climate change and the wealth of scientific data suggest that this time the causes are largely "anthropogenic"—made by humankind.

Principal among these is an increased level of carbon dioxide in the atmosphere caused by a dramatic increase in the burning of fossil fuels and by deforestation (forests absorb carbon dioxide). Gases such as carbon dioxide and methane are known as "greenhouse gases" because they reduce the rate at which heat is radiated from the Earth, therefore causing it to warm up.

Reducing emissions is seen as the key to slowing and, if possible, reversing climate change, and the Kyoto Protocol, adopted in 1997, set international targets for emissions reductions. Although some European countries have succeeded in cutting emissions significantly, those of the United States and Canada have increased by more than 20 percent since 1990.

SUMMARY

Climate change is a global process that includes warming of the land, seas, and atmosphere, as well as changes to the world's weather patterns, melting of ice caps and glaciers, rising sea levels, and an increase in extreme weather events. It is probably largely due to an increased concentration of carbon dioxide (CO_2) in the atmosphere as a result of the burning of fossil fuels.

What *Started World War I?*

Most historians would say that there were three causes of World War I. Depending on your point of view, it began because of a single individual, a questionable alliance system, or—and this was the official answer at the end of the war—it was Germany's fault.

FACT: A total of eight alliance treaties and agreements were signed by European states between 1879 and 1914.

The individual who could be accused of starting World War I was a young man named Gavrilo Princip, a Serbian nationalist. At the time, young men like him felt that they had a good case for hating the Austro-Hungarian Empire, which had held sway over the Balkans for a couple of hundred years. In Bosnia and Herzegovina, the Serb community wanted to leave the Austro-Hungarian Empire and unite with Serbia. The ruling powers of the empire feared that such a move would trigger all sorts of secessionist movements, leading to the breakup of an already declining empire.

The Black Hand

Gavrilo Princip belonged to the Black Hand, a group that plotted to kill the heir to the Austro-Hungarian Empire, Archduke Franz Ferdinand, when he visited Sarajevo. An attempt to bomb the royal cortege went wrong, killing and wounding members of the crowd but leaving the archduke unharmed. Advisors of the archduke wanted to bundle him out of the city as quickly as possible, but he wouldn't leave before visiting the hospital where the injured lay. This gave the Black Hand a surprise second chance. Gavrilo was able to fire his revolver into the car carrying the royals, killing them both.

The Austro-Hungarian Empire was outraged by the assassinations and set out to punish Serbia. Russia prepared to support the Serbians, with whom there were close cultural links. Germany feared that their security was threatened by Russian mobilization—and it all began from there. So, the shots fired by Gavrilo Princip could be described as the opening salvo of the war.

FACT: The Treaty of Versailles (1919) forced the German government to accept that Germany had been responsible for starting World War I. This caused lasting resentment and later fueled support for extremists such as Adolf Hitler.

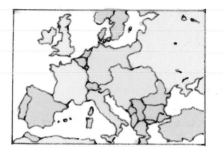

Triple Entente

Neutral countries

Triple Alliance

Russian allies

The Alliance System

Europe at the time was a complex web of alliances. Germany, Italy, and Austria-Hungary formed the Triple Alliance, and Britain, France, and Russia the Triple Entente. The opposing forces were so evenly balanced that war would be a catastrophe and therefore was less likely to occur, or so it was thought.

Both alliances had sophisticated plans for different eventualities. When Germany saw Russia mobilizing her armed forces in support of Serbia, the Schlieffen plan was undermined. Having banked on knocking France out of the war before turning on the vastly bigger but much less advanced forces of Russia, the plan relied on Russia being slow to mobilize. If Russia was already prepared, the plan would collapse and the Serbian justification might even be a cover for a joint Franco-Russian attack. Far from deterring war, the alliance system may have created an inescapable chain reaction, culminating in war.

The Kaiser

Kaiser Wilhelm II was eager for Germany to join the ranks of the great imperial powers, but most of the choice prizes had already been snapped up. Instead of looking to Africa and Asia, the German government saw potential in Eastern Europe. As the first decade of the twentieth century concluded, the Kaiser shifted from using the alliance system to maintain the status quo to pressing for change in the balance of power. Maintaining a large and technologically impressive land force, while matching British naval power, placed a great strain on the German economy. As a result, 1914 was make-or-break time for Germany. Either the Kaiser would achieve his ambitions in one dazzling stroke, or there would be a humiliating acceptance of the existing order.

FACT: The naval arms race of the early twentieth century was similar to the nuclear arms race of the Cold War. Ships such as the Dreadnought class were cripplingly expensive.

SUMMARY

The causes of World War I have long been the source of academic debate. They can be defined in terms of the great forces of history, such as imperialism, militarism, and nationalism, or the ambitions and actions of individuals such as Kaiser Wilhelm II and Gavrilo Princip. In the end, however, you might agree with Britain's Queen Mary when she said: "For such a stupid reason, too."

<u>**Who**</u> Was the Worst Dictator of the Twentieth Century?

There are three main contenders for this appalling title: Adolf Hitler, Joseph Stalin, and Mao Zedong, not to mention a host of other tyrants from around the globe. If you ever hear the twentieth century referred to as "history's bloodiest century," these people are the reason why.

The Führer

The figure of Adolf Hitler continues to be of global fascination, and many people around the world see him as the pre-eminent dictator of the twentieth century. In the wake of World War I, Germany was mired in debt, had lost territory, and its military was strictly limited. The impoverished population resented these conditions, and Hitler rode a groundswell of nationalism, eventually coming to power in 1933. As the '30s progressed, he stripped away the vestiges of democracy from the German state and began to work toward a new world order. As Europe and the world once more spiraled toward war, Hitler's campaign against those he considered "undesirable"—Jews, homosexuals, disabled people, and many more—gathered pace, culminating in the death camps of the Holocaust. Undoubtedly, the atrocities committed in Hitler's name were terrible, and estimates for the combined military and civilian dead of World War II and the Holcaust generally exceed fifty million. But the question remains: Was Adolf Hitler the worst dictator of the twentieth century, or simply the one with whose savagery Westerners are most familiar?

✳

Adolf Hitler, ex-painter and decorator; dictator of the Third Reich.

QUOTE: "

"Terrorism is the best political weapon for nothing drives people harder than a fear of sudden death." Adolf Hitler (1889–1945)

Uncle Joe

Although on the side of the Allies in fighting fascism in general and Hitler's Germany in particular, Stalin nevertheless stakes a very strong claim to being the worst dictator of the twentieth century.

Compared to Hitler's atrocities, those of Stalin are less well known because they largely took place away from the eyes of the West. However, that does not diminish their scale. Having become General Secretary in 1922, Stalin strengthened his grip on power until it was absolute, ruling with an iron fist until his death in 1953.

Many fell victim to Stalin's political purges that stripped the upper echelons of government, the Communist Party,

Josef Stalin, ex-seminary student; dictator of the Union of Soviet Socialist Republics.

✳

*FACT: Josef Stalin is often believed to have said, "One death is a tragedy, a million is a statistic." This phrase was, in fact, written by the author of **All Quiet on the Western Front**, Erich Maria Remarque.*

SUMMARY

Hitler, Stalin, or Mao could be considered the worst dictator of the twentieth century. In part, who you choose depends on the criteria you employ, but the secretive nature of single-party states also means that there is little agreement about the numbers of deaths for which they were responsible.

and the armed forces of anyone perceived to be a threat to Stalin or his ideals. A wide variety of estimates exist for those who died in the *gulag* prison system, but they number in the millions and possibly tens of millions. To these must be added those who died during forced deportations, as well as those who starved as a consequence of misguided farm collectivization.

There can be no doubt that Stalin was responsible for the deaths of tens of millions of people; however, the cloak of secrecy that surrounded the Soviet Union makes it difficult to estimate the exact cost in human lives.

The Chairman

Like Stalin, Mao fought on the side of the Allies during World War II, but he had already been at war for a number of years before that. As the head of China's communist movement, Mao fought a civil war, against the nationalist Kuomintang, that lasted until 1950.

In the decade that followed the communist victory on the mainland, Mao became obsessed with the need for China to join the ranks of the great industrial powers. In 1958 he launched "The Great Leap Forward." This policy, like those of Stalin in Russia, was intended to turn agriculture into vast collectives while at the same time striving for a massive increase in the productivity of heavy industry. Within a few years, even the teams of investigators sent out by the Communist Party had to conclude that famine was widespread, but national pride was at stake and Mao continued to insist that agricultural export orders were met and industrial productivity targets attained. Tens of millions died of starvation and disease.

That was not the end of Mao's wrongs. Like Stalin he employed purges and labor camps to deadly effect, killing many more millions of his own people. However, as is the case with the Soviet Union, the secrecy of the state has hidden the true extent of these crimes from the world, and estimates vary wildly.

*FACT: In 1964, Chairman Mao published a collection of his quotations, known in the West as **The Little Red Book**. It is possibly the most printed book in history, with between 5 and 6.5 billion copies produced during the Cultural Revolution.*

Mao Zedong, ex-library assistant; dictator of the People's Republic of China.

<u>Why</u> Was an Atomic Bomb Dropped on Hiroshima?

It was one of the iconic moments of the twentieth century, but why did it happen? There is an official set of reasons for dropping an atomic bomb on Hiroshima, and an unofficial set; these are sometimes referred to as the contemporary and revisionist views. Despite a wealth of information about the development and use of the world's first atomic bomb, debate still rages about the real motives.

The official explanation for why the atomic bomb was used against Japan is based on the differences between conflict in Europe and conflict in the Pacific. Despite fears to the contrary, the Nazis did not continue a guerrilla war after the capture of Berlin. A few fanatical units fought on, and there were some isolated incidents of political violence, but Germany as a whole capitulated. The war in the Pacific, on the other hand, showed every sign of being the reverse. The slow subjugation of the Pacific islands was achieved at an ever-increasing human cost. The closer the Allies came to the Japanese home islands, the more determined became the resistance that they encountered.

A Swift End

The infamous invasion of Iwo Jima caused the deaths of 6,200 American servicemen. At Okinawa, another 13,000 lost their lives. This led the U.S. military to propose appalling estimates for the casualty rates if the Japanese home islands had to be invaded. The use of kamikaze attacks on Allied shipping and the willingness of Japanese soldiers and civilians to die rather than be captured convinced many in the military that American casualties could be as high as 150,000 before Japan was vanquished. President Truman, therefore, took the decision to use the atomic bombs as a swift and decisive method for achieving the unconditional surrender of the Japanese.

The decision was popular at the time. The end of the war in Europe had created an intense desire to bring the war in the Pacific to a swift conclusion. The sacrifice had been too high already, and the prospect of war dragging on for years seemed unbearable. There was also an inclination among some people—recalling the sudden attack on Pearl Harbor—to punish Japan in a manner that would have been less acceptable against a European nation.

The two nuclear bombs that concluded World War II were dropped on Hiroshima and Nagasaki in the southwest of Japan.

Hiroshima

Nagasaki

Tokyo

FACT: *The Allied program to develop an atomic weapon was called the Manhattan Project. Initially, it was believed that Nazi Germany was actively working on the creation of a similar weapon.*

FACT: *Albert Einstein was one of the initial proponents of an Allied atomic bomb project, but he warned other scientists: "You realize, once the military have this, they will use it, no matter what you say."*

A Show of Power

The unofficial explanation for the bomb's use at Hiroshima explores motivation and political intent. With the war in Europe coming to a close, the USSR began to take a more active interest in the Pacific conflict. Winston Churchill and Harry S. Truman were acutely aware of Joseph Stalin's aspirations for a dominant communist bloc. By employing the atomic bomb against the Japanese, the United States was able to secure victory on its own terms and without Russian intervention. This incentive was strong enough to override any alternative proposals, for example, to demonstrate the power of this new weapon by unleashing it on a deserted island. It might also explain why two cities were targeted in quick succession, because this demonstrated that the United States had the capacity to deliver more than a single attack and that the government had the will to employ such a terrible weapon.

Although his discoveries were central to its development, Einstein was deeply troubled by the implications of the atomic bomb.

QUOTE:

"From Stettin in the Baltic to Trieste in the Adriatic, an iron curtain has descended across the Continent."

Winston Churchill in 1946

Whether or not this was the real motive, the influence of the USSR in Asia and the Pacific was curtailed. In Europe, the numerical advantage of the Red Army suddenly appeared less influential. The atomic bomb appeared to create a line that was to become permanent in the form of the Iron Curtain. The shape of the postwar world was established.

FACT: *The Hiroshima bombing killed 66,000 people and the Nagasaki bombing, three days later, killed another 39,000. Conventional bombing raids on Japan's six largest cities killed up to 250,000 people in total.*

SUMMARY

The reasons for the dropping of an atomic weapon on Hiroshima in 1945 will never be settled because so much depends on the reading of intentions and motivations. It can be interpreted as an unnecessary act of inhumanity based on a cold political calculation. It can equally be interpreted as a brave act of leadership that swiftly concluded World War II and prevented the immediate outbreak of new hostilities between the victorious allies.

Where Was the First Female Head of Government Elected?

There are two potential candidates who could claim to be the first female head of government to be elected to that position. You may not have heard of them, but they can each claim to have taken an important step in the emancipation of women. They are Khertek Amyrbitovna Anchimaa-Toka from the Tuvinian People's Republic and Sirimavo Ratwatte Dias Bandaranaike in Sri Lanka.

Human history records a wide range of powerful and influential women. Queens and empresses have been at the center of some of history's most decisive moments. However, women have often been excluded from positions of power, and this continued even as democracy became more widespread. In most countries the right to vote was restricted to men alone. It was only in the twentieth century that increasing numbers of women won the right to vote, often after a long and painful struggle. With the right to vote the potential to become an elected leader has developed, but in all too many democracies that possibility has yet to become reality.

FACT: *The Tuvan Republic is located south of Siberia. Turkic peoples make up its ethnic majority. They are closely related to the neighboring Mongols.*

Tuva can claim to be the location of the first elected female head of government. Khertek Anchimaa was elected to the leadership of the parliament, or Little Khural, of the Tuvinian People's Republic in 1940. She served in that capacity until 1944. At the height of World War II, Khertek Anchimaa, a strong communist and graduate of the Communist University of the Toilers of the East, played a part in the process that witnessed Tuva become a full member of the USSR. A remarkable woman, she was born into poverty, taught herself to read and write, became involved in communist politics, and remained politically active until 1972. She lived in retirement until her death in 2008. The only difficulty with her claim is that she was the representative of a one-party state. It was an election in name only.

Khertek Anchimaa, the first elected female head of state.

FACT: *Sri Lanka is an island state south of India. The country is ethnically divided between Tamils and Sinhalese.*

Sirimavo Bandaranaike became the Prime Minister of Sri Lanka in 1960. She had a lifelong involvement in the Sri Lanka Freedom Party that lasted until her death in 2000. Like Khertek Anchimaa, she was attracted to left-wing politics. She encouraged her party to work in a coalition with the Marxist Lanka Sama Samaja Party, which created tensions within the government. Bandaranaike was also anxious to encourage developing countries to opt out of Cold War politics. Rather than joining alliances with East or West, she promoted the concept of nonalignment, arguing that developing countries should find their own international voice. She served as the Chairperson of the Association of Non-Aligned Nations. Bandaranaike served two terms as Prime Minister, the first from 1970 to 1977 and the second from 1994 to 2000. The first term was not a success. Inspired by left-wing ideals, her government nationalized important industries and attempted to restructure the economy. The result was economic hardship. This, combined with increasing ethnic tensions, led to a crushing defeat in the 1977 elections. Her United Front coalition was demolished and her own party virtually disappeared from parliament, winning only 8 of a possible 168 seats. Nevertheless Sri Lanka can rightly claim the honor of the being the first multiparty democracy to elect a female head of government.

✳

The island of Sri Lanka is home to about 20 million people (2009).

More Firsts

There are several notable firsts in different countries. The first woman to be in the line of succession to the U.S. presidency was Secretary of Labor Frances Perkins, who took up her post in 1933. India, the world's largest democracy, elected Indira Gandhi in 1966. Both Gandhi and Bandaranaike served as prime minister. The first female president was María Perón, who took up the leadership of Argentina after the death of her husband in 1974, albeit through succession rather than election; so Simone Weil could claim to have been the first elected president when she became president of the European Parliament in 1979; or, if you insist on a nation-state, then Vigdis Finnbogadottir, elected president of Finland in 1980. The list has continued to grow, but is still in no way representative of the total population.

SUMMARY

Although there are are a number of better-known female leaders—Golda Meir, Benazir Bhutto, and Margaret Thatcher, for example—the two claimants to the title of first female elected head of government remain relatively obscure: Khertek Amyrbitovna Anchimaa-Toka of the Tuvinian People's Republic and Sirimavo Ratwatte Dias Bandaranaike of Sri Lanka.

When Did the Cold War End?

That should be a fairly straightforward question, shouldn't it? But perhaps it happened after your school days. There are three potentially correct answers: three dates for the conclusion of the Cold War, each of which can claim to be valid, and all of which are interlinked.

The Cold War developed quickly after the conclusion of World War II. The wartime alliance between the USSR and the Western Allies had always been a marriage of convenience. As the war drew to a close, the differences became more threatening. Stalin was determined to establish Soviet influence in Eastern Europe. In countries liberated by the Red Army, governments sympathetic to Russia were put in place; the liberators became occupiers. In the West, the North Atlantic Treaty Organization (NATO) was founded. By 1949 the USSR had created its own atomic bomb. This created a strategic standoff rationalized as the doctrine of "mutually assured destruction" (MAD). The superpowers waged a Cold War through technological competition and a series of proxy wars.

Glasnost and Perestroika

President Leonid Brezhnev, like the USSR in general, appeared increasingly outdated and vulnerable. On December 7, 1979, Soviet forces invaded Afghanistan in support of its failing communist government, and the Cold War began to heat up. By the early 1980s the stability of the superpower standoff was under threat. In 1980, the fiercely anticommunist Ronald Reagan had become president. His administration injected new ideological energy into the politics of the West. The following year, martial law was imposed in Poland in response to popular unrest focused on the Solidarity movement. A new arms race was underway, and the Reagan administration was promoting innovations such as the Strategic Defense Initiative. The USSR was bogged down in an intractable war in Afghanistan, its economy was failing to deliver, and its leadership was in crisis with the death of three heads of state in as many years.

The Brandenburg Gate, closed between 1961 and 1989, was emblematic of a divided Berlin, a divided Germany, and a divided world. ✳

On March 11, 1985, the youngest member of the politburo, Mikhail Gorbachev, became General Secretary of the Communist Party of the Soviet Union, another date that could be considered as the end of the Cold War. Gorbachev began a process that culminated in the peaceful dismantling of the USSR. He came to power as the head of a vast Communist state and within four years oversaw statewide contested elections. Fully

"The end of the Cold War is our common victory."

Mikhail Gorbachev (b. 1931)

In reality, identifying any single date for the end of the Cold War is artificial because, like its beginning, the end was a process rather than an event. If one date has to be given, it should be the one that still lives in the popular imagination: November 9, 1989, the day the Berlin Wall came down.

aware of the challenges facing the USSR, Gorbachev launched a program of reform with two themes: openness (*glasnost*) and restructuring (*perestroika*). He began the disengagement of the Red Army from Afghanistan, and at a summit meeting in Reykjavik, Iceland, reversed the arms race with a daring proposal to halve the nuclear arsenals held by the two superpowers.

The Wall

On November 9, 1989, the world witnessed some of the most remarkable scenes ever televised. Young people clambered on top of the iconic Berlin Wall, beating it with sledgehammers and embracing each other as bewildered border guards stood by helplessly. Germany had begun the process of reunification that was to be formally ratified in the following year.

The division of Germany at the end of World War II was one of the first acts of the Cold War, and the collapse of the Berlin Wall is perhaps the most appropriate date for its conclusion. The reforms introduced by Gorbachev had dramatically weakened the hold of Russia over Eastern Europe. The populations of Czechoslovakia, Poland, Hungary, and the German Democratic Republic pressed for change. On November 4, 1989, upward of a million people protested in East Berlin, the government neared collapse, and Gorbachev did not intervene. With no state resistance, the way was open for the Berlin Wall to be pulled down by the inhabitants of the city.

An Attempted Coup

In August 1991, a group of hardline Communists attempted a coup in response to Gorbachev's reforms. However, Boris Yeltsin, then mayor of Moscow, led a popular movement against the coup, and thousands of Muscovites surrounded the parliament building.

It was clear Yeltsin had the popular support that the leaders of the coup lacked. Their resolve crumbled and arrests followed within days. Yeltsin took advantage of the situation to press for the end of the Soviet Union and the creation of a Russian republic. With the collapse of the coup, the USSR was doomed, and the Cold War thawed.

* The Cold War divided Europe and much of the world beyond it.

NATO members

Warsaw Pact countries

Neutral countries

Communist Yugoslavia

Communist Albania

Knowledge: *the ability to recall information*

1) Where was the home of the Greek gods?
- **a.** Athens
- **b.** Atlantis
- **c.** Olympus
- **d.** Cloud nine

2) Who was the Roman god of fire?
- **a.** Jupiter
- **b.** Mars
- **c.** Vulcan
- **d.** Venus

3) Which of these was not a symbol of Zeus/Jupiter?
- **a.** The thunderbolt
- **b.** The oak tree
- **c.** The bull
- **d.** The cross

4) What is the collective name given to the four sacred texts of the Hindu religion?
- **a.** The Bible
- **b.** The Tanakh
- **c.** The Torah
- **d.** The Vedas

5) In which modern-day country is the Indus Valley located?
- **a.** Iran
- **b.** Tibet
- **c.** Pakistan
- **d.** China

6) Approximately how many Buddhists are there worldwide?
- **a.** 100 million
- **b.** 1 billion
- **c.** 1.6 billion
- **d.** 2.5 billion

7) Which year do most western historians believe Buddha was born?
- **a.** 303 B.C.E.
- **b.** 563 B.C.E.
- **c.** 961 B.C.E.
- **d.** 623 B.C.E.

8) In what year did John Toland first coin the word "pantheism"?
- **a.** 1650
- **b.** 1689
- **c.** 1702
- **d.** 1705

9) What are the *two* main forms of pantheism?
- **a.** Mysticism
- **b.** Hinduism
- **c.** Spiritualism
- **d.** Theomonisticism

10) What does the word philosophy mean?
- **a.** Love of truth
- **b.** Love of money
- **c.** Love of wisdom
- **d.** Love of honor

11) Which of these figures was not a Father of Western Philosophy?
- **a.** Socrates
- **b.** Plato
- **c.** Galen
- **d.** Aristotle

12) Who was the first philosopher?
- **a.** Socrates
- **b.** Plato
- **c.** St. Thomas Acquinas
- **d.** Thales of Miletus

Understanding: *the ability to interpret information and make links between different aspects of it*

1) Why did the early Roman pantheon lack a strong narrative?

2) Why is it so difficult to identify the origin of Hinduism?

3) In what way is the traditional theory of Aryan migration weak in explaining the birth of Hinduism?

4) Why is dating the life of Buddha so difficult?

5) What is the point of pantheism?

6) What is the connection between western philosophy and Islam?

Knowledge: *the ability to recall information*

1) For how long did the dinosaurs populate Earth?
- **a.** 10 million years
- **b.** 65 million years
- **c.** 150 million years
- **d.** 250 million years

2) What group of living things is thought to have evolved from the dinosaurs?
- **a.** Birds
- **b.** Fish
- **c.** Mammals
- **d.** None

3) The word "dinosaur" comes from two Greek words meaning:
- **a.** Giant reptile
- **b.** Killing machine
- **c.** Cold-blooded
- **d.** Terrible lizard

4) In which century did Carl Linnaeus live?
- **a.** 16th
- **b.** 17th
- **c.** 18th
- **d.** 19th

5) Which of these Kingdoms comprises single-celled organisms without a nucleus?
- **a.** Protists
- **b.** Monerans
- **c.** Plants
- **d.** Fungi

6) What was the name of the ship on which Charles Darwin made his important journey to South America?
- **a.** HMS *Beagle*
- **b.** The *Mayflower*
- **c.** HMS *Pinafore*
- **d.** The *Golden Hind*

7) Who first discovered the structure of the DNA molecule?
- **a.** Abbott and Costello
- **b.** Franklin and Wilkins
- **c.** Thomson and Thompson
- **d.** Crick and Watson

8) How many base pairs does human DNA contain?
- **a.** 3 billion
- **b.** 64
- **c.** 46
- **d.** 1 million

9) The Latin name for modern humans is *Homo sapiens*. What does *sapiens* mean?
- **a.** Upright
- **b.** Modern
- **c.** Wise
- **d.** Handy

10) It is thought that *Homo sapiens* evolved as a separate species in:
- **a.** China
- **b.** Africa
- **c.** Australia
- **d.** Java

11) What kind of image helped researchers determine the structure of DNA?
- **a.** Electron microscope
- **b.** Photographic
- **c.** Optical microscope
- **d.** X-ray diffraction

12) Where is the crater made by the meteorite that is thought to have caused the extinction of the dinosaurs?
- **a.** South Africa
- **b.** Mexico
- **c.** Antarctica
- **d.** Russia

Understanding: *the ability to interpret information and make links between different aspects of it*

1) What is the K-T boundary, and how might it be related to the extinction of the dinosaurs?

2) What advantage does the binomial Latin system of naming have over the use of common names?

3) In the Linnaean classification system, each Kingdom of the living world is repeatedly subdivided. What are the names of those subdivisions down to the subspecies level?

4) By what mechanism is evolution thought to occur?

5) Can you name the four bases that make up the rungs in the DNA ladder, and say which pairs with which?

6) What name is given to the theory that humans evolved in one place, and what is the main alternative theory?

Knowledge: *the ability to recall information*

1) The most powerful earthquake ever recorded occurred in:
- **a.** Chile in 1960
- **b.** China in 1556
- **c.** Canada in 1946
- **d.** Turkey in 1999

2) The greatest number of people killed by a single earthquake is:
- **a.** 6,000
- **b.** 17,000
- **c.** 250,000
- **d.** 830,000

3) The magnitude of an earthquake can be measured on the:
- **a.** Beaufort Scale
- **b.** Moh Scale
- **c.** Richter Scale
- **d.** Scoville Scale

4) Dark tourism encourages:
- **a.** Visits to nightclubs and theater land
- **b.** Tours of sites linked with death
- **c.** Blindfolded mystery tours
- **d.** Guided tours of sewers and underground tunnels

5) How old is the world's oldest known map?
- **a.** 20,000 years old
- **b.** 8,000 years old
- **c.** 2,000 years old
- **d.** 500 years old

6) What 18th century invention enabled mariners to calculate latitude accurately?
- **a.** Global positioning systems
- **b.** Globes
- **c.** Clocks
- **d.** Sextants

7) The U.S. city with the largest population is:
- **a.** Chicago
- **b.** New York
- **c.** Phoenix
- **d.** Houston

8) Which administratively defined city has the largest population?
- **a.** Mexico City
- **b.** New York
- **c.** Moscow
- **d.** Mumbai

9) What was the first city to have a population of over one million?
- **a.** Alexandria
- **b.** Rome
- **c.** Athens
- **d.** London

10) What caused the rapid expansion of London in the 1800s?
- **a.** A gold rush
- **b.** The Industrial Revolution
- **c.** Immigration from other countries
- **d.** The building of Heathrow Airport

11) What is the main cause of present-day climate change?
- **a.** Increased solar activity
- **b.** Movements of Earth's tectonic plates
- **c.** Increased levels of carbon dioxide in the atmosphere
- **d.** Depletion of the ozone layer

12) Which of the following are already occurring?
- **a.** Warming of the oceans
- **b.** Rising sea levels
- **c.** Sea ice retreating in the Arctic
- **d.** All of these

Understanding: *the ability to interpret information and make links between different aspects of it*

1) What form of tectonic activity causes earthquakes?

2) Why does tourism often fail to have economic benefits for the host region?

3) Why is Mercator's map projection less useful as one approaches the North and South Poles?

4) What human activity is primarily responsible for climate change and how?

Knowledge: *the ability to recall information*

1) What was the name of the Serbian nationalists who killed Archduke Franz Ferdinand of Austria?
- **a.** Black Foot
- **b.** Black Hand
- **c.** Black Head
- **d.** Black Heart

2) When was the Treaty of Versailles signed?
- **a.** 1914
- **b.** 1918
- **c.** 1919
- **d.** 1921

3) In what year did Adolf Hitler take power?
- **a.** 1930
- **b.** 1932
- **c.** 1933
- **d.** 1935

4) Who was Uncle Joe?
- **a.** Joseph Goebbels
- **b.** Joe McCarthy
- **c.** Emperor Franz Joseph
- **d.** Josef Stalin

5) In what year did Mao initiate the "Great Leap Forward?"
- **a.** 1950
- **b.** 1955
- **c.** 1958
- **d.** 1960

6) What was the U.S. program called that sought to develop the atomic bomb?
- **a.** The Manhattan Project
- **b.** The Marshall Plan
- **c.** The Molotov Plan
- **d.** The Final Solution

7) Who described the descent of an "iron curtain" in Europe in 1946?
- **a.** Harry Truman
- **b.** Winston Churchill
- **c.** Josef Stalin
- **d.** Adolf Hitler

8) In what year did Sirimavo Bandaranaike become Prime Minister of Sri Lanka?
- **a.** 1960
- **b.** 1958
- **c.** 1965
- **d.** 1962

9) Who was the first elected female President of a nation state?
- **a.** Simone Weil
- **b.** Sirimavo Bandaranaike
- **c.** Maria Estela Martinez de Peron
- **d.** Vigdis Finnbogadottir

10) What does the strategic stand-off doctrine MAD stand for?
- **a.** Mad and dangerous
- **b.** Massive and destructive
- **c.** Mutually assured destruction
- **d.** Mutually aided development

11) What does "Glasnost" mean?
- **a.** Openness
- **b.** Restructuring
- **c.** Economic restriction
- **d.** Censorship

12) On which date did the Berlin Wall come down?
- **a.** November 20, 1981
- **b.** November 1, 1995
- **c.** December 1, 1989
- **d.** November 9, 1989

Understanding: *the ability to interpret information and make links between different aspects of it*

1) Why did Germany press to alter the balance of power?

2) Why are Mao and Stalin's atrocities less well known than Hitler's?

3) What was *The Little Red Book*?

4) Why was the decision to drop the atomic bomb relatively popular at the time?

5) Why is Khertek Anchimaa's claim to be the first elected female head of government disputed?

6) What makes identifying a single date for the end of the Cold War difficult?

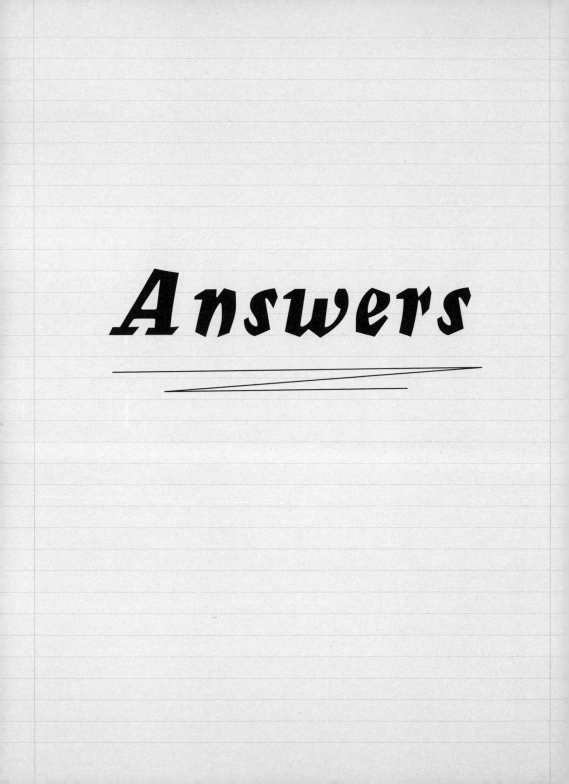

Answers

Scores
(per test)

15-18 out of 18

Excellent!

You have outstanding factual recall and an ability to discern the significant information in a topic. You may wish to do some further research. The Library of Congress has an interesting exhibition about major documents in the history of the United States on its website (www.loc.gov). You can also view online facsimiles of documents such as the Magna Carta on the website of the British Library (www.bl.uk).

8-14 out of 18

Not bad

If most of your marks were for knowledge, you may want to think about how you absorb information. Perhaps you are looking for details like dates and names, and forgetting that a subject is just as much about interpretation as it is about facts.

Under 8 out of 18

Oh dear . . .

Extra homework for you tonight! Try reading more about the subject; there are lots of good resources online. This might help you realize how important the subjects in this book are, and how they affect you and the world you live in.

Lesson 1 - Earth Sciences

Knowledge:

1) **b.** 4.6 billion years

2) **b.** The outer core

3) **c.** 5

4) **d.** A woolly mammoth

5) **d.** All of these

6) **c.** Continental drift

7) **a.** Divergent

8) **c.** Two tectonic plates colliding

9) **d.** Mount Tambora

10) **b.** The Ring of Fire

11) **c.** 130

12) **a.** Carried by glaciers

Understanding:

1) The Moon was formed when the molten Earth was struck by a massive object that knocked off a large quantity of molten rock. This formed a sphere that cooled and remained in orbit around our planet.

2) Ice ages are major fluctuations in Earth's temperature caused by variations in the amount of energy received from the Sun, the movements of Earth's tectonic plates, and the concentration of carbon dioxide in the atmosphere.

3) Alfred Wegener and his supporters suggested that the world's continents were being dragged across the globe by the rotation of Earth and by the Moon's gravity, but if the continents were plowing through a crust of solid rock, these factors were clearly not strong enough.

4) As new crust is formed at divergent boundaries, tectonic plates are pushed against each other. At convergent subductive boundaries, one crust is forced down beneath the other. As it descends, the heat beneath Earth's crust causes it to become molten, and it returns to the mantle.

5) It is thought that each island in the Hawaiian chain was formed by a "hotspot" forcing liquid rock up through the crust. As the tectonic plate moved over the stationary hotspot, a chain of islands was created over time.

6) The seven continents are commonly thought of as North and South America, Africa, Asia, Antarctica, Europe, and Australia. These do broadly correspond with the main tectonic plates, except that Europe and most of Asia are on a single plate. The Indian and Arabian plates are separate.

Lesson 2 - History

Knowledge:

1) **b.** The Sumerians

2) **d.** 3500 B.C.E.

3) **c.** The land between rivers

4) **a.** 399 B.C.E.

5) **c.** 500

6) **b.** Hemlock

7) **b.** Split the empire in two

8) **c.** Bread

9) **a.** The 8th century C.E.

10) **c.** The Tang Dynasty

11) **b.** Recording data

12) **a.** A pictorial alphabet

Understanding:

1) By the time distinct civilizations had developed, the human race had migrated across much of the globe and it is difficult to pinpoint just one origin for all these peoples.

2) Writing extended memory provided a means of recording events and became the platform for developments in areas such as religion, politics, and commerce.

3) This is partly because of Socrates' contribution to the study of western philosophy (posthumously entitled the Socratic Method) and partly because the philosopher Plato recorded the final stages of Socrates' life and then immortalized him as a character in his dialogues.

4) The Roman Empire had been founded upon military conquest as is evident in its name. The size of the empire meant that military leaders controlled many soldiers and were extremely powerful. Consequently, Rome was only as strong and united as its legions.

5) The Chinese alchemist Wei Boyang had experimented with some of the components of gunpowder as early as the first century B.C.E. when he was charged by the Emperor to explore ways of attaining immortality. When gunpowder spread to Western Europe it also came to be associated with the alchemists' second objective: transforming base metals into valuable ones.

6) The Empire did not fall all at once. In the West it fell during the early 6th century, but in the East it survived almost another thousand years. And in many ways its legacy still lives on today in areas such as law, architecture, and religion.

Lesson 3 – Mathematics

Knowledge:

1) **a.** 674

2) **d.** It is still in use.

3) **d.** 10,000,000 digits

4) **c.** 60

5) **a.** India

6) **d.** Mayans

7) **b.** 12th century

8) **d.** None of the above

9) **c.** π is an irrational number.

10) **a.** They occur in the structure of some living things.

11) **b.** A number whose divisors all add up to the number itself

12) **a.** The position of a number determines its value.

Understanding:

1) A prime number is a natural number (the whole numbers that we use for counting) that has only two natural number divisors. In other words, it can be divided only by two numbers—one and itself. The first three prime numbers are 3, 5, and 7. The number 1 has only one divisor, so it is not a prime number.

2) The Fibonacci sequence is generated by starting with 1, adding it to itself to get 2, and then adding together the last two numbers to get the next. This gives us 1, 2, 3, 5, 8, 13, 21, 34, etc.

3) The golden ratio is the ratio between two lengths when the ratio of the shorter length to the longer one is the same as the ratio of the longer length to both lengths added together. This ratio is approximately 1:1.62. In other words, if a rectangle has sides of 1 unit and 1.62 units, the sides are in the golden ratio, because the ratio of 1:1.62 is the same as 1.62:(1 + 1.62).

4) The decimal system that we use today came from the Arabic world, and it was brought to Europe by Fibonacci, who learned about the system when he was living in Algeria. He published a book, *Liber Abaci*, that led to the adoption of this system in the Western world.

5) An irrational number is a number that cannot be expressed as a fraction that is made up of one integer divided by another integer. Pi is an irrational number, and so is the square root of 2. When expressed as a decimal figure, an irrational number never ends and does not repeat—it has an infinite number of decimal places and shows no pattern in the numbers.

6) Fibonacci received that name because of his father. After his death, Leonard of Pisa became known as Filius Bonaccio, "son of the good-natured one," later abbreviated to Fibonacci.

Lesson 4 – Religion

Knowledge:

1) **c.** Buddhism

2) **d.** Over 2,000

3) **a.** Isaac

4) **b.** Sikhism

5) **c.** The Tanakh

6) **a.** 27

7) **d.** St. Jerome

8) **d.** 4 billion

9) **b.** Saudi Arabia

10) **a.** Oil

11) **a.** St. Peter

12) **d.** Avignon, France

Understanding:

1) Because in some apparently polytheistic religions, such as Hinduism, though many gods are worshipped they are all seen as being different manifestations of the same god; and in some faiths traditionally regarded as monotheistic, such as Christianity, a belief in one god incorporates a belief in a tripartite godhead (the Trinity).

2) Whereas in polytheism specific gods may be called upon for help with specific matters, in monotheism the same god is the focus of all prayer and worship.

3) Abraham's smashing of all but one of his father's idols was symptomatic of Abraham's change in belief from polytheism to monotheism—the victory of the one true god over the many false ones.

4) It is difficult because there is no single agreed-on version of the Bible. The books included within these texts were all written at different times and originate from different historical traditions, and there have been (and continue to be) many revisions and alterations made to them.

5) The prophet Muhammad is said to have been born in Mecca around the end of the sixth century B.C.E. Mecca was also the place that Muhammad established the Islamic faith, and though he was forced to flee Mecca, Muhammad later returned and reconquered the city.

6) The papacy was important because during the medieval period it had the power to validate kingship (through divine kingship theory) and also to devalidate it (through excommunication).

Lesson 1 - Science

Knowledge:

1) **b.** Fred Hoyle

2) **a.** 14 billion years

3) **b.** 1990

4) **c.** The speed of light

5) **d.** The Manhattan Project

6) **c.** Both particles and waves

7) **a.** Energy and momentum

8) **a.** Isaac Newton

9) **c.** Big Rip

10) **d.** The question is meaningless.

11) **b.** Bends light

12) **c.** 100 billion years

Understanding:

1) The four fundamental physical forces are gravity, electromagnetism, and the strong and weak nuclear forces. It is thought that they had their present values about one trillionth of a second (one pico second or 0.000000000001 of a second) after the Big Bang.

2) The answer is "Both." At the start of World War II, Einstein feared that Germany would develop a nuclear weapon and he encouraged the President to fund research in this field, but he later changed his mind, refusing to work on the Manhattan Project and opposing nuclear weapons.

3) A prism splits light because light is composed of various wavelengths. The light changes direction (or is "refracted") as it passes into and out of the prism, and light of shorter wavelengths (the violet end of the spectrum) is bent more than the longer wavelengths (e.g., red), and this splits the wavelengths.

4) The galaxies are not moving through space—space itself is expanding and moving the galaxies apart. The more space there is between two galaxies (i.e., the further apart they are), the more rapidly they will move away from each other as space expands, and this can produce a rate of separation that is greater than the speed of light.

Lesson 2 - Art

Knowledge:

1) **b.** 30,000–28,000 B.C.E.

2) **d.** Red and black

3) **d.** 1994

4) **c.** Bishop Odo

5) **c.** 70 m

6) **c.** Rebirth

7) **d.** The photographic camera

8) **c.** John Stuart Mill

9) **a.** 1452

10) **d.** The wife of a Florentine silk merchant

11) **c.** Pissarro

12) **b.** A Monet painting

Understanding:

1) Animals roamed wild and lived alongside these early cave dwellers; consequently, they were an important part of people's lives. They may well have been linked to certain human attributes and even held a ceremonial or religious significance.

2) The victorious Normans commissioned the tapestry and most likely designed it to tell their side of the story. It can be regarded, therefore, as a Norman account.

3) The tapestry was a piece of propaganda, which reminded people of France's power and success in past victories.

4) It is not a term that contemporaries would have recognized, rather one that historians have later attached to the period. Whereas some historians see a clearly defined period of rebirth, others argue that the concept is flawed and belittles the achievements of the "Middle Ages."

5) The *Mona Lisa*'s smile continues to provoke debate because of its ambiguity. The lady in the portrait possesses an unusual half-smile. Whether this is deliberate and, if so, whether it was the result of artistic technique, contemporary fashion, or a medical problem is much debated.

6) They were hoping to capture a snapshot of everyday life. This meant often painting relatively ordinary objects or scenes and encapsulating the impression or feeling this had rather than attempting to attain photographic-style realism.

Lesson 3 - Mathematics

Knowledge:

1) **d.** 10110

2) **c.** A Latin word for "pebble"

3) **b.** Gottfried Leibniz and Isaac Newton

4) **d.** A right-angled triangle

5) **a.** Arabic

6) **b.** The Greek island of Samos

7) **c.** The meter

8) **d.** French Revolution

9) **b.** The United States

10) **c.** Differential calculus

11) **d.** Swiss

12) **b.** Clay

Understanding:

1) The four basic operations of arithmetic are addition, subtraction, multiplication, and division. They were being used by the Sumerians of Mesopotamia more than 4,000 years ago.

2) The correct order of operations is first to deal with anything inside parentheses (or brackets), then exponentials (or orders), and then sequentially take care of division, multiplication, addition, and subtraction. The acronym PEDMAS (or BODMAS) is helpful for remembering this order.

3) Pythagoras's theorem is: "The square of the hypotenuse of a right triangle is equal to the sum of the squares of the lengths of each of the other two sides." It can also be stated as: "In any right triangle, the area of the square whose side is the hypotenuse (the side opposite the right angle) is equal to the sum of the areas of the squares whose sides are the two legs (the two sides that meet at a right angle)."

4) The seven base units of the International System of Units are:

- the meter (m), for length
- the kilogram (kg), for mass
- the second (s), for time
- the ampere (A), for electric current
- the kelvin (K), for thermodynamic temperature
- the mole (mol), for amount of substance
- the candela (cd), for luminous intensity

Lesson 4 - Literature

Knowledge:

1) **b.** Mid 7th–mid 8th centuries C.E.

2) **a.** To say

3) **d.** Samuel Coleridge

4) **d.** *Daffodils*

5) **a.** April 26, 1564

6) **c.** Anne Hathaway

7) **b.** Stratford

8) **a.** Japan

9) **c.** Matsuo Bashō

10) **a.** 5-7-5

11) **c.** Stopping place

12) **d.** Limericks

Understanding:

1) The Vikings sought land overseas partly because their native land in Scandinavia was harsh and of limited agricultural potential; partly because they sought to trade and establish new colonies; and partly because they were now able to travel overseas more easily as a change in climate had caused ice levels to decrease and allowed their longboats to make such voyages with greater ease.

2) They heavily influenced the English saga tradition and provided inspiration for figures such as Richard Wagner and J.R.R. Tolkien.

3) The translator has to decide whether to translate the text directly or to alter it slightly in order in order to preserve the rhyme or feeling of the original poem.

4) The first collection of his works was published only after his death and some were interpolated from working drafts.

5) Because haiku was born out of the Zen Buddhist tradition, many make seasonal references or use a word with seasonal connotations.

6) Haiku originated in Japan and was designed for the Japanese language, in which syllables are much shorter than in English; therefore, it was easier to comply with haiku's strict syllabic system.

7) Stanzas can take a huge variety of forms. There is no line, word, or syllable limit and they don't have to rhyme or really follow any conventions at all.

Lesson 1 - Civics

Knowledge:

1) **b.** 1787

2) **d.** 1688

3) **a.** 1789

4) **c.** 22nd

5) **b.** So that the office did not become the preserve of the wealthy

6) **d.** 1,700 years

7) **b.** 1946

8) **c.** HMS *Prince of Wales*

9) **a.** October 24th

10) **d.** Friedrich Engels

11) **c.** 30,000

12) **a.** 1847

Understanding:

1) The British form of constitution consists of written documents such as the Magna Carta and written laws and precedents. Rather than "unwritten," it can be better described as a constitution not embodied in a single document.

2) To define and restrict the powers of the three branches of state power—the executive, the legislative, and the judiciary—and to provide procedure for its own amendment.

3) He sought to appeal to all the electorate, and affiliation with one party threatened to cause division, which would harm the power and purpose of government.

4) It was a combination of successive conflicts and the shift of power away from Damascus to Baghdad.

5) Many industrial achievements improved both transport and communication between countries and therefore increased the capacity for new diplomatic bodies to operate.

6) Communists like Lenin hoped that through an active communist party, the moment of revolution and overthrow of capitalism would be reached earlier.

Lesson 2 - Earth Sciences

Knowledge:

1) **d.** Anadromous

2) **b.** Monarch

3) **c.** Impenetrable wetlands

4) **a.** John Hanning Speke

5) **d.** 2006

6) **c.** Australia

7) **b.** Both benefit

8) **d.** All of these

9) **c.** They are in Antarctica.

10) **a.** Katabatic

11) **c.** Arizona

12) **b.** Sedimentary

Understanding:

1) Creatures that need to feed near the surface, such as zooplankton and fish, avoid predators by feeding at night and going down to the safety of the deep in the daytime. Microscopic plants come to the surface to get sunlight in the daytime and go deep to find nutrients at night.

2) The main reasons that animals migrate are to find suitable breeding habitats and food for themselves or their offspring, and to avoid extreme weather, especially the cold.

3) The ancient Egyptians had a writing system, well-developed architecture and construction methods, mining, trade over a wide area, and a complex religious life. They also ruled a large empire. This was only possible because the River Nile provided the area with enough water and fertile soil for agriculture in what is a desert area.

4) Coral polyps look like tiny sea anemones, with a tubular body and stinging tentacles around the mouth that capture plankton and small sea creatures. Some build hard shells of calcium carbonate, and these accumulate to form coral reefs.

5) Deserts form because:

a) Warm wet winds from the Equator have already sunk in the atmosphere, cooling and causing the moisture to fall as rain before the air reaches the tropics.

b) Some areas are just too far from the sea for moist air to reach them.

c) On coasts, cold ocean currents cool the air and cause the moisture to fall as rain before the air reaches the land.

d) High mountain ranges cause moist air to rise, cool, and precipitate the moisture as rain, so land on the downwind side of the mountains is in a dry "rain shadow."

6) The walls of the Grand Canyon are striped because the rock is composed of layers laid down over hundreds of millions of years. The different colors are the result of minerals that are present in the rock.

Lesson 3 - Science

Knowledge:

1) **d.** Alchemy

2) **b.** Paracelsus

3) **c.** 1898

4) **a.** Henri Becquerel

5) **c.** Poland

6) **d.** Carbon

7) **a.** Unconquerable

8) **d.** Any color reduces the value.

9) **c.** Raises the boiling point of a liquid

10) **d.** The ends of the molecule have slight positive and negative charges.

11) **a.** Water is a solvent and table salt is a solute.

12) **d.** All of these

Understanding:

1) The alchemists in Medieval Europe were trying to change base metal into gold, discover the formula for an elixir that would cure all ills and confer immortality, and find the universal solvent that would dissolve anything.

2) The most significant finding that Curie made was that the amount of radioactivity coming from a sample of uranium compounds was directly proportional to the amount of uranium present. It was not affected by the other chemicals present. This proved that radioactivity was a property of the uranium atoms and was unrelated to chemical bonding.

3) The weight of a diamond is expressed in units called carats. Originally the carat was the weight of a carob seed, but since these can vary, the carat is now fixed at a value of $\frac{1}{142}$ ounces or 0.2 grams.

4) Extra energy must be put in for a substance to change its phase from solid to liquid and from liquid to gas, even though the temperature does not change. "Latent heat of fusion" is the energy needed to change from a solid to a liquid, and "latent heat of vaporization" is the energy needed to change from a liquid to a gas.

5) Although melting point and freezing point are theoretically the same (a solid changing to a liquid at the same temperature that its liquid form freezes), some substances will remain liquid below their freezing point if they are kept very still. This is called "supercooling."

6) Grease molecules are nonpolar, so they can't dissolve in water. Each detergent molecule has a polar end that bonds with water and a nonpolar end that bonds with grease molecules. Detergent molecules surround globules of grease, bonding to them. The "tails" of the detergent molecules bond with water, removing the grease and keeping it suspended in water.

Lesson 4 - Phys Ed

Knowledge:

1) **c.** 2,000 years ago

2) **d.** France

3) **b.** Roger Bannister

4) **c.** The Romans

5) **d.** Nothing at all

6) **a.** Francis I

7) **c.** Fairground wrestling

8) **d.** Running

9) **a.** Crawl/freestyle

10) **c.** Captain Matthew Webb

Understanding:

1) The main reasons for continued improvement by athletes are the development of professional sports (which has meant that more time can be devoted to training), longer athletic careers (meaning more time for improvement), and technological advances in the equipment that is being used.

2) The main advantage of a round ball is that its behavior is predictable when kicked, rolled, or bounced, making it suitable for a kicking game. The oval ball, on the other hand, is easier to throw, catch, and hold on to when running, and these are the qualities needed for games such as American, Australian, and Rugby football.

3) Glima, the Icelandic national style of wrestling, differs from other forms of wrestling in that the combatants wear belts around their waists and thighs that are connected by straps. The aim is to grab hold of these straps and use them to throw your opponent to the ground.

4) The breaststroke is not the most efficient stroke because during the recovery (i.e., while the arms are being moved into position to start the power stroke), the arms must be extended forward through the water, which slows the swimmer down.

5) Versions of the crawl and the breaststroke, in which the head is kept above the water, are used when rescuers are searching for a person in difficulty. Sidestroke or an "on the back" version of the breaststroke using only the legs is used when a rescuer needs to swim while holding onto another person.

Lesson 1 - Literature

Knowledge:

1) **c.** Unhappy

2) **a.** Russia

3) **a.** The Napoleonic war

4) **c.** Eric Arthur Blair

5) **b.** India

6) **b.** Spanish Civil War

7) **a.** The United States

8) **b.** Ahab

9) **c.** *Iron Heel*

10) **b.** The first

11) **a.** 22,000 items

12) **a.** President Thomas Jefferson

Understanding:

1) Tolstoy used the historical backdrop of the Napoleonic war to explore issues that were very important to the Russia of his day. There was a tension between those who believed that Russia had its own distinctive future and those who believed that Russia should become more western in outlook and culture.

2) The novel *Nineteen Eighty-Four* explores the implications of a totalitarian government with sufficient technological power to control all aspects of society. The fear and tension created by near constant warfare is used to justify the brutal crushing of individual will.

3) *Moby Dick* has been seen as an allegory for the decline of democracy in the United States. More recently it has also been portrayed as an allegory for the systematic destruction of the natural world by industry.

4) Informal censorship tends to occur when members of a community feel that a book has become inappropriate. A text such as *Gone with the Wind* might be viewed as racist in its portrayal of some characters. This objection might encourage some communities to withdraw the book from the shelves of their local library or school. Formal censorship is usually conducted by the government. Formal censorship usually occurs because a text is believed to be politically, morally, or socially unacceptable.

5) The Library of Congress had a false start because the first collection and the building that housed it were destroyed in 1814 by the British army. In prosecuting its war against France, the British navy had attempted to blockade the country. The interception of American ships and the pressing of sailors from those ships raised tensions to the point of warfare in 1812.

6) The Library of Congress is currently working with other major libraries and UNESCO to create the World Digital Library. It will become the largest repository of human knowledge in history and a project that will never be completed.

Lesson 2 - History

Knowledge:

1) **a.** Pigs

2) **d.** Fleas

3) **b.** 25 million

4) **c.** Great Charter

5) **d.** Runnymede in 1215

6) **b.** Strasburg

7) **a.** The production of the Bible

8) **c.** The Caribbean

9) **b.** The Spanish Monarchy

10) **c.** The *Golden Hind*

11) **c.** 100,000

12) **c.** 1792

Understanding:

1) Improved global trade links, a thriving pilgrimage tradition, a number of large conflicts, and increased levels of migration.

2) The barons did not believe that King John would honor his promises and were more concerned with other issues contained in the document. John saw it simply as a negotiating tool to buy him time.

3) The American colonists argued that King George III had broken the traditional freedoms guaranteed by the Magna Carta and that this, therefore, justified their rebellion against his authority.

4) It meant that books became less expensive and more available. This meant that literacy levels rose, and also that ideas could now be promulgated further than ever before.

5) America had been home to native indigenous tribes for centuries, Viking ships had landed in America almost five hundred years earlier, and Columbus himself never landed in America.

6) In France he lost popularity after opposing the execution of Louis XVI and the ultra-revolutionary Jacobins. This unpopularity was exacerbated by his book the *Age of Reason*, which criticized organized religion in general and Christianity in particular. This caused many of his remaining supporters to distance themselves from him.

Lesson 3 - Art

Knowledge:

1) **a.** Summer 1826

2) **c.** 8 hours

3) **b.** Christmas Eve 1888

4) **d.** Gauguin

5) **b.** Epilepsy

6) **c.** Popular art

7) **c.** Salvador Dali

8) **d.** Tsar Nicholas I

9) **c.** 365

10) **a.** Antonio Gaudí

11) **c.** He was hit by a tram.

12) **b.** 2025

Understanding:

1) He died before his achievement was officially recognized and it was left to Daguerre to claim this honor. It also did not help that Niépce's first photograph was then lost for over fifty years.

2) Digitalis, which was used to treat epilepsy, sometimes caused yellow-tinted vision, which it has been suggested caused the prevalence of yellow in Van Gogh's paintings. Similarly, lead poisoning from lead paints could have caused halo-like vision, which is also reflected in his painting.

3) What started as an approach critical of artistic elitism and popular culture gradually became elite and popular itself, therefore losing its impact.

4) From a reference by the reclusive Catherine the Great to her little retreat.

5) It contains art work forcibly seized from German industrialists as reparations by the Red Army after World War II.

6) One reason is its huge size and ambitious design, another is that it is being financed entirely by donations, and a final reason is that the Spanish Civil War impeded the speed of progress.

Lesson 4 - Civics

Knowledge:

1) **b.** France

2) **a.** Winston Churchill

3) **d.** The U.K. House of Lords

4) **d.** The Netherlands

5) **c.** The directive branch

6) **c.** Charles de Montesquieu

7) **c.** Britain

8) **c.** 1918

9) **c.** Troublemaker

10) **b.** 1993

11) **c.** 1848

12) **c.** 1783

Understanding:

1) Voters may feel increasingly detached from the political system, they may not want to give the current political system any legitimacy, they may not like any of their options, or they may feel scared to vote the wrong way.

2) Case law is the legal framework created by courts, and the accumulation of judicial precedents.

3) It has greater theoretical power than it exercises in practice. Though such monarchies possess constitutional power, it is expected that this power will not be exercised.

4) The ANC was the African National Congress and, inspired by the example of Gandhi in India, it sought to promote human rights in a peaceful and legal manner.

5) Apartheid is a legal structure that determines citizens' rights and opportunities by their race.

6) Triangular trade was a profitable trade route that involved the transportation of African slaves to the Americas, where they produced cheap goods to sell in Europe.

Lesson 1 - Religion

Knowledge:

1) **c.** Olympus

2) **c.** Vulcan

3) **d.** The cross

4) **d.** The Vedas

5) **c.** Pakistan

6) **c.** 1.6 billion

7) **b.** 563 B.C.E.

8) **d.** 1705

9) **a.** Mysticism *and* **d.** Theomonisticism

10) **c.** Love of wisdom

11) **c.** Galen

12) **d.** Thales of Miletus

Understanding:

1) The Roman pantheon was in the early stages of its development. In addition, their gods were more expressions of powerful natural forces than figures of personality.

2) Unlike most other religions, Hinduism has no central and charismatic figure, and the origins of their holy texts is shrouded in mystery.

3) There is a lack of archaeological or cultural evidence to suggest that either horses or chariots made any impact on the Indus Valley during this period, and both would have been necessary for Aryan migration.

4) With no single leader or institution, much regional variation has emerged and with it a number of different scholarly traditions.

5) It is an attempt to unite the divine and physical worlds.

6) When the Western Roman Empire collapsed, the teachings of western philosophers became disjointed and even lost. It was the Islamic scholars of the Middle East who ensured that these philosophers' works were not lost.

Lesson 2 - Science

Knowledge:

1) **c.** 150 million years

2) **a.** Birds

3) **d.** Terrible lizard

4) **c.** 18th

5) **b.** Monerans

6) **a.** HMS *Beagle*

7) **d.** Crick and Watson

8) **a.** 3 billion

9) **c.** Wise

10) **b.** Africa

11) **d.** X-ray diffraction

12) **b.** Mexico

Understanding:

1) The K-T boundary is a geological boundary between the Cretaceous and Tertiary Ages. The existence of a layer of the element iridium in the rock at this boundary suggests a meteor impact, which might have caused the extinction of the dinosaurs by raising vast quantities of dust and blocking out the sunlight.

2) The binomial system gives every organism its own individual two-part Latin name. Whereas common names can be vague and differ between countries and in different languages, the binomial system is recognized around the world.

3) The subdivisions of each Kingdom of the living world are:

Phylum (plural *phyla*)

Class

Order

Family

Genus (plural *genera*)

Species

Subspecies

4) Evolution is thought to proceed through by scientists the mechanism of natural selection. Within a species there is a certain level of variation in the genetic makeup. Some variations will increase the individual's chances of surviving and having more offspring, and this leads to the variation becoming more widespread within the population, eventually leading to the development of a new species.

5) The four bases are cytosine, guanine, adenine, and thymine. Guanine will bond only with cytosine. Adenine bonds only with thymine.

6) The theory that *Homo sapiens* evolved in one place is the Recent African Origin, or RAO, theory. An alternative, but less commonly supported, theory suggests that we evolved in several locations around the globe at approximately the same time from various groups of *Homo erectus*, giving rise to the visibly distinct regional populations that we see today.

Lesson 3 - Earth Sciences

Knowledge:

1) **a.** Chile in 1960

2) **d.** 830,000

3) **c.** Richter Scale

4) **b.** Tours of sites linked with death

5) **b.** 8,000 years old

6) **c.** Clocks

7) **b.** New York

8) **d.** Mumbai

9) **a.** Alexandria

10) **b.** The Industrial Revolution

11) **c.** Increased levels of carbon dioxide in the atmosphere

12) **d.** All of these

Understanding:

1) Earthquakes are caused by the movement of tectonic plates that are moving past each other at a transformational boundary. Friction at the boundary causes stresses to build up in the rock, which deforms. When movement finally occurs, enormous energy is released. This sends seismic waves out through Earth's crust, and tsunamis across the oceans, and these can be highly destructive.

2) Although tourism leads to investment and the creation of jobs, work for local people is often low paid and seasonal, and the investment can lead to higher costs for local people. Much of the money that is spent by tourists goes to outside companies and investors rather than to benefit the host communities.

3) Because the lines of longitude are parallel in Mercator's projection (when in reality they converge at the Poles), the representation of area becomes more and more distorted as distance north and south from the equator increases. This reduces the usefulness of the map as one approaches the Poles, which are shown as occupying the whole width of the top and bottom of the map.

4) The principle human activity that is causing current changes in Earth's climate is the burning of fossil fuels—coal, oil and its derivatives, and gas. This has raised the amount of carbon dioxide in the atmosphere. Carbon dioxide is known as a "greenhouse gas," because it reduces the rate at which heat is lost from the planet, causing the average temperature of the atmosphere, Earth's surface, and the oceans to rise.

Lesson 4 - History

Knowledge:

1) **b.** Black Hand

2) **c.** 1919

3) **c.** 1933

4) **d.** Josef Stalin

5) **c.** 1958

6) **a.** The Manhattan Project

7) **b.** Winston Churchill

8) **a.** 1960

9) **d.** Vigdis Finnbogadottir

10) **c.** Mutually assured destruction

11) **a.** Openness

12) **d.** November 9, 1989

Understanding:

1) They wanted to become an imperial power on the world stage and felt they could not under the present geopolitical circumstances.

2) Mao and Stalin's atrocities were carried out within their respective countries and away from the eyes of Western Europe. Stalin and Mao were also on the allies' side during the war and remained popular and in power afterward. They were, therefore, able to keep the scale of their atrocities secret.

3) Published in 1964 by Chairman Mao, *The Little Red Book* was a collection of communist quotations. It is possibly the most printed book in history.

4) Partly because it swiftly ended a long and bloody war; partly because it did so in a manner which saved the lives of many American servicemen, without the assistance of Russia; and partly because the full brutal effects of the bomb had not yet been realized.

5) Because she was elected in name only. In reality Tuva was a one-party state and Anchimaa was effectively nominated leader.

6) Because of the nature of the Cold War as a symbolic term for the period of tension and animosity between the Soviet Union and the West, especially America, after World War II. Its end was as gradual, accumulative, and unofficial as its beginning.

Index

About the authors . . .

Stephen Evans has a career in education that spans twenty years. In that time he has taught history, geography, politics, sports, and English to students between eight and eighteen years old. Stephen holds a Masters degree, has worked as a senior lecturer in education studies at graduate and postgraduate levels, and is a contributor to the prestigious *Times Educational Supplement*. He is currently an assistant principal at a highly successful school, where he is devoted to making learning effective, productive, and fun.

Ian Whitelaw is an editor and writer currently living on Vancouver Island, in Canada, where he and his wife run a small farm. Ian's university studies included chemistry, physics, and biology, as well as anthropology, in which he graduated from the University of Durham, U.K., with an Honors degree. As an author, contributor, and editor, he has been involved in numerous books, and his published work includes *A Measure of All Things: The Story of Man and Measurement*. He also coauthored (with Dr. Michael Picard) *This Is Not a Book: Adventures in Popular Philosophy*.

Credits